IMPRESSIONISTS AND SYMBOLISTS

BOOKS BY LIONELLO VENTURI

_____

Painting and Painters

Modern Painters

Impressionists and Symbolists
    (*Modern Painters, Volume II*)

_____

CHARLES SCRIBNER'S SONS

LIONELLO VENTURI

IMPRESSIONISTS
AND
SYMBOLISTS

*MANET, DEGAS, MONET, PISSARRO,
SISLEY, RENOIR, CEZANNE, SEURAT,
GAUGUIN, VAN GOGH,
TOULOUSE-LAUTREC*

Translated from the Italian by
Francis Steegmuller

CHARLES SCRIBNER'S SONS · NEW YORK
CHARLES SCRIBNER'S SONS · LTD · LONDON
1950

The translator warmly thanks Dante Negro,
of Brooklyn College, for his valuable assistance.

Contents

Plates

PLATES

PLATES

Fig. 23. MANET: *The Model for A Bar at the Folies-Bergère*, 1881
Dijon Museum
Photo Giacomelli

Fig. 24. DEGAS: *The Bellelli Family*, 1860–62
Museum of Impressionism, Louvre, Paris
Photo Archives Photographiques

Fig. 25. DEGAS: *Portrait of a Young Woman*, 1867
Museum of Impressionism, Louvre, Paris
Photo Archives Photographiques

Fig. 26. DEGAS: *M. and Mme. Morbilli*, 1867
Museum of Fine Arts, Boston
Photo Museum of Fine Arts

Fig. 27. DEGAS: *War Scene in the Middle Ages*, 1865
Museum of Impressionism, Louvre, Paris
Photo Archives Photographiques

Fig. 28. DEGAS: *The Office of a Cotton Firm*, 1873
Pau Museum
Photo Bulloz

Fig. 29. DEGAS: *The Carriage at the Races*, 1870–73
Museum of Fine Arts, Boston
Photo Bulloz

Fig. 30. DEGAS: *At the Races*, 1877–80
Museum of Impressionism, Louvre, Paris
Photo Archives Photographiques

Fig. 31. DEGAS: *The Orchestra of the Paris Opera*, 1868–69
Museum of Impressionism, Louvre, Paris
Photo Braun

Fig. 32. DEGAS: *Café-Concert, Les Ambassadeurs*, 1876–77
Lyons Museum
Photo Bulloz

Fig. 33. DEGAS: *Ballet Classroom, Paris Opera*, 1872
Museum of Impressionism, Louvre, Paris
Photo Bulloz

Fig. 34. DEGAS: *Ballet Rehearsal*, 1875–77
Tate Gallery, Sir William Burrell Collection, London

PLATES

Fig. 35. DEGAS: *Rehearsal in the Ballet Classroom,* 1875
Harry Payne Bingham Collection, New York
Photo Vizzavona

Fig. 36. DEGAS: *Ballet Dancers Tying Their Slippers* (after 1890)
Cleveland Museum of Art
Photo Gemeente Museum, Amsterdam

Fig. 37. DEGAS: *Women Combing Their Hair, c.* 1876–78
Formerly Carstairs Collection, New York
Photo Vizzavona

Fig. 38. DEGAS: *Diego Martelli,* 1879
Jacques Seligmann Collection, New York
Photo Gemeente Museum, Amsterdam

Fig. 39. DEGAS: *Absinth,* 1876
Museum of Impressionism, Louvre, Paris
Photo Archives Photographiques

Fig. 40. DEGAS: *Women Outside a Café, Evening,* 1877
Museum of Impressionism, Louvre, Paris
Photo Archives Photographiques

Fig. 41. DEGAS: *Women Ironing, c.* 1884
Museum of Impressionism, Louvre, Paris
Photo Archives Photographiques

Fig. 42. DEGAS: *The Tub,* 1886
Museum of Impressionism, Louvre, Paris
Photo Archives Photographiques

Fig. 43. DEGAS: *End of the Bath, c.* 1895
Victor Lyon Collection
Photo Bulloz

Fig. 44. DEGAS: *Breakfast after the Bath, c.* 1895–98
Formerly A. Vollard Collection, Paris

Fig. 45. DEGAS: *After the Bath,* 1899
Formerly A. Vollard Collection

Fig. 46. MONET: *Mouth of the Seine at Honfleur,* 1864
Formerly Bottenwieser Collection, New York

Fig. 47. MONET: *Camille, or the Lady in the Green Dress,* 1866
Bremen Museum
Photo Durand-Ruel

PLATES

PLATES

PLATES

PLATES

Fig. 85. SISLEY: *The Route de la Princesse, Louveciennes, Evening,* 1875
Formerly Durand-Ruel Collection, Paris
Photo Durand-Ruel

Fig. 86. SISLEY: *Landscape,* 1876
Formerly Durand-Ruel Collection, Paris
Photo Durand-Ruel

Fig. 87. SISLEY: *The Boat during the Flood,* 1876
Museum of Impressionism, Louvre, Paris
Photo Archives Photographiques

Fig. 88. SISLEY: *The Seine at Suresne,* 1877
Museum of Impressionism, Louvre, Paris
Photo Archives Photographiques

Fig. 89. SISLEY: *A Cottage at Les Sablons,* 1885
Formerly Durand-Ruel Collection, Paris
Photo Durand-Ruel

Fig. 90. SISLEY: *Sunset on the River Loing, St. Michel, Moret,* 1889
Formerly Durand-Ruel Collection, Paris
Photo Durand-Ruel

Fig. 91. SISLEY: *The Bridge at Moret, c.* 1894
Formerly Durand-Ruel Collection, Paris
Photo Durand-Ruel

Fig. 92. RENOIR: *Portrait of Mlle. Romaine Lacaux,* 1864
Cleveland Museum of Art

Fig. 93. RENOIR: *Lise,* 1867
Folkwang Museum, Essen
Photo Folkwang Museum

Fig. 94. RENOIR: *La Grenouillère, c.* 1867
Museum of Modern Western Art, Moscow

Fig. 95. RENOIR: *The Pont Neuf,* 1872
Marshall Field Collection, New York
Photo Wildenstein

Fig. 96. RENOIR: *Bathing Woman,* 1876
Museum of Modern Western Art, Moscow

Fig. 97. RENOIR: *The Moulin de la Galette,* 1876
Museum of Impressionism, Louvre, Paris
Photo Archives Photographiques

PLATES

PLATES

Fig. 111. RENOIR: *Paul Durand-Ruel,* 1910
    Durand-Ruel Collection, Paris
    Photo Durand-Ruel

Fig. 112. RENOIR: *Landscape, c.* 1910
    Frank Baer Collection, Woodlands Corner, West Byfleet,
    Surrey

Fig. 113. RENOIR: *Woman's Torso,* 1905
    Formerly Prince de Wagram Collection, Paris
    Photo Durand-Ruel

Fig. 114. RENOIR: *After the Bath,* 1913
    Formerly Ambroise Vollard Collection, Paris

Fig. 115. RENOIR: *Gabrielle at the Mirror, c.* 1910
    Albert Skira Collection, Geneva
    Photo Giacomelli

Fig. 116. RENOIR: *Bathing Women, c.* 1918
    Formerly Claude Renoir Collection, Cagnes

Fig. 117. CEZANNE: *Portrait of a Monk,* 1865–67
    Frick Collection, New York
    Photo Basel Museum

Fig. 118. CEZANNE: *Pastoral,* 1870
    J. V. Pellerin Collection, Paris
    Photo Bernheim-Jeune

Fig. 119. CEZANNE: *Melting Snow at L'Estaque, c.* 1870
    J. V. Pellerin Collection, Paris
    Photo Bernheim-Jeune

Fig. 120. CEZANNE: *The House of the Hanged Man, Auvers-sur-Oise,*
    1872–73
    Museum of Impressionism, Louvre, Paris
    Photo Bernheim-Jeune

Fig. 121. CEZANNE: *The Black Clock,* 1869–71
    Edward G. Robinson Collection, Beverly Hills
    Photo Paul Rosenberg

Fig. 122. CEZANNE: *The Boundary Wall,* 1875–76
    Durand-Ruel Collection, New York
    Photo Durand-Ruel

PLATES

Fig. 123. CEZANNE: *Still Life,* 1873
Mme. Jacques Doucet Collection, Neuilly-sur-Seine
Photo Vizzavona

Fig. 124. CEZANNE: *Portrait of Victor Chocquet,* 1876–77
Victor Rothschild Collection, London
Photo Vizzavona

Fig. 125. CEZANNE: *The Little Bridge,* 1882–85
Gaston Bernheim de Villers Collection, Paris
Photo Durand-Ruel

Fig. 126. CEZANNE: *The Bridge over the Marne at Créteil, c.* 1888
Museum of Modern Western Art, Moscow
Photo Museum of Modern Western Art

Fig. 127. CEZANNE: *Houses at L'Estaque,* 1882–85
Mrs. Virginia Harrison Collection, New York
Photo Paul Rosenberg

Fig. 128. CEZANNE: *The Montagne Sainte-Victoire, near Gardanne,* 1885–86
Loeser Collection, Florence
Photo Giacomelli

Fig. 129. CEZANNE: *The Montagne Sainte-Victoire with Tall Pine,* 1885–87
Duncan Phillips Memorial Gallery, Washington
Photo Paul Rosenberg

Fig. 130. CEZANNE: *The Bay of Marseilles, Seen From L'Estaque,* 1883–85
Metropolitan Museum, New York
Photo Metropolitan Museum

Fig. 131. CEZANNE: *The Montagne Sainte-Victoire,* 1894–1900
Lord Ivor Spencer Churchill Collection, London
Photo M. Knoedler & Co.

Fig. 132. CEZANNE: *The Kitchen Table,* 1888–90
Museum of Impressionism, Louvre, Paris
Photo Archives Photographiques

Fig. 133. CEZANNE: *Portrait of Paul Cézanne,* 1890–94
J. V. Pellerin Collection, Paris
Photo Pellerin

Fig. 134. CEZANNE: *Madame Cézanne in the Greenhouse, c.* 1890
Stephen C. Clark Collection, New York

PLATES

Fig. 135. CEZANNE: *Woman With a Coffee-Pot,* 1890–94
J. V. Pellerin Collection, Paris
Photo Pellerin

Fig. 136. CEZANNE: *The Card Players,* 1890–92
J. V. Pellerin Collection, Paris
Photo Bulloz

Fig. 137. CEZANNE: *Still Life,* 1895–1900
Museum of Modern Art, New York
Photo Paul Rosenberg

Fig. 138. CEZANNE: *Lake of Annecy,* 1896
Courtauld Institute, London
Photo Paul Rosenberg

Fig. 139. CEZANNE: *The Montagne Sainte-Victoire,* 1904–06
A. H. Buhrle Collection, Zurich
Photo Venturi

Fig. 140. CEZANNE: *Portrait of Vallier* (water colour), 1906
Formerly Paul Rosenberg Collection, Paris
Photo Durand-Ruel

Fig. 141. CEZANNE: *Bathing Women,* 1900–06
Formerly Paul Cézanne, Jr. Collection, Paris
Photo Venturi

Fig. 142. SEURAT: *Suburb,* 1883
Formerly Félix Fénéon Collection, Paris
Photo Vizzavona

Fig. 143. SEURAT: *Peasant with a Hoe, c.* 1884
Solomon R. Guggenheim Foundation, New York
Photo Vizzavona

Fig. 144. SEURAT: *A Bathing Party, Asnières,* 1883–84
Tate Gallery, London
Photo Vizzavona

Fig. 145. SEURAT: *The Seine at Courbevoie,* 1885
Mme. Charles Cachin-Signac Collection, Paris
Photo Vizzavona

Fig. 146. SEURAT: *The Island of the Grande Jatte, Study for the Picture,*
1884
Formerly Lefevre Gallery

PLATES

PLATES

PLATES

IMPRESSIONISTS AND SYMBOLISTS

Chapter One

EDOUARD MANET

WHEN WE approach the best works of Manet today, we are accustomed to see in them a perfect art, easy to understand and even familiar. We marvel at the struggle that he had to maintain throughout his life to secure recognition of his value as an artist and at the hostility which constantly beset him, continued after his death, and even today sporadically revives. By these considerations a critic is led to suspect that admiration may not be a sufficient basis for a complete understanding of the art of Manet and that it may be profitable to examine the controversy that it caused in its day. Perhaps in this way it will be possible to understand it in its two aspects—the eternal aspect, which we enjoy, and the other aspect of its relation to the moment in which it arose.

For six years, from 1850 to 1856, Manet studied painting with Couture, whose then celebrated canvas, *Romans of the Decadence*, had enjoyed great success because it fully satisfied the taste of the public, of the critics, and of the Academy. It was a "classical" painting of a subject from ancient history. From the foundation of the Academy in the seventeenth century, that type of French painting which drew its inspiration from Italian art of the Renaissance, especially from the Carracci and their school, was considered classical, and it alone obtained official favor and recognition. It is true that some of the best painters, Watteau, Chardin, Delacroix, the landscape painters of 1830, had chosen other paths, following the tradition of the Venetians, of Rubens, and of the Dutch, but they had not succeeded in changing the official taste, which remained bound to the classicist tradition.

Just as Napoleon I had favored the neo-classicism of David, so Napoleon III favored the reformed neo-classicism which was that of Ingres. By 1850 the romantic impulse in painting had been reabsorbed into a hybrid classicism, which was continuing by force of inertia. It inspired not a single real artist, but it fully satisfied both the Academy, which approved its observance of codified forms, and the public, which was interested in its subject matter—historical scenes theatrically depicted.

The Academy and the public would have been perfectly content had it not been for one discordant note: realism, as personified in Courbet. In 1855, just at the moment of Ingres's greatest triumph, Courbet's private exhibition had scandalized all properly thinking persons. The scandal was caused by the painter's subjects: to depict peasants and stone-breakers with the epic pretension that had hitherto been accorded only to ancient Romans was artistic blasphemy. The innovation also contained an implied social and political threat to which the middle class was very sensitive. Still, to one aspect of Courbet's painting no one could object: his drawing, chiaroscuro, and colour all conformed to the rules of the classicist tradition. It was therefore admitted with good or bad grace that he was the possessor of a good technique, master of his tools.

Edouard Manet, who was born in 1832, had at the age of nineteen participated in the uprising against Louis Napoleon's

1851 coup d'état and had spent a night in the hands of the police. He belonged to one of those upper middle-class families that seem destined for the civil service, and in order to devote himself to painting he had had to revolt against his father's wishes. Every intelligent young man in Paris under the Second Empire was a rebel, and it is natural that Manet, lacking deep social and political interests, entirely absorbed in art, should have been a rebel in painting. In Couture's studio he rebelled against the methods of the master, stirring up the enthusiasm of his fellow students.

Even so he continued to work with Couture, and at the Louvre and in Italy he copied various paintings by old masters, according to academic custom. He also visited Germany, Belgium, and Holland, thus acquiring an unusually broad pictorial culture. The realists of 1850 were principally land-scape painters, but not until many years later was Manet to display any real interest in landscape. The realism of Courbet he felt to be alien to his nature; no doubt Courbet's spirit, with its leaning towards the people, seemed vulgar to one who possessed not only the worldly "distinction" of the upper mid-dle class but also the wide acquaintance with pictures that Manet had gained in his travels. Nevertheless, in the decade between 1850 and 1860 a young rebel could not escape being a realist, and even Manet felt himself to be one, that is, with rare exceptions he painted what he saw as he saw it. Still, his manner of seeing had an entire culture behind it: in Manet's work Velasquez and Goya, Raphael and Franz Hals are always more or less present by implication. His was thus a cultural manner of interpreting and transcending the reality which he represented. Courbet considered that he represented reality objectively, and he identified his own reality with truth. Manet, on the other hand, achieved art by means of a transformation of reality which was inspired by the works of the past.

Detesting the Academy and for various reasons feeling himself distant also from Delacroix, from Courbet, and from the landscapists of 1830, Manet quite naturally followed his own path, not from any conscious wish to play the part of the rebel, but because he was inexorably driven by his own inner need.

In 1867, when he organized a private exhibition of his works (close to one of the entrances of the Exposition Universelle, which had refused to show them), he wrote as a preface to his catalogue:

> Monsieur Manet has never desired to protest. Quite the contrary: to his surprise, others protested against him. There is a traditional way of teaching forms, methods, visualization, painting: those who are trained in such principles admit no others, and thus acquire a naïve intolerance. Anything outside their formulas must be without value, and of it they become not only critics, but enemies, active enemies. . . . M. Manet has always recognized talent where it is to be found, and he has never claimed to overthrow an old form of painting or to create a new one. He has merely tried to be himself, and no one else.[1]

After the hesitancies natural to a young man, Manet reached the crucial turning point of his life at the age of thirty-one in

[1] Tabarant, *Manet*, 1947, p. 136.

4

1863, when he exhibited *The Picnic* (*Le Déjeuner sur l'herbe*) (fig. 1) at the Salon des Refusés, and immediately afterwards painted what would in another age have been his Venus—his most famous picture, perhaps his masterpiece, the *Olympia* (fig. 2).

* * *

Let us consider for a moment beautiful nudes by great masters: by Giorgione, Titian, Velasquez, Goya, Delacroix, and Courbet. It has been said that Manet was inspired by Goya. An affinity between them may be admitted, but it is a moral affinity. Goya conceived the *Maja nuda* as a woman who offers herself, with a hint of irony in her pretended modesty. Olympia also offers herself; she is without modesty of any kind, offering herself quite naturally, or rather naturalistically. With that exception affinities between Maja and Olympia do not exist. Giorgione, Titian, Velasquez, Delacroix, and Courbet all painted nude women more or less realistically, all with the definite intent to picture the woman's beauty in accordance with the age-old opinion that distinguishes the beautiful woman from the other members of her sex. Goya obeyed this same convention. But Manet ignored it. His model, Victorine Meurend, was probably considerably more beautiful in the nude than he painted her in the *Olympia:* she appears again, apparently closer to life, in *The Picnic.* In the *Olympia* the nude is angular, posed to bring forward the entire length of the body, not in full or half relief, but as though modelled in light relief, and the mass of the substance (*matière*) in the area in relief is thicker than it seems. This conception of the nude is consistent with the manner of con-

5

structing the other light areas of the painting: the cushion, the sheets, the flowered scarf, the dress of the Negress. In these there is a variation, or rather a dance of light and shadow, which is naturally not present in the nude, and which serves to lighten and make more brilliant the total effect, but whose form is again that of a relief of light on dark—of whites veined with blue, yellow, green, and pink on the background of black and brown. And since there are no transitions from light to dark, the light relief is, as it were, in a coloured setting, in which black and brown act on the imagination of the spectator with as much force as the lightness of the images.

Thus in the *Olympia* Manet's style is coherent: the woman, the bed, and the background are all reduced to an effect of colour; the subject, a nude woman, is transposed into a chromatic motif—too present in the artist's mind not to take the form of a relief, even though the relief be light. The result is poetry, not translatable into words, because it depends solely on the vitality, energy, and coherence with which the image is presented. Other painters have transformed what they saw according to an ideal of beauty; even Courbet transformed what he saw according to an ideal that he believed to be the naked truth; Manet transformed, not to attain to beauty or to truth, but to obtain a plastic-chromatic coherence of his own.

It need scarcely be said that the other above-named painters also painted with their own plastic-chromatic coherence, but in their case this was a natural thing, the result of traditional technique. For Manet the coherence was a new ideal, something to be created at every new step. For it he sacrificed in his painting the femininity to which in life he was so sensitive; for it he made his Victorine into something that smacks at

6

once of the idol and of the marionette. Beauty, truth, life—all were absorbed into his art. Not for the purpose of producing "art for art's sake," à la Théophile Gautier (Gautier used his formula to sacrifice art to the beau ideal of Ingres and therefore despised the *Olympia*), but to achieve autonomy of vision. Thus, unaware or almost unaware of what he was doing, by substituting an ideal for a practice Manet discovered the direction of his own creative fancy. And he discovered it not only for himself. With the *Olympia* he introduced the principle of the autonomy of vision into art, and all modern art has used it as a basis and as a banner.

Manet's originality consists precisely in his having given this direction to his way of imagining and executing a picture: the origin of this direction is to be found in himself alone.

The masters of the past whom he had studied and copied, especially Velasquez and Goya, were present in his mind at the moment of creation, not as models to be followed but as material to be used. He used it as a point of departure, and his attitude in doing so was one of irony transcending any practical purpose, with a detached indifference towards nature and truth. Certain critics, such as Francastel and Waldemar George, have emphasized Manet's relationship with the past in support of their claim that he was a great executant rather than a creator. Their error lay in not understanding the difference between invention and creation.

Indeed Manet did not invent myths in painting, as did Delacroix with his *28 July 1830* or Courbet with his *Stone-Breakers*. There are no myths in Manet. He hints at one—the myth of modern life—in *Concert in the Tuileries Gardens* (fig. 3), but this had already been treated by Courbet,

7

and Manet did not stress it. When he painted *The Execution of Maximilian,* an entirely contemporary event, he drew his inspiration from Goya's *Firing Squads of the Third of May.*

But though he invented no myths, Manet did something greater: he created images, admirable purely in and for themselves. These exist by means of their artistic life, which parallels the life of natural things but is not to be confused with it. They are in no way active; they do not communicate specific emotions or passions; as we have said, their message is not a message at all in the sense of expressing something; their value consists purely in their own existence; they are precious simply in so far as they possess aesthetic life.

Thus it is quite true that Manet did not possess an inventive imagination. Utterly absorbed by his fancy, which constantly created images, he had eyes for nothing else: not for nature, not for action, not for moral significance, not for beauty, not even for the representation of space. From those elements— the very elements with which painters and critics were commonly concerned—he cut himself off as completely as possible.

Manet was a man of the world, a Parisian boulevardier, and he lived during the Second Empire, in the optimistic atmosphere of the "age of progress." Had anyone remarked to him that his concentration of painting in the image was a return to a mediaeval concept, he would doubtless have been offended. And yet mediaeval art had been, precisely, a *presentation of images;* and it had ended when the Renaissance and the modern age substituted the *representation of reality.* By an irony of history, at a moment when the representation of reality had become more objective than ever before, to the point of being photographic and mechanical, a brilliant Parisian

8

who desired to paint realistically was forced instead, by the strength and the nature of his marvellous genius, to lead art back to its function as creator of images.

Such a development had scarcely been expected by the Academy or the critics or the public of 1863 or 1865. Then as now those persons always needed some sort of a crutch to lean on in approaching a work of art, and they found their crutches in concepts extraneous, even though close, to art: in nature, in historical and poetic subject matter, in beauty, in the ability to create illusion.

The *Olympia* was not an imitation of nature; it was not a model of beauty; it did not arouse interest by means of its subject (the title, suggested by a literary man after the picture was finished, perplexed the critics and made them suspicious); it did not dazzle by sheer brilliance. In short, it had absolutely nothing to recommend it, no merit whatever, and yet it was impossible to be indifferent to the *Olympia;* young artists spoke of nothing else and the public was spellbound. There was thus an enchantment about it that had to be exorcized; people felt that they were in some way being made the victims of a swindle, and in order to escape from this humiliating role they felt it necessary to become indignant and insult the man who was disturbing the public peace.

Everyone in Paris knew Manet, a charming, attractive, elegant dandy, smiling, perhaps a trifle ironic—a sunny soul, as Renoir said. But the dandy now turned out to be a painter who broke all the rules of good society—and therefore he was a barbarian, an uncivilized man, a violent revolutionary, a bad boy who threw stones through windows, a guttersnipe.

It is easy to understand the bewilderment of the public but

9

less easy to excuse the critics' inability to explain the reasons
behind the conflict. Baudelaire, who was a friend of Manet
and kindly disposed toward his art, encouraged him in his
"Spanishness" (one of the most transient elements in his
art), defended him when he was accused of being a maker of
pastiches, and insisted that his affinities with Goya were
merely coincidental; but when he wrote him in 1865 to
encourage him to stand up against the fury of his detractors
he proposed to him as models Chateaubriand and Wagner,
whereas "you are pre-eminent only in the decrepitude of your
art." By that he meant that Chateaubriand and Wagner belonged to the future, Manet to the past. Today, when Manet
is far more a man of the moment than either of the others, it is
sad to think that Baudelaire's critical genius should so err.
Again, shortly thereafter, writing to Mme. Paul Meurice,
Baudelaire said of Manet, "He is so brilliant, so light in his
touch, that it would be unfortunate should he become discouraged. He will never completely fill the gap in his temperament. But he has a temperament." [2] What—one can only
wonder in reply to that—was the gap in Baudelaire's own
thinking, that he should so go astray? He did not appreciate
realism, and perhaps he felt in Manet a lack of those literary
qualities which he found in Delacroix. For us today that very
lack is an immense virtue.

With much greater courage and conviction, in which he
was supported by his friend Paul Cézanne, Emile Zola wrote
of Manet in 1866 and 1867. His profession of faith is well
known: "The word 'realist' means nothing to me. The real
must be made subordinate to temperament. Create things

[2] Tabarant, *Manet*, p. 110.

that are true, and I will applaud; but above all, create things that are individual and living—I will applaud even louder." [3]

Zola thus emphasized the subjectivity of creation, at the moment of transition from realism to naturalism. And he went on to particularize concerning Manet's individual way of seeing and its translation into painting:

> The first impression created by one of Edouard Manet's pictures is a trifle harsh. We are not accustomed to see such simple and sincere translations from reality. Furthermore . . . there is a certain elegant stiffness which is surprising. The eye perceives at first only colours, broadly laid on. Soon the objects become outlined and take their places; after a few seconds, the ensemble seems vigorous, and we experience a real charm in contemplating this clear, sober painting, which renders nature with tender brutality, if I may so express myself. On drawing near the picture, we see that the technique is delicate rather than brusque; the artist uses only the brush, and makes use of it very prudently. There are no spots of thick colour, but a unified surface. This daring artist, who has been so mocked at, has very intelligent ways of doing things, and if his works have a special look about them it is entirely owing to his completely personal way of seeing and translating objects. [4]

All that is quite finely observed and stated, but it does not go far enough. Zola's concept of nature (for him nature was the fixed element, the individual being the variable) prevented him from understanding Manet's ideal creation, which

---

[3] Zola, *Mes Haines*, 1902, p. 281.   [4] *Ibid.*, p. 345.

constituted the fundamental difference of his art from any-thing that is known in nature—a difference that is present in the art of all true artists in all periods.

A further contrast with Courbet is appropriate at this point. Courbet was a realist in so far as he painted only what he saw and refused to paint ancient Romans or angels: his was a realism of subject, his form, as we have said, being traditional even though personal.

Such is not the case with Manet. His revolt against the Academy was a revolt of form. He felt the necessity of con-sidering line a division rather than merely a contour, of re-ducing chiaroscuro to a minimum, of giving little considera-tion to three-dimensional space. In this way he obtained great precision in his images and colour that is precious even in his blacks, and his images, instead of being in relief, are detached from the background and made more compelling by being pushed forward, the space behind them being non-articulated and therefore infinite. Plastic form reduced to light relief and detached from the atmosphere, colouring that is jewel-like and intense because its harmonies are achieved outside the chiaroscuro, and surface composition—those are the three pivotal elements in the style of Manet, and from them are born images which impress the observer with their vivid presence and immediacy.

This effect caused by Manet's images is closely bound up with his manner of execution. His friend Antonin Proust recalls:

Dear Manet—his eye was so keen that Paris has never known an idler who idled so usefully. . . . He would sketch a mere nothing in a notebook—a profile, a hat, a fleeting impression—and the next day a friend, catching sight of it, would say, "You ought to finish that." Manet would laugh. "Do you take me for a historical painter?" "Historical painter" was in his mouth the most damning insult that could be hurled at an artist. "There is nothing more ludicrous," he would say, "than to reconstruct historical figures. Do you paint a man according to the description given on his hunting license? There is only one thing that is real: to put down immediately, with one stroke, what you see. When you get it, you have it. When you don't get it, you try again. Everything else is nonsense." [5]

This does not mean that Manet was a "quick sketch artist." On the contrary, he is known to have required his models to sit for him repeatedly, and he constantly redid his canvases, rubbing them out and beginning again. But the point is that he did rub out; he did not complete his pictures, did not over-finish them. He made endless studies on the canvas, until he was satisfied by the sudden appearance of the image. He was the opposite of an improviser, but he wished to give and he did give his images the character of improvisations. The finish demanded by the Academy and the public was for him simply falsehood. And it is enough to glance at a nude by Courbet to understand how the value of presence and immediacy possessed by the *Olympia* depends on the unfinished finish, if one may so put it, that is characteristically Manet.

His non-finishing of his pictures is, of course, related to his

[5] Antonin Proust, *Edouard Manet—Souvenirs,* 1913, pp. 29–30.

personal character and to his position in society. He was impulsive and brilliant, and he hid the deepest impulses of his life, and his indomitable courage, behind a worldly lightness of spirit; his soul was full of sunlight, but his lips had an ironical twist. Constable and Corot were capable of finishing their landscapes (which for themselves they preferred to leave "unfinished") out of respect for academic opinion, bowing humbly before it even when they felt themselves in the right. Manet bowed to no one, was quite incapable of finishing, for if he had paid homage to popular opinion he would have felt himself ridiculous.

Thus he revolted against both tradition and nature, and he made use of both to do with as he pleased; he understood neither the limitations of what he did nor his own reasons for doing it, but he did it with a seemingly carefree jauntiness, in which were combined the dandy and the street urchin.

The result of this paradoxical fusion of contrasting elements was that Manet cut himself free from tradition not only without any intention of doing so but even remaining unaware that he had done so. Once free, he found himself face to face with reality. And of reality he made use—but simply as a pretext for doing as he wished. Since he was Manet, doing as he wished resulted in the production of images that transcend and transfigure reality, precisely because they are images, pure forms, which serve no purpose, but which we look at with never-ending surprise.

Both before and after painting the *Olympia,* Manet frequently indulged his liking for depicting Spanish motifs and costumes. *L'Espagnolisme*—Spanishness—was fashionable in

Paris, and Manet enjoyed it, either because it was fashionable, or because of his sympathy for Velasquez and Goya, or simply as a pretext for using brilliant colours. The most famous of his Spanish canvases is *Lola de Valence,* 1862 (fig. 4), which inspired a quatrain of Baudelaire's. The figure is solidly constructed, the head vivacious and provocative, the arm perhaps too beautiful in itself for the style of the whole, and the dress too multi-coloured to accord with the rest. It seems more a vivacious tour de force than a complete work of art.

Concert in the Tuileries Gardens, 1860 (fig. 3), is a scene of fashionable modern life and an attempt to harmonize a landscape, a series of quickly sketched portraits of friends, and the surrounding crowd. It is a timid and at the same time a controversial work; it shows Manet's wish to achieve surface images even though the garden is represented with a certain depth and his wish to give casualness to the composition in order to affirm its realism. Despite a few happy passages the total result is confused.

Finding himself one day with Antonin Proust on the banks of the Seine at Gennevillers, where the Manet family owned some property, Edouard declared, "I have to paint a nude. Well, I am going to paint one . . . in the transparency of the atmosphere, with people like those we are looking at now. I shall be harshly criticized, but people can say what they please."[6] It was shortly thereafter that he painted his large picture *The Picnic,* 1863 (fig. 1).

The idea of composing a scene showing a nude woman and fully clothed men in the open air came from Giorgione's *Concert Champêtre,* and the composition of the three princi-

[6] Antonin Proust, *op. cit.,* p. 43.

pal figures was suggested by an engraving by Marcantonio after a drawing by Raphael. The engraving had a linear rhythm which uncoiled in depth, and which Manet suppressed because of his desire to avoid full relief and to separate his images by means of flat areas of colour. And indeed his colour effect is quite successful in its contrast of pure blue tones and shaded greys and yellows. The landscape is interesting in its rapid and summary execution, the still life marvellous in its colour. The figures are vivacious, the head of the man at the left is quite strong, the nude well modelled without shadows; but the figures do not harmonize with the landscape, which is neither a background for them nor a setting. Therefore, although certain sections are excellent, the picture does not exist as a whole. The failure of this canvas is easily explained by reference to what we have noted above concerning the quality of the image characteristic of Manet's art. *The Picnic* is a compromise between the representation of reality, as the Renaissance had conceived it, and the mediaeval presentation of the image, as Manet felt it. The two visions are juxtaposed but not blended, and hence the composition is unbalanced. *The Picnic* may be considered the crisis of Manet's career, and the resolution of the crisis is the *Olympia,* which was painted immediately after, in the same year, 1863.

The significance of this resolution, this liberation, is clearly apparent in *The Fifer,* 1866 (fig. 6), in which the dark blue image emerges with such exceptional energy from its light grey background. Jamot thought he saw in the face of the fifer the features of Victorine Meurend, and a harmless, unimportant trick of this kind would be perfectly in keeping with Manet's style. The important thing here is the value of the image, so immediate and rapid, a result of the singing of the colours in their harmony of dark on light. This picture is strikingly different from the *Lola,* with its effect of chiaroscuro. And noteworthy also is the way in which a few synthetic tones are concentrated in the vitality of the image, whereas the varicoloured tones are scattered. *The Fifer* is all pure creation, the work of a happy moment, a magical achievement that goes beyond all trickery and all reality.

A confirmation that Manet found his perfection in the image and only in the image comes to us from the artist himself, in his frequent dissatisfaction concerning his large compositions, as contrasted with his higher opinion of certain of the individual images in them. His *Episode of a Bullfight* had been considerably criticized in the Salon of 1864 because of a deformation of perspective, and Manet cut the picture into several pieces; one fragment, the *Dead Bullfighter,* in the Widener Collection in Philadelphia, is a magnificent pictorial bit. Again, on June 18, 1867, the Emperor Maximilian was shot by a firing squad in Mexico; the theme appealed to Manet, and he used it five times, in three paintings, a sketch, and a lithograph. The composition was never happy, however, not even in the latest of the paintings, which is in the museum of Mannheim, and the canvas that would seem from its fragments to have been the most elaborate was cut into several pieces by the artist. The fragment known as *Soldier Examining His Rifle* (fig. 5) in the National Gallery of London is a miraculously vital example of pictorial power, of pure creativity.

Manet felt no such need to cut up the canvas known as *Lunch in the Studio* (fig. 7). Here the total effect is most successful. There is no action, merely a presentation of images. The seated man smoking at the right and the old weapons and armor at the left are incidental: one's chief attention is given to the young man in the foreground and the woman in the background. Their position and their proportions tell us that they are on two different planes in depth, planes that are well defined and evident, and yet not natural, that is, not so represented as to create an illusion. By this means the appearance of the two images is given a character of unreality which nevertheless captures our attention as though it were actual and present, a character that is magical and poetic.

The colour accentuates this quality: in the foreground the black of the jacket, farther back the mauve grey of the woman's dress, still farther back the white of the vase. All the rest is a muted accompaniment. Thus there is a relationship of dark tone on light, not for the purpose of fusing the images, but on the contrary to separate them, emphasizing their presence and vitality.

Of Manet's portraits, the best are those in which the artist tried least to be objective, to produce a finished effect, but rather allowed himself to be carried away by his need for style. A comparison between the portrait of *Zola* in the Louvre (fig. 8) and that of *Berthe Morisot with a Muff* (fig. 9) is instructive. The vitality of Mlle. Morisot's irrepressible grace belongs in the realm of that second nature which is art; in the picture of Zola vitality is attenuated by accurate finish and superfluous detail.

The Salon, preparation of pictures for the Salon, determination to win the battle of the Salon, discouragement following refusal to be admitted, failure of pictures that were admitted—all those things hampered Manet in his creation. As relaxation he painted flowers and still lifes, executing particularly large numbers of such canvases in 1864 and 1866. They are usually masterpieces.

Towards the end of the 1870's Manet's interest in open-air scenes became more pronounced. There are beach scenes, effects of light on boats in crowded harbours, scenes of hills and houses. He had been present at the fall of Paris in 1871 and had later gone to the South of France, and this, too, had encouraged him in open-air painting.

The Bordeaux Harbour of 1871 (fig. 10) is a perfect fusion of surface and depth effects, of image and representation. The dark tones are in blue, the light tones in sky blue and white; there are a few strips of green, a few slight touches of red. Colours are few but quite rich in tone. In both foreground and background form is identical with the effect of light, which transcends the confusion of forms.

As early as 1866 Claude Monet had begun to paint in the open air—not following the usual practice of preparing scenes in the open to be finished in the studio, but completing even his large pictures out of doors in order to achieve that unified treatment of figures and landscape which had eluded Manet in *The Picnic*. Monet painted his *Women in the Garden* (fig. 49) in a garden of Ville d'Avray, and Courbet visited him while he was at work on it. Manet gave no thought to this problem but concerned himself with varying and intensifying his light-effects, with the result that he gradually lightened his plastic form. For such studies seascape or landscape served better than the human figure.

As early as 1864 he had painted *Races at Longchamp* (fig. 11), in which the distribution of light and dark areas not only results in perfect harmony between surface and depth but also gives the image a mobility which suggests the vibrancy of light.

This effect of light may be compared with that in *The Croquet Game,* Paris, 1873 (fig. 12). Here the reflections of the light strike the foliage of the trees, the ground, and even, almost completely, the figures, in such a way as to unify the vision. There are no longer light and dark areas, but the lights and shadows interpenetrate each other and become the protagonists of the picture.

Similarly, in *On the Beach,* 1873 (fig. 13), the transparencies in the feminine figure and the reflections in the sea make the entire canvas vibrant with inner life.

Unquestionably the predominance of light-effects in a painting does not harmonize easily with the ideal of the image, and *The Croquet Game* and *On the Beach* clearly show a radical change of style from the *Olympia.* This change would be inexplicable were it not for impressionism. Among the impressionists it was Monet and Renoir who interested Manet. He was attracted by their light-effects, their divided colours, and their light, jewel-like tones.

Monet and Renoir had founded impressionism on the principle of outdoor painting, and it is well known how in 1874, unable to exhibit in the Salon, they and Pissarro, Sisley, Berthe Morisot, Cézanne, and Degas organized a private exhibition, which caused a scandal and gave them the name impressionists.

Manet did not wish to be identified with them, and he

continued his own battle with the Salon. In 1873 he was represented there with *The Good Beer* (fig. 14), which brought him his first great public success. The year before, Durand-Ruel had bought in one purchase twenty-three of his pictures, almost the entire contents of his studio. He was understandably particularly happy at this time: success was his; he was sought after in the Salon and in society, and he enjoyed it all.

It was natural that he should attribute to his style this success which was really due to his virtuosity, and since he was perfectly sincere, he tried to prolong his success by employing the impressionistic qualities which seemed to him advanced. The success was short-lived, but in the meantime he had enriched his taste with jewel-like brush strokes, with graduated and diffused light, with light colours, and especially with a greater confidence in nature.

Full of optimism, he easily achieved in his compositions of human figures the necessary accord between the supremacy of light and his need of images.

Meanwhile he painted several marvellous landscapes. *The Grand Canal, Venice,* 1875 (fig. 15), and *The Road Menders, rue Mosnier,* 1878 (fig. 16), are among his most brilliant impressionistic effects. In both pictures he abandons himself to the vibrancy of the light, participates in the vitality of everything in nature, and makes a style of reflections in water and their extension to figures and houses; both pictures are brilliant with divided colours, synthesized by the human eye. Manet is by now a perfect master of the impressionistic technique. But he is far from abandoning his personal preferences. These can be perceived in certain contrasts of tones, certain dark areas, which emerge from the fusion of the whole—the black of the gondola in *The Grand Canal,* the dark patches of the carriages in *The Road Menders.* These contrasts, these interruptions of the total fusion, are a residue of Manet's earlier preference for the opposition of lights and darks. But they have their function in the new style as well. They accentuate the delicacy of the gradations of light, the tenuous harmonies of precious colours. And under the cosmic vibrancy of light are to be found broken, witty lines revelatory of Manet's irrepressible and all but unconscious liking for the controversial.

The impressionist style was also fruitful for Manet in his flower paintings, of which he did many during the last months of his life in 1882 and 1883. *Peonies in a Vase,* 1883 (fig. 17), is a miracle of pinks and reds detached from their dark background and of reflections in the transparencies of the glass vase.

Landscapes, flowers, still lifes, portraits—Manet could not be content with these. At no time did he realize that his creative force was concentrated in the image, and the idea of composition, which had obsessed him in 1863 and led him to paint *The Picnic,* continued to appeal to him. In this his assimilation of the impressionist style was no obstacle, but his fusion of figures and landscapes always achieved more satisfactory results in sketches than in his large-scale paintings with human figures in the foreground.

The Railroad, 1879, *Argenteuil,* 1874 (fig. 18), *M. and Mme. Jules Guillemet in the Greenhouse,* 1879, all have magnificently painted figures in the foreground and more or less developed landscapes in the background. Unity of figure and landscape is lacking, and lacking also is any magic in the appearance of the images. Perhaps they are too real, perhaps the light and the emphatically drawn lines that determine the images are imperfectly harmonized. These are works of prime importance in the development of Manet's taste, but not of his art.

In *The Restaurant of Père Lathuile,* 1879 (fig. 19), his mistake becomes graver. It is a genre scene, an illustration for a story that might have been written by Maupassant, with an accent of vulgarity hitherto unsuspected in Manet. Perhaps this results from the attitude in which the young man is posed (which gives the impression of having been taken from a snapshot), perhaps from the relation between the actions of the two figures, perhaps from Manet's wish to depict their psychological relationship—all of which are elements utterly extraneous to his fancy.

Fortunately his instinct led him to other, more masterly solutions of the relationship between images and setting.

In the Boat, 1874 (fig. 20), *The Waitress,* 1878 (fig. 21), *A Bar at the Folies-Bergère,* 1881 (fig. 22), are the greatest masterpieces of Manet's last decade of activity.

In the Boat is a complete success. The cutting off of the boat at each side of the picture, the pose of the figures and their relation one to the other—suggestive of space even though they remain in the foreground—give the sense of the swift passing of a vision. And the dark brown of the boat, the tan of the flesh, the blue of the woman, and even the white of the man, considerably shaded with blue, stand out in tone against the light blue-green water, resulting in a unity of dark on light. The group thus constitutes a single image. The rapidity with which it is revealed to the spectator and its magical, apparitionlike character differ from these same qualities in the works prior to 1870.

In *Argenteuil,* on the other hand, although the vision of the Seine is magnificent and the figures are treated impressionistically with consummate ability, the group is static and without true relation to the background; thus unity of vision and rapidity of effect are lacking. Instead of a swift, all-embracing vision, there is concentration on single parts of the picture, the result of the excessive attention demanded by their masterly execution.

The happy composition of *The Waitress* is due to the fact that the various figures in the foreground form a compact group, extremely varied in light, shadow, and contrasts, organized as a single image of light and shadow transcending the single figures. In this picture the blacks are numerous, and take on a colour value whose dark solidity contrasts with the transparencies floating lightly about it. The distant background is light—hence the unity of the vision of dark on light is perfectly achieved.

A Bar at the Folies-Bergère is certainly the most phantasmagorical work ever painted by Manet. Out of his mastery of the play of light he devised an unreal setting for the barmaid who is his central figure. She is shown standing, directly facing the spectator, but there is nothing static about her. The ornaments, the bottles, the flowers in the vase suffice to give her a phantomlike appearance. And this effect is infinitely increased by the mirror behind her, in which we see that she is talking to a customer and see also the crowd sitting at tables in the bar—all of this scarcely hinted at, as in a day-dream. No painter before or since Manet has transposed reality into such a phantasmagoria of lights. The girl's image is magical precisely because she is a phantom among phantoms, with a grace that is extremely attractive.

In the last years of his life Manet no longer felt the urge to struggle. His enemies never ceased their attacks, and some of his best friends (among them, unfortunately, Zola himself) drew away from him because of their dislike of his lack of finish, but he enjoyed the esteem and the admiration of a sufficient number of people to be able to forget the others.

During his last long illness he found that the technique of pastel fatigued him less than that of oil, and in his last years he drew in pastel numerous heads of women with infinite grace, never accentuating the peculiarities of his style, never insisting on impressionistic light-effects, but simply abandoning himself to the pleasure of contemplation. For example, *The Model for A Bar at the Folies-Bergère,* 1881 (fig. 23), seems to us far less phantomlike in pastel than in the large oil—more the natural woman, exquisite in her grace, delicate and flowerlike in her youth, and possessed of a highly civilized elegance.

On April 30, 1883, Manet died. A large number of persons were present at this funeral. "He was greater than we thought," Degas said. In January, 1884, a great exhibition of his work opened in—of all places—the Academy of Fine Arts.

In 1890 Claude Monet initiated a public subscription, which purchased the *Olympia* and offered it to the state. And in 1907 Clemenceau directed that it be exhibited at the Louvre. By that time, Manet belonged to the eternal life of art.

Chapter Two

EDGAR DEGAS

ANET HAD to combat other artists, the critics, and the public, and in his struggle he was sustained by his inner certainty and his carefree nature. Degas isolated himself in order not to have to combat the opinions of others. He looked down on most men and their opinions from the height of his pride—a pride of which he was fully conscious. But he had to combat *himself*—his education and his prejudices—and in his struggle he was urged on by a never-ending doubt and a heroic will that were those of a seeker.

He came from a family of bankers, of a reactionary tendency that had been accentuated by the danger which the painter's grandfather had run during the Terror; he had had to flee to Naples and there had founded a flourishing bank and a family, which intermarried with Italian nobility.

Edgar Degas, born in 1834, grew up in an environment in which there was a keen interest in art and in particular an admiration for Ingres. When he finished the lycée and registered at the School of Fine Arts he entered the studio of Louis Lamothe (1822–69), one of Ingres's favorite pupils. He was introduced to Ingres, his god, who gave him words of advice that have since become celebrated: "Draw lines, young man, many lines, either from memory or from nature; that

is the way you will become a great and noble artist." Since
Ingres himself was continually inspired by the masters of the
Italian Renaissance, since Degas's father considered Lamothe's
drawing somewhat soft, and since many relatives—grandfather, aunts, and cousins—lived in Naples and Florence, it
was natural that the young painter should make frequent
visits to Italy. There he spent the greater part of the years
1857 and 1858 copying many paintings and drawings of the
fifteenth and sixteenth centuries, and he returned to Paris
master of a sure, strong, fine line, in the best taste of the school
of Ingres. It was the classic line, more or less that which
Manet had learned in the school of Couture, and which at
that time almost every young painter was taught in the
schools. Manet, Renoir, and Cézanne quickly rebelled against
it. Not so Degas. Neither his family and social background
nor the excellence of his artistic models are sufficient to explain
fully his enthusiasm for the classic line. He had a natural
talent for drawing; he took pleasure in the subtle, continuous,
pure outline; he saw in it a source of nobility, and the only
means of achieving the beauty which he worshipped; line
became for him a passion, and he succeeded so completely
in possessing it that no one among the direct or indirect followers of Ingres drew as well. Had he continued to follow
this path, he would have become an academic painter, certainly the greatest of the academic painters after Ingres.

But Degas, with his powerful talent, realized that something was raging about him which was not in complete
harmony with Ingres, something called realism. Courbet's
art inevitably seemed too vulgar to him, and he seems to
have been attracted rather by the theory of realism as pro-

pounded by Louis-Emile Duranty (1833–80) in his news-paper, *Réalisme*, beginning in 1856. Duranty urged the abandonment of formulas and the antique, in order that the artist might reproduce simply and sincerely what was before his eyes. The only means which Degas had at his disposal were his extremely pure line and the consequent practice of chiaroscuro—two abstractions from reality which tended to lead to the attainment of ideal beauty. To depict the real, it was necessary to employ those means in such a way as to individualize images; in portraiture, for example, it was quite permissible to give nobility to one's subject, but not to such a degree as to cause them to lose their individual char-acter. The young Degas began to paint himself and members of his family: except for his copies of old paintings and his academic studies, he painted almost exclusively portraits be-tween 1853 and 1859.

Degas was sensitive to colour, as is shown not only in the softly harmonious colours of his first pictures but also in the notes made during his stay in Italy. But the same reason that caused him to strive to attain to the line of Ingres, so rooted in the Renaissance taste, resulted in his being in-spired by the colour of the old masters: his desire to attain "the spiritual impulse of a Mantegna with the verve and colour of a Veronese." [1] Even in the last years of his life he continued to search for the "secrets" of Venetian colour—without finding them, naturally, since they were not secrets but merely ways of seeing which could not be revived in the nineteenth century.

Those, then, were the three irreconcilable terms against

[1] Lemoisne, *Degas*, I, p. 13.

which Degas's iron will had to contend: a realistic aim, idealized line, and colouring that was rooted in the past.

Several of his mental attitudes made his struggles all the more difficult. Vasari would have said that Degas had a strong liking for the difficulties of art—and, it may be added, for the difficulties of life, as well. He rejected any easy solution, always preferring to look beneath the surface, to burrow deeply into any problem. From this his spontaneity suffered, and of spontaneity he took all too much pleasure in defiantly disavowing any trace. "No art is as lacking in spontaneity as mine. What I do is the result of reflection and of study of the great masters; as for inspiration, spontaneity, temperament—I know nothing of them." [2] If one remembers that in the second half of the nineteenth century, and especially in realistic circles, art was given a social and humanitarian function and gave rise to much rhetoric on the subject of "temperament," the new *deus ex machina*, the barbed, controversial character of Degas's attitude can be understood. The more jealously he hid his passion for art the greater it grew, and to it he dedicated, indeed sacrificed, his life. At moments he even seemed to be an enemy of art: "Art is vice. It is not to be embraced in lawful wedlock, but raped. He who says art, says sacrifice. Art is treacherous and cruel." It goes without saying that in his best paintings Degas's creativity goes beyond this state of mind, which is expressed only in controversy; however, a substratum of controversy exists in all his work, giving it a particular accent. His passion for art was certainly a fever, but an intellectual fever.

The sincerity of his attitude toward art is proved by its

[2] *Ibid.,* p. 117.

consistency with his life. Even as a young man he took pleasure in isolation. At the age of twenty-four in Assisi he felt momentarily drawn to religion, which would allow him to lead an isolated life. That moment was fleeting, however: he preferred to continue in his proud cynicism.

His pride was the result of the quality of his mind, which was on a higher level—more serious and rigorous—than those of the persons with whom he came in contact. The humiliation of the defeat of 1871 led him to hold his contemporaries in low esteem, and since he had no political or social interests, he isolated himself in a proud egotism, which toward the end of his life became tragic. His isolation and his caustic tongue gained him a reputation for cruelty, which has been exploded by Ernest Rouart and others. There is no doubt, however, that the legend originated in the care which Degas took to hide his own affectionate and kindly qualities.

The portraits of his youthful period clearly mirror his faith in drawing, his unbounded ability, his refinement, his moral rigour.

The Bellelli Family (fig. 24), which represents one of Degas's aunts, an uncle, and two cousins, was executed in Paris about 1860–62 after numerous studies made in Naples and Florence between 1856 and 1860. Its size (two and half metres wide) and the complexity of the theme (a group of figures in their setting) indicate the zeal with which Degas applied himself to the task. It is a realistic scene, but representation of space is lacking, and for this reason even the very fine drawing does not succeed in giving a sense of volume, nor does the very delicate and harmonious colour (sky blue,

white, and black) achieve an effect of tone. The attention of
the painter is concentrated on the images. These relatives of
Degas have no particular expression and are engaged in no
activity; they merely display the "distinction" peculiar to
their aristocratic class, their desire for order (shared also by
the painter), their strong-willed, unamiable natures which
protect them against familiarity. In the face of his aunt Degas
has captured the refinement which for him took the place of
beauty, but he has not achieved any great vitality. As Degas
saw them, these people were more inspiring of respect than
anything else, and thanks to the very rare quality of its drawing the picture has the same effect, but in the presence of so
much respect artistic response is weak.

About seven years later, in 1867, Degas painted the portrait
of *M. and Mme. Morbilli,* his sister and brother-in-law (fig.
26). The drawing is still Ingres-like, but it has achieved far
greater energy; thanks to this the images stand out powerfully even though volume and space are still largely absent.
The colours, especially, have an intensity not present in *The
Bellelli Family*: the black and grey of Morbilli's clothing contrast with the yellow of the wall, and the contrast of yellow
and black is continued in the table cover, while the figure of
the woman harmonizes with the blue grey of the hanging in
the background. The effect is not one of tone but a perfectly
realized, vivacious harmony of contrasting colours. In this
portrait the fusion of Ingres-like drawing and realistic intent
can be said to be achieved, and yet we continue to feel a lack
of life in the dourness of the people depicted.

To find a pure masterpiece, with no residuum of intellectualistic stylism, we must look at the small *Portrait of a Young*

Woman, 1867 (fig. 25). The chestnut hair and the brown-black dress are perfectly harmonized as tones with the grey background. Although the colours are not intense, the light that caresses the face reveals Degas's concern for the beginning of a formal value in which Ingres's line is barely suggested. Everything that the painter knows, everything that he desires, is extraneous to the sensitivity which quivers in that caress of light and opens the way to the creation of absolute art. It is a sublime moment of pause along Degas's path of constant, painful search.

The Ingres tradition approved of the historical picture, and Degas tried his hand at several before realizing that it was a blind alley. His last attempt was the *War Scene in the Middle Ages or the Misfortunes of the City of Orleans* (fig. 27). The composition is parallel to the plane of the background; the figures are not seen in space and display no action; the colour is dead except for one spot of yellow in the archer bending his bow; the dramatic contrast of lights and darks in the landscape is completely unsuccessful. Several preliminary drawings of the nude victims are very beautiful but transferred to canvas they become purely academic.

After this unsuccessful attempt Degas turned elsewhere. Knowing that he was successful with portraits, he resolved, according to the realistic formula, to tell the story of his own time. During the Franco-Prussian War he had served in the artillery, and later, depressed by the defeat, he gave himself a change of scene by going at the end of 1872 to New Orleans, where an uncle and two brothers were in the cotton business. There he found the family affection which he prized, but he felt out of his element and after a few months returned to

Paris. A letter from New Orleans dated December 5, 1872, to his friend Henri Rouart, tells us of what his aspirations must have continued to be on his return to France: "I am staying at home and beginning a regular life such as has never been led by anyone except Bouguereau, whose energy and workmanship I do not expect to equal. I am thirsty for order.... I dream of something well painted, well ordered in all its parts (something in the style of Poussin and the late Corot)." [3] Even if the reference to Bouguereau be considered a bit of bravado, it is clear that in 1872 order and the Academy were still synonymous in Degas's mind.

The pictorial result of his trip to New Orleans is *The Office of a Cotton Firm*, 1873 (fig. 28). It aims to be a scene of contemporary life, the kind of scene made fashionable by Manet and by Degas's other realist, soon-to-be-impressionist friends; actually it is a collection of family portraits with space and surrounding objects developed in a way hitherto unknown in Degas. In a scene of this kind colour has an important function, and this seems to exasperate Degas: his colour becomes banal, as in the red of the wall. The form, on the other hand, is so precise and portraitlike in the various images and their arrangement is so casual that no composition of any kind results. It is evident that although Degas wished to paint a realistic scene he did not believe in realism and that he exaggerated the banality of the effect.

Nevertheless he persisted, and he treated another naturalistic subject à la Zola in *The Rape*, 1874 [4]—the gravest error of taste he ever committed. The objectivity and ability of the execution show all the more clearly the lack of style, the lack of

---

[3] *Lettres de Degas*, p. 11.   [4] Lemoisne, *op. cit.*, p. 348.

emotional participation in the scene. One could even imagine that the artist felt a repugnance for his own work.

The Office of a Cotton Firm and *The Rape* close one period of Degas's style, the period which can be called academic-realist, and in which he was a prisoner of form. During the past several years he had been hinting at the motifs and the ways of seeing which were to liberate him and which were to be developed in his next period.

Before mentioning the external factors—Manet, the impressionists, the Japanese—which encouraged Degas's new style after 1873, it is interesting to look inside the artist himself for reasons underlying the change. About 1873 that very sensitivity which had made it possible for him to step outside the academic style even in his first period and to surpass every academician of his time took the upper hand over what he had learned. His continuing passion for precise, incisive line had to adapt itself to new demands, imposed by two elements: movement and the effect of light and shadow. The struggle between line and these other elements was a bitter one, and Degas never ceased to be proud of his accomplishments as a draftsman. But after 1873 line was never again the absolute victor. At times it even seemed that light and shadow might triumph, but this was illusory. The effect of light and shadow was for Degas an expansion of line, and because of this it never sprang naturally out of his colour as it did for Titian, Tintoretto, Rembrandt, Manet, and Cézanne; in his case it was more intellectual, more tormented, more limited. But for this very reason it assumed in his work a value that was particularly rare and rigorous, incomparable

in energy and finesse. Degas's struggle to maintain simultane-
ously two contradictory principles and to dominate them both
is the reason for many of his failures, but it is also the reason
for many of his masterpieces.

Several years before the war of 1870, Degas had become a
friend of Manet and a frequenter of the Café Guerbois, where
the future impressionists and naturalist writers foregathered;
and after 1870 he continued to frequent the same group at
the Café de la Nouvelle Athènes. In the company of those
who were to revolutionize the world of painting (and not of
painting only) Degas felt himself isolated. One of his remarks
to the painter Sickert explains the reason, "I always tried to
persuade my colleagues to seek new effects according to the
principles of drawing, which I consider more fruitful than
colour. But they refused to listen to me and did otherwise."

Furthermore, he was indifferent to nature in the open
country, which was at once the delight and the moral support of the impressionists. In 1873 he wrote Henri Rouart,
"Cane in hand, but without a parasol, I shall be studying
values and the curves of roads on little hills. . . . Nature! I
expect to find a less mad joy in it than you would; only a
little rest for my eyes, and some relaxation." [5] In that year
Degas did make an effort to share the other impressionists'
interest in Cézanne's beloved "curving roads," but his scepti-
cal inhibition was too strong for him. In 1887 he admitted
this to Henry Lerolle: "When we love nature, we can never
know whether she loves us in return." (At this point it is
impossible not to think of Ruskin, who was well aware that

[5] *Lettres de Degas*, pp. 14, 15.

nature does not return man's love but who loved her desperately none the less.)

Degas told Moreau-Nélaton in 1907 that he was irritated by the thought of landscapists who paint *"from nature,* as if art did not live by conventions. Don't speak to me of those fellows who clutter up the fields with their easels." [6] He would have liked to be a tyrant, with the power to shoot them all.

With such ideas as that, any community of work with the impressionists was impossible. Degas frequented them and at times admired them, but he felt that he and they were in opposite camps. He wished to portray the same motifs as they but by the use of line.

In 1882 he wrote Henri Rouart about the Salon, "The Manet is stupid and fine, like a playing card; it makes no impression; it is a Spanish *trompe l'oeil;* he is a painter who ... Well, you'll see for yourself." [7] But a year later, after Manet's death, he confessed, "He was greater than we thought." He reproached Renoir for making his pictures of women beautiful. He did not spare Monet an occasional shaft, such as, "The weather is beautiful, but much too Monet for my poor eyes," [8] though he subsequently said to Sickert, "Damn that fellow Monet, everything he does turns out right the first time, whereas I always give myself so much trouble and it isn't what I want at all." [9] Degas had a particular sympathy for Pissarro, of whom he wrote on one occasion, "He is delightful in his ardour and his faith."

When the group of painters later called impressionists was inaugurated in 1874 for the purpose of exhibiting outside the

[6] *L'Amour de l'Art,* July, 1931.
[7] *Lettres de Degas,* p. 44.
[8] Lemoisne, *Degas,* p. 155.
[9] *Burlington Magazine,* November, 1917.

Salon, Degas joined the rebels even though he had not been refused by the Salon like the others and had even received a half promise of an honorable mention; indeed he was one of the most active organizers of the exhibition, obtaining numerous recruits. Manet, on the other hand, who was much closer to the impressionists than Degas, remained faithful to the Salon.

Degas participated in all the succeeding impressionist exhibitions (which ended in 1886) except that of 1882, when he stipulated as a condition of his exhibiting the exclusion of Monet, Renoir, and Sisley, who had committed the crime of showing at the Salon.

Degas's willing participation in these secessionist exhibitions was at once generous, courageous, and clever. Generous because he gave the impressionists undoubted support, courageous because he defied the pharisaical critics and the official painters, making himself a rebel against the conventional order of the Salons to attain to a truly artistic order. But he also profited from his abstention from the Salon. Zola wrote in 1880:

> M. Degas alone has derived a true profit from the private exhibitions of the impressionists; and the reason for this must be sought in his talent. M. Degas was never one of those persecuted by the official Salons. He was accepted, and even relatively well shown. But since his artistic temperament is a delicate one, since he does not have an impressive power, the crowd passed before his pictures without seeing them. Quite understandably the artist was annoyed, and he realized that he would gain

certain advantages by showing in a small group [*petite chapelle*], where his fine, carefully executed pictures could be seen and studied by themselves. And indeed, as soon as he was no longer lost in the crowd of the Salons, he was known to everyone: a circle of fervent admirers gathered around him.[10]

Whatever the truth of that may be, there is no question that Degas derived one other advantage from his collaboration with the impressionists: an impulse to renew his art.

Since 1862 Degas had been interested in horse-races as a motif and had painted several more or less finished pictures of the subject. Between 1870 and 1873 he painted *The Carriage at the Races* (fig. 29), in which the linear style is still evident, exceptional in its refinement, with its images set in a rarefied atmosphere in which it is impossible for them to breathe. The brown of the horses, the black of the carriage, the grey and the pale purple of the dresses, the acid green of the field, and the grey of the sky—all the colours are precious, but they do not make up into any relationship of light and shadow. The off-center composition indicates the artist's capricious will, and the diagonal position of the carriage occupies no space and seems to have the function of causing one horse partially to emerge from the canvas. One senses the artist's sharp eye, his sensitivity for nuance, his boldness in affirming his own subjectivity; but his vision is piecemeal.

If we compare this work with *At the Races* of 1877–80

[10] L. Venturi, *Les Archives de l'Impressionnisme*, II, p. 278.

(fig. 30), we see how completely Degas's vision has changed. Line is implicit, but it does not disturb the relationship between the colours, which are ordered according to the effect of light and shadow and constitute a unified vision; for this reason the tone which gives form to a jockey is the equivalent of that which suggests distant houses; and from the unity of the vision, from the pictorial lack of finish, springs the feeling of the atmosphere, in which every image breathes. It is true that the images lack volume, as does the representation of space, but these are not defects because they are not necessary to the unity of the vision. The foreground figure with its back turned, cut by the frame, is a superfluous bit of eccentricity; the jockeys, on the other hand, pick up and revivify the colour effect with their multi-coloured uniforms of yellows, pink, red, and sky blue, which harmonize perfectly with the green, grey-blue, and grey-yellow areas of the background. In this picture Degas has finally immersed his form in a coloured, breathable atmosphere. He certainly painted his picture from memory, rather than in the open air, and his memory had retained not an abstract form but a vision concrete both in form and colour.

We have already mentioned Degas's determined indifference to nature and his irony concerning landscapists. About 1869, however, he had executed a number of pastel studies which include many beach scenes. He never showed them, and they were all found in his studio after his death. Later he painted some landscapes with contrasts of light and shade, but those of 1869 seem to me more indicative of how Degas saw nature. With a few rather summary but very fine touches, with a horizon line drawn from memory, and with a few nuances, he succeeded in giving a sense of amplitude, of distance, of ecstasy communicated by sky and land, without any precise indication of place.

Degas did not derive inspiration for his light-effects from the country or the sea, but from the theatre, from the café-concert, and from ballet dancers.

Theatre scenes first attracted Degas's attention for other reasons. *The Orchestra of the Paris Opera,* 1868–69 (fig. 31), was painted for the purpose of portraying one of his friends, Désiré Dihau, and his fellow musicians. It is a crowded group of players, well individualized, seen against a number of dancers on a stage, the latter serving as background without participating in the composition. He repeated the motif several times, gradually paying greater attention to light, until in the *Café-Concert, Les Ambassadeurs,* 1876–77 (fig. 32), the stage with its multi-coloured spectacle becomes a protagonist of the picture instead of remaining a background. It is a pastel on monotype, that is, Degas first determined his lights and darks and then thought of his colours. The foreground is out of focus, to direct the attention to the singer, and the apparent disorder of artificial lights and shadows gives a fantastic vivacity to the scene.

Degas's chief fame with the public is as a painter of ballet dancers, and indeed no other subject pleased him as much, and perhaps with no other subject did he find a way of identifying his style. In the theme of dancers there was an infinite number of opportunities to make use of his exquisite line and at the same time to harmonize it with effects of artificial light. Even with this theme, however, he proceeded gradually, not at first renouncing line: it was as though line served to enable him to discover the field in which he was later to find such freedom.

Ballet Classroom, Paris Opera, 1872 (fig. 33), is a delightful miniature, well balanced, realized in space, in which the line of Ingres clearly delineates the beauty of the dancers, but quite delicately, without too much insistence. The dominating tones are greys, blue greys, pale yellows. But though we begin by admiring this as a jewel, we soon feel that we are looking at a pretty toy.

Some years later, about 1877, Degas painted the *Ballet Rehearsal* (fig. 34). Light plays an active part in the scene, but it is magic light—its origin remains unexplained. The excellent drawing is still present, but in this picture it does more than tell of the grace of each dancer: it is functional within the light—the skeleton, so to speak, of the light.

To use light that was impressionistic and colours that were not—that was a program in itself, a motif for masterpieces; Degas knew it, and with changes in details he painted many. Among them is the *Rehearsal in the Ballet Classroom,* 1875 (fig. 35), in which because of the pilasters and the windows the contrast of darks and lights is still more definite and fantastic, with a tone of mystery.

The effect of light revealed to Degas the value of movement. Indeed all pictorial light is a perpetual, cosmic vibrancy, which eliminates every static quality of outline; and quite rightly it transformed pose into movement, giving the dancers that lightness which is their charm.

Although the series of dancers in light and shadow is long and rich in masterpieces, Degas, the eternal seeker, was not content. *Ballet Dancers Tying Their Slippers* (fig. 36) seems to have been painted after 1890, during a period when life seemed tragic to Degas. This motif, so many times repeated, he now executed with his own tragedy in mind; and he expresses tragedy not, of course, in the gestures but in the outlines, which are veritable furrows, and in the contrasts of lights and shadows, all quivering with vital energy and with imprecations against fate. The dominant grey becomes silver, with some touches of green and orange on a brown background. The colour deepens and has greater resonance; movement is more definite; light and shadow are in sharper contrast; the form is more synthetic; life springs more intense than before. Between the *Ballet Classroom, Paris Opera* and the *Ballet Dancers Tying Their Slippers* lies the entire development of Degas's style, from pre-impressionistic realism, through a diffident and almost unwilling approach to impressionism, until he realized a kind of expressionism.

Expressionism, in a broad sense, is a style which simplifies forms to the extreme in order to accentuate expression. Degas liked Japanese prints for their synthetic outlines and for the manner in which they pulled to the surface any suggestion of foreshortening and perspective. On the other hand, for a short time he became obsessed with naturalistic themes à la Zola and impressed them with a dramatic content unknown in his previous work. Both simplification of forms and dramatic content drew Degas toward his kind of expressionism.

The process of simplification is typically represented by *Women Combing Their Hair* (fig. 37), painted about 1877. The horizon line is so high that the pinkish yellow sand of

42

the beach constitutes a unified background against which are stretched the whites of the slips and the chestnut reds of the hair. It is a syntheticism that anticipates Gauguin. The effect is bizarre, but with an undoubted formal and realistic seriousness.

From the elevation of the horizon line Degas derived his best results in *Diego Martelli,* 1879 (fig. 38). The colours are more lively than those which he had used previously. The background has three areas: in grey, purple green, and orange yellow. The floor is blue-grey yellow. The sofa is blue, and on the table are masses of papers in grey, brown, yellow, and black. Martelli is depicted in tones of brown and grey. Here Degas has plunged headlong into colour. But the figure of the man, although placed to one side of the composition, is the center of the artist's interest, and the entire setting is felt to revolve around the portrait. Martelli, well characterized and given considerable solidity of volume, is a mass which emerges from the picture and draws with it everything surrounding it. Thanks to this homogeneous treatment the vision is unified: there is none of the isolation of the image which is always produced by relief. Volumes and intense colouring, those two pictorial qualities had previously been lacking in Degas, and for them one wonders whether he is perhaps indebted to Cézanne. The same motif in a picture in the National Gallery of Scotland, Edinburgh,[11] has greater finish and less energy.

The other aspect of Degas's art, connected with naturalistic themes, appears in *Absinth,* 1876 (fig. 39), and in the *Women Outside a Café, Evening,* 1877 (fig. 40). Here he is seeking

[11] Lemoisne, *Dégas,* p. 519.

subjects which will express his caustic pessimism, express his moral condemnation of what he sees about him.

Thus in *Absinth* he transforms a graceful actress, Ellen Andrée, and his friend Marcellin Desboutin into a prostitute and a derelict, that is, Degas has imagined a subject à la Zola. Nevertheless, light and shadow give this work an exceptional impressionistic pictorial value, even though the colours are not vivid but full of fine nuances.

In the *Women Outside a Café,* a pastel, the effect of artificial light is still more complex, and the caustic intent is all the more evident since the appearance of viciousness is attributed to women who do not belong to a low class.

In those two works and a few others Degas touched on social caricature, which, had he persisted in it, would have made his art anecdotal. But now new impulses drove his spirit towards different ideals.

From 1886, when he participated in the last exhibition of the impressionists, until his death in 1917 Degas did not exhibit. Painting became for him an increasingly private affair. Durand-Ruel and others purchased from him paintings and pastels which disappeared into collections; the public never saw them. The more numerous Degas's admirers became, the greater the distance he kept from them. The abhorrence which he had always felt for the crowd caused him to seek increasing isolation, only occasionally interrupted by the visits of a few trusted friends. He also showed an interest, naturally a despotic one, in a few young painters. He lived alone, without a family, surrounded by countless paintings and sketches and drawings which he kept jealously hidden from all, and by a very choice collection of the works of others, from Ingres and Delacroix to Cézanne and Gauguin. In 1893 he realized that he was on the verge of blindness, but he continued frantically to draw and paint, all the more passionately since he knew that he was working for himself alone. It is natural that in these circumstances his character, which had always been of a cruel severity even towards himself, should become dangerously embittered.

In a letter of 1890 to his friend De Valernes, whom he feared he had offended by harsh criticisms, there emerges a sense of self-pity: "I was, or I seemed to be, harsh with everyone, through a kind of involuntary brutality which sprang from my doubts and my bad humour. I felt myself so poorly endowed and equipped, so weak, whereas it seemed to me that my artistic theories were so right. I glowered at every one and at myself." [12]

In 1884 he wrote to Henri Lerolle, "If you were a bachelor and fifty years old, you would experience such moments, when you close yourself like a door, and not only to your friends. You suppress everything around you, and once alone you annihilate yourself, kill yourself out of disgust. I have made too many plans; here I am, blocked, powerless. . . . I piled all my plans in a cupboard and always carried the key; and now I have lost that key." [13]

It is precisely this self-pity that makes Degas's art more human in the last period of his life.

It is not mere coincidence that from 1880 on, as his art grew freer, Degas used chiefly pastel, often mixed with tempera

---

[12] *Lettres de Degas*, p. 181.   [13] *Ibid.*, pp. 64–65.

and water. From youth he had experimented with this technique, although at that time he preferred painting in oil: this parallels his wish to remain faithful to the tradition of Ingres and yet at the same time to assimilate the impressionism which he mistrusted. But pastel allowed him to paint while doing the drawing that remained his innermost passion, and to obtain colour effects without covering the drawing.

His character as a seeker and his absolute mastery of the human form benefited greatly from the improvisational quality inherent in the technique of pastel; he was able to alter forms and positions by means of successive tracings on different sheets of paper, rather than by constant corrections on the same canvas.

Moreover, pastel gave him the chance to use scintillating colours in drawing in such a way as to cause them to seem what Gromaire has called "irradiations of form"; by means of parallel strokes he obtained even that division of colours which he had previously always avoided.

From 1880 on, therefore, Degas cultivated those pictorial qualities which had appeared in the portrait of Diego Martelli, that is, intense colours and volumes. He abandoned all Japanese influence except for an occasional compositional motif, and he also abandoned the refinement of careful outlines dedicated to ideal beauty, now preferring above all else the expression of vitality and energy.

If we compare with the *Women Combing Their Hair* the picture of the *Women Ironing* of about 1884 (fig. 41), the difference is obvious. The new conception of volume, the naturalness of appearance, the richness of colouring, the objective sureness of execution, the substitution of energy for capricious fancy—these are the effects which Degas still seeks but which he now finds easily. The picture is painted in oil but seems to be pastel: more precisely, his use of pastel is evident in his colour. Against the sky-blue-grey wall are displayed in rounded form the reds, pinks, yellows, whites, and blues of the women. There is no composition of light, but the light adheres to the colours and gives them a plastic appearance.

The theme which chiefly preoccupied Degas in the last years of his life was that of the feminine nude. He has contributed more than anyone else to emancipate the nude from the academic tradition. His nudes are researches into form, into light and movement, into the mechanism of the body and of its action. He aims to be the portraitist of the *bête humaine,* but his enthusiasm for the action and energy of the human mechanism is such that intellectual coldness disappears from the images. Indeed his whole passion, and sometimes his desperation, are reflected in them.

Thus in 1886 he exhibited a series of pastels entitled, "Series of Nudes: Women Bathing, Washing, Drying Themselves, Combing Their Hair, or Having Their Hair Combed." But the mocking tone of the title detracts not at all from the painter's earnestness. Among the hundreds of pastels of nudes, the following four well indicate two aspects of this last vision of Degas.

The Tub, 1886 (fig. 42), is a masterpiece of form and light. More than ten years later Degas painted a similar motif, the *End of the Bath* (fig. 43), in which the strokes of the crayon are less fused, the form less modelled, and the colours are richer and deeper. The image seems to appear under a

47

rain of jewel-like sparks of white, yellow, blue, and purple. Thus in the last two decades of his activity Degas not only acquired a richness of colour that he had previously not known but proceeded to create his form by means of chromatic touches, liberating it from isolation, immersing it in a bath of colour.

A pastel, *Breakfast after the Bath, c.* 1895 (fig. 44), and an oil, *After the Bath,* 1899 (fig. 45), reveal the drama of the painter twisting his nudes into impossible positions, tormenting himself to find new ways of balancing them, making inanimate objects as well as human bodies vibrant with light, and finding serenity in soft pinks and other tender colours.

In these works there is an absolute creative liberty and, despite all the torment, a joy that is not present in the pictures of his early years. It was the joy of creation before the darkness descended over his eyes.

Chapter Three

CLAUDE MONET

I T IS clear to anyone who at this distance of time follows the development of Monet's career that in him destiny and personality were one—until the day when his personality sprang forward and created its own destiny. Favourable external conditions and an unyielding will explain his becoming the principal promoter of that taste which was later called impressionism and his being recognized as the leader of his comrades, several of whom were more completely unfettered artists than he. Impressionism, of course, was a revolution in the way of feeling and seeing, which changed not only painting, but also sculpture, music, literature, and even criticism, and which even today, after seventy years, still retains a certain power of suggestion.

The new taste which Monet did more than anyone else to create is of such breadth that in comparison with its total significance his own artistic achievement, authentic though it is, seems of minor dimensions. Renoir and Cézanne also contributed to the creation of impressionism, but unlike Monet each of them looms large in his own personality against the general backdrop of the coming of the new taste. And when Monet reformed impressionism and attained a kind of symbolism of light, everyone believed (he himself being the first) that that symbolism was still impressionism. And at the end, in an atmosphere of triumph he buried his own creation.

Born in Paris in 1840, Monet passed his early youth in Le Havre, where instead of following a regular schooling he attained local fame as a caricaturist. He attracted the attention of Eugène Boudin (1824–98), a modest man and a fine and sincere landscapist, of whom Baudelaire wrote in 1859 that his sketches of waves and clouds "always carry on the margins a note of the date, the hour, and the prevailing wind. . . . Hide the notes with your hand, and you will *guess* the season, the hour, and the wind." [1]

Although his intentions and method were different from Boudin's, Monet also, thirty years later, was to make precise records of the season and of the hour in painting. One of Boudin's bits of advice to Monet was, "Everything painted on the spot always has a strength, a power, a vivacity of touch which are never recaptured in the studio." That was the whole theory of *plein air*, of outdoor painting.

A little later, Monet was inspired by Johan-Barthold Jongkind (1819–91), a Dutch painter who liked to paint bridges, villages, river banks, and shapeless huts with a nervous, spirited, lively touch, more vibrant than that of his French contemporaries. From Boudin and Jongkind Monet derived the principal elements of his artistic culture.

In Paris, where he went in 1859, he saw and appreciated the work of Courbet, Corot, Daubigny, and later of Manet, and he profited from it surprisingly quickly, although always maintaining a detached attitude, more that of a rebel than of a follower. He did not wish to pursue regular studies at the

[1] *La peinture romantique,* ed. Faure, p. 177.

official Academy or in that of Gleyre, where he spent some time in 1863. There he met those who became his companions, Bazille, Sisley, and Renoir, and he dissuaded them from following academic studies. After the closing of Gleyre's studio Monet took them to Chailly, on the edge of the forest of Fontainebleau, to paint in the open.

Instead of broadening his rather limited artistic culture, Monet devoted himself with complete faith to his happy intuitions concerning the life of nature. These were checked by none of the considerations that he might have derived from an intellectual system, and he rapidly developed his instinctive way of seeing. Manet, studying with Couture and in the Louvre, and Degas, assimilating the line of Ingres and the Italian Renaissance masters, were based very firmly on tradition as compared with Monet.

The drawing and chiaroscuro that are studied in the schools develop the plastic sense of things. Monet was all his life indifferent to the plastic, considerably more so than Renoir or Pissarro, not to mention Cézanne. As Jacques-Emile Blanche has said, Monet "established" rather than drew. But Degas admitted to Sickert that a painting by Monet was always solidly constructed—that he had a sure perception of planes. The pictorial realists headed by Courbet enjoyed painting bodies in relief, or rather they found in modelling the measure of their ability to create illusion. But Monet, since he knew little of the plastic, found it easy to represent not the illusory reality of the object but its simple appearance, and thus he went beyond realism.

Even in his later years Monet was with all but his few intimates serious and taciturn, and he loved solitude and disliked society. Thus the appearance he gave things in his pictures was never vitiated by the desire to please or by flattery. Making no concession, he insisted in the face of everything and everyone on the validity of his interpretation of appearances, until at long last the public agreed that he was right.

He neither wrote nor spoke of art theory, and indeed did not have the intellectual equipment to do so. And yet the production of both his first and last periods is marred by an intellectualistic defect. Perhaps he frequently lacked sufficient reflection, which might have preserved his intuitions in their purity and prevented his rushing into improvised projects that disturbed the artistic result. What he considered important was to arrive at extreme consequences more often than anyone else and before anyone else. These traits brought him the allegiance of his companions, especially Bazille and Renoir, and caused him to become the leader of the impressionists.

The first works which Monet exhibited in the Salon were considerably less novel than those of Manet, and for that reason were received with favour; but in 1869 the jury, the critics, and the public became aware of his revolutionary force, and immediately the doors of the Salon were shut in his face.

He was never content to paint what he saw as he saw it, as were Pissarro and Sisley; he felt the need to create an exceptional effect, to attempt the painting of the impossible. He liked what was *ébouriffant* (startling), and he gave his images of water, sky, houses, and trees a surprising vitality and vibrancy. With his limitless verve, this convinced realist was by nature a visionary.

Monet was represented in the Salon for the first time in 1865, with a painting done the previous year—*Mouth of the Seine at Honfleur* (fig. 46), which enjoyed a notable success. Paul Mantz [2] appreciated its "harmonious colouring in the play of analogous tones . . . a bold way of seeing things and of seizing the attention of the spectator." And it is easy to see that this picture should have been found pleasing. Its motif and its composition are inspired by a painting by Jongkind, painted in the same place and in the same year,[3] and its colour has the rich nuances of Courbet's low, restrained colour range. The representation of deep space is successfully achieved by means of the shore lines, which indicate the middle and distant planes in traditional style. What Monet adds of his own is the "bold way of seeing things and of seizing the attention of the spectator," and this is evident in the brush strokes in the foreground water and in the clouds, which intensify the traditional effect rather than diminish it.

Although Monet had painted, in the open air, a large composition, the *Picnic,* bolder than the similar motif by Manet which had already caused such a scandal, it did not satisfy him, and the picture which he exhibited in the Salon of 1866 was *Camille, or the Lady in the Green Dress* (fig. 47), a portrait of the woman who was to become his wife, completed in a few days. Although its merits were disputed, *Camille* enjoyed a success, and it was compared with Manet. It was really inspired by Courbet, both in colour and in the position of the image, which recalls the woman in the group of society amateurs in the *Studio.* Nevertheless it reveals Monet's per-

[2] *Gazette des Beaux Arts,* XIX, 1865, p. 26.
[3] Moreau-Nélaton, *Jongkind,* Fig. 73.

sonality: his indifference to the plastic allows him to make convincing the movement of the image and the vibrancy of light in the skirt, thus giving the whole an effect of rapidity and immediacy that is lacking in Courbet and quite different from similar effects in Manet.

In the same year he exhibited *St. Germain l'Auxerrois* (fig. 48), which is of far greater importance for his future style. Painted from a terrace of the Louvre, it is an outdoor vision whose principal subject is the shining of light on the foliage of trees. Light is yellow green and shadow is green black, and both are achieved by means of juxtaposed brush strokes that represent the quivering of the atmosphere. The brush strokes are already impressionistic, but the colours are not and lack transparency. Even the blue shadows are opaque, used as though they were black. The church and the houses are stiff, without any of the vitality of the foliage. Unity of vision is lacking, but the manner of painting the foliage reveals Monet's ideal.

Camille was a figure painted in the studio, *St. Germain l'Auxerrois* a landscape done in the open: it was necessary to fuse the two visions. Such a fusion had not turned out successfully for Monet in the *Picnic,* but it did succeed in the *Women in the Garden* of 1867 (fig. 49). The scene is taken from a photograph—an indication of Monet's indifference to composition, which he is willing to leave rather fortuitous. The photograph aimed to suggest deep space, but to this too Monet is indifferent. He has eyes only for plane surfaces and contrasts of colours.

Because of the very lack of volume and modelling in the images, the colours can display all their brightness and variety.

54

The ornamentation of the dresses, the flowers in the lawn, the leaves which stand out from the mass of the foliage, the appearance of the sky through the leaves, the lights which break the shadows, all give the impression of a coloured mosaic. Tonal effect is lacking, lights and shadows are on the same surface as the figures, and thus the light does not penetrate the bodies, does not become formal substance. Local colours are too insistent. In everything there is plan rather than reality of visualization, but the plan is one of unheard-of boldness. Once these traces of effort and plan will have disappeared, once the light begins to be vibrant within the penumbras, every brush stroke will be permeated with life and the vision will be unified; and at that moment art will spring forth, and impressionism will be of age.

To understand the prophetic importance of the *Women in the Garden* it is enough to compare it with a picture painted the same year by Jean Frédéric Bazille (1841–70), the *Family Gathering*. Bazille, Monet's most intimate friend and admirer, was a gifted, cultivated painter, with a richer pigment than Monet, and he had taken over more than Monet from the teachings of Gleyre. In the *Family Gathering* the plastic is not discarded, and although light colours are used, Bazille does not draw such extreme consequences from them as does Monet; and for these reasons, no sooner was Bazille's picture painted than it immediately belonged to the past.

In 1867 Monet worked feverishly on no less than twenty pictures—figures, gardens, regattas, views of Le Havre—and the next year he wrote to Bazille from Fécamp, "Determined as one may be, in Paris one is too taken up with what one sees and hears; and what I shall do here will at least have the merit of not resembling anyone else's work, since it will be simply the impression of what I alone have experienced. The further I go, the more I regret even the little I know; that is what troubles me the most." [4] Except for Renoir, all the impressionists shared this preference for the country; they avoided Paris, with its companionship and theoretical discussions, to preserve their personal manners of seeing.

In the Salon of 1868 one picture by Monet was accepted, but by those of 1869 and 1870 he was inexorably rejected despite outspoken protests from various quarters. Meanwhile his poverty grew pitiless. He ate bread when Renoir brought him some; he had no colours with which to paint; he was desperate, even attempting suicide. When war broke out he went to Holland and then to London, where Daubigny and Durand-Ruel bought a few of his pictures.

In 1871 he returned to France by way of Holland and settled at Argenteuil near Paris, where he had already spent some time in 1868.

Meanwhile he had painted several pictures which were less ambitious than the *Women in the Garden* but more spontaneous and homogeneous.

Argenteuil-sur-Seine, 1868 (fig. 50), is a more unified vision because the dark of the foreground and the light of the background are integrated. Representation of space is not lacking even though reduced to two planes—one near, one distant—and the reflections in the water already suggest vibrancy—still slight but sufficient to give life. Moreover, in the figure there is an exceptional hint of volume, resulting from the relations of colour entirely without chiaroscuro.

[4] Paulain, *Bazille et ses amis,* p. 131.

In 1869 Monet (as well as Renoir) painted *La Grenouillère* (fig. 51), a bathing place on the Seine at Bougival, a motif particularly suited because of the importance of the reflections in the water to accomplish the unity of the impressionistic style. Monet made many sketches of it but was satisfied with none of them. The brush strokes convey the vibrancy of the light, rid objects of their static form, and juxtapose colours in order to achieve an effect of synthesis at a distance, but side by side with the blues a residuum of black keeps the penumbra from being transparent. The foliage of the background, despite the intensity of the yellow green, constitutes a backdrop that does not form part of the unity of the vision.

This attempt to consider the vibrancy of the light as the dominant motif of the picture continues to a greater or lesser extent in the works of 1870 and 1871, several of which, however, under the influence of Turner in London and Jongkind in Holland, mark a moment of pause and reflection.

In 1867 Monet and Bazille had planned an independent exhibition of a group of friends following the refusal of some of them by the Salon, and in 1873, Bazille having died in the war, Monet revived the project in the hope of improving his financial condition, which was increasingly precarious. The next year, against the advice of the critic Duret and of Manet, Monet and his companions together with Degas and other painters opened in 1874 that exhibition of independent artists which was to pass into history as the first exhibition of the impressionists. The name was bestowed on them in derision, inspired by a picture by Monet called *Impression—Rising Sun*.

Everyone has read of the various events connected with the impressionist exhibitions, which were repeated in 1876 and

1877, scandalizing the critics and the public, failing to achieve any financial success, but at least attracting attention to the novelty of the impressionistic way of seeing things. It is also well known how the group of painters, which had been formed in 1874, disintegrated little by little after 1877 although the exhibitions continued until 1886.

Meanwhile, between 1874 and 1877 Monet worked tranquilly despite his financial difficulties; he felt growing up around him the approval of several authentic artists, among them Manet; and he reaffirmed his faith in himself and matured his style to the point of perfection.

Cézanne's phrase, "Monet is only an eye, but what an eye!", although it is not enough to justify Monet's art indicates clearly his function in the history of taste. And Monet himself confessed to Clemenceau, "One day, finding myself beside the death-bed of a woman who had been very dear to me, I surprised myself in the act of watching the colour effects which death was imposing on her still face. There were tones of blue, yellow, grey—tones I cannot describe. That was the point to which I had come. The appearance of these colours of death had shocked me for a moment, but then my reflexes made me resume the activity which was part of my daily life. It was like a farm animal mechanically turning its millstone." [5]

Monet was unquestionably an inventive genius of visualization; he was able to see in relationships of lights and colours what had been seen by no one before him.

By his concentration on light and on colours he found the form most adapted to light-and-color values, abstracting these

[5] Clemenceau, *Claude Monet,* pp. 19–20.

58

values from the other elements of painting and glorifying them. And he did more. Painting with the precise intent to represent light and colour, he excluded spontaneously, almost without being aware of it, every external, literary, and social element, even more radically than Manet. Thus on the occasion of the exhibition of 1877 Georges Rivière was able to write the prophetic sentence: "Treatment of a subject for the tones and not for the subject itself is what distinguishes the impressionists from other painters." [6]

We have seen that Monet's eye was that of a genius, inventive, unique. But what was behind the eye? What was the relation between what Monet saw and what he felt or imagined?

These questions are triumphantly answered in the paintings executed at Argenteuil between 1874 and 1878. These show the pure artist, the creator at his happiest. For example: *Sailboat at Argenteuil,* traditionally believed to be of 1873 (fig. 52); *The Bridge at Argenteuil,* 1874 (fig. 53); *River Banks,* 1874 (fig. 54); *Boats at Argenteuil,* 1875 (fig. 55).

Every trace of controversial intent that still remained in *La Grenouillère* has disappeared from the *Sailboat at Argenteuil.* Instead of contrasts there are gradations of tone, achieved not by the fusion of tints but by their division and juxtaposition, which create optical synthesis. Black has disappeared from the painter's palette, and it is the prismatic colours alone that create the lights and shadows and become the substance of the form. Nothing—neither distance nor nearness, nor objects, nor water, nor sky—interferes with the pictorial style, which flows naturally, transforming everything into an ideal

[6] L. Venturi, *Les Archives de l'Impressionnisme,* II, p. 309.

vision. The representation of space, not articulated, without precise planes, unites nearness and distance. There are purples and yellows in the blue of the water as in the blue of the sky, and yet their difference of tone distinguishes the liquid substance from the ethereal in such a way as to make the mirror of the river a base for the sky. Geometric perspective is abandoned, to reveal the infinite fluidity of atmospheric life. Each of the colours is softened, but their total effect is intense, revealing the painter's contemplation of the day which is dying in a blaze of light on the horizon, while the great sail assumes cool tones in the grey penumbra. It is the contemplation of a visionary who is participating in the very life of the light, in its slow dying in the sunset, in its drawing of a veil of melancholy over the whole of nature.

In *The Bridge at Argenteuil* the colour becomes more intense within a limited, definite space. The greens, yellows, blues, and purples are no longer local colours, but live by the transition of each into the others, and the light is but their continual vibrancy, their participation in cosmic life. The form is solid and well established, like a truth that is self-evident. It is a feast of nature, and this feast, this joy of contemplation, has been created by art, with absolute harmony of colour and self-evident truth of form.

In the *River Banks* the motif is obviously chosen by a virtuoso who is not content with transparencies of light and of penumbras but wants the very things of nature to be themselves transparent. The delicacy of the house and of the tones in general, and the successful framing, communicate the magic of Monet's creative fancy.

Boats at Argenteuil is even more fantastic. Monet feels the need of rigorously enclosing space in order to make luminous lines rise towards the sky—the masts of the sailboats and their reflections in the water. Were they not so pure, so intimate, they would look like rocket flares. This picture, with its light though intense tones, shows the painter's need for a discipline of forms, which anticipates Seurat.

These are Monet's moments of grace, his fairy-tales of colour, his contemplations of the marvel of the world. It is enough for him to look at his own garden or at the river flowing near-by; he feels no need to test his strength, to tame his enemies. But this dream was of brief duration; this happy moment never returned—for his desire for conquest was soon again upon him.

In 1877 he painted a series of scenes of the St. Lazare Station, among them that in the Art Institute of Chicago (fig. 56). At that time a locomotive was still a fascinating object, a miracle of science: to paint a locomotive in a station was to set the reality of modern life against traditional forms and compositions, the diabolical force of life against false gods. More than that, Monet wished to show that even a black machine and a black shed could be effectively represented in blue, that the dirty grey of a platform could be seen in green, that smoke itself could become a motif of light. Values of energy, space, contrast, and pictorial motion (even though the subject is static) are fully realized. Still, the effect is one of controversial intent rather than pure contemplation, and the picture is thus reminiscent of those painted before 1870 although the virtuosity is greater. The very idea of painting a series of the same subject, even though in different lights and at different times and from different angles, is indicative of a program, and a program is always stifling to creative liberty.

Although the 1877 impressionist exhibition was, like its predecessors, a financial failure, it succeeded in securing for the impressionists a certain lessening of public and critical hostility, and Monet knew how to profit from this to escape from his financial difficulties. Durand-Ruel and Duret both became aware of his flair for finding buyers for his pictures. In 1880 his abandonment of the impressionist group to exhibit at the Salon brought down on him the wrath of Degas, who reproached him for his "unbridled publicity." In an interview with Taboureaux in 1880, Monet displayed aloofness and pride: "I am an impressionist . . . but now I rarely see my companions. . . . The little church has become a banal school, which opens its doors to the first dauber." [7]

Also in 1880 Zola remarked that the group of impressionists seemed to have "outlived itself," and he explained as follows what he considered their failure: "The great misfortune is that not a single artist of this group has brought to any powerful and definitive realization the new formula which they have all stated in a scattered way in all their works. The formula is there, infinitely split up, but nowhere, in none of the pictures, does one find it applied by a master." [8] What that supposed "master" *should* do, Zola indicates six years later in his novel *L'Oeuvre* when he speaks admiringly of the artist Langier, who wants to paint "all of modern life. Frescos as lofty as the Pantheon. A marvellous series of canvases that would burst the seams of the Louvre."

[7] L. Venturi, *Les Archives de l'Impressionnisme,* II, p. 340.
[8] L. Venturi, *op. cit.,* p. 280.

Monet considered himself to be that kind of "master," capable of achievements that others could not equal, but only at the end of his long life, with the series of water-lily panels in the museum of the Orangerie (his gravest artistic error), did he accept the idea of decoration. In the years immediately following 1880 he well knew that his style and that of all the impressionists could not be extended to decoration. But he continued to conceive of series of variations on the same theme —as already exemplified in the series of the St. Lazare Station—as collections of cantos, each collection making up into a great poem. At Argenteuil he had found artistic totality in a reflection in water or in the quivering of a leaf, now he sought it in vain in precise recordings of the hour of the day, of the season, of the temperature, of atmospheric conditions.

In 1880 he painted the series of *Ice Floes at Vétheuil,* of which one canvas is *The Breaking of the Ice* (fig. 57), all in grey, white, and blue, with soft tonal transitions which from a distance give a sense of empty coldness, of the death of things. But the impression remains vague because the form was established in advance and does not spring out vitally from the light itself. Here is proof that Monet's sharp eye is not enough in itself, that his entire being must participate, must be concentrated in his fancy. In this picture his fancy is not at work.

Indeed, after 1880 the pictures are either evanescent or violent. In *Boats in Winter,* 1885 (fig. 58), non-essential details are rigorously excluded; effects are suggested by means of contrast. The purple of the huts, the earth, the boats, and the house is contrasted with the green of the sea. The sky is a mere strip of purple grey. The lifting of the horizon line and the consequent foreshortening of all the images from above are inspired by Japanese prints. And the angry colour scheme, which is stronger than the nuances of light, was perhaps invented by Monet, following his discovery of the Mediterranean sun at Bordighera the year before. Like Van Gogh in 1886, Monet here uses colours arbitrarily to express himself more strongly. But whereas Van Gogh was to derive from this practice the basis for his style, Monet passed rapidly on to new experiments, content in this picture and others of the same character merely to establish the foundations on which fauvism was to arise twenty years later.

In 1891 he exhibited a series of pictures of haystacks, among them the *Haystacks, Late Summer* (fig. 59). It is a series notable for the painter's increasing indifference towards the subject depicted, his search for very simple forms, mere pretexts for the study of light—a light which becomes a veil of gleaming particles.

The poplar pictures exhibited in a series of 1892, among them the *Poplars beside the River Epte* of 1890 (fig. 60), tend, on the other hand, to refined, decorative composition, prophetic of the general end-of-the-century trend towards decorativeness.

Then follow the cathedrals, the Thames series, and finally the water lilies. Monet seeks unusual motifs, attempts the impossible, professes disgust for anything that can be achieved with ease, and he produces marvels of technical skill. The nuances are all in the same key, rigorously harmonized. But the more refined the nuances, the greater their loss of vitality; the greater the care and research given to the light, the less it liberates itself from the all-enveloping mist that obliterates the objects. What is felt is the painter's concern for grandeur, power, heroic effort. The study of light in these series is certainly a scientific project, but the pictures tend to be sentimental. The expression of the inexpressible, of mystery, of sentiments so general that they lose concrete character and artistic truth—these show Monet possessing the same taste which gave birth to symbolism. But in this direction he was blocked: the qualities of impressionism which he retained prevented him from fully realizing his new ideal.

Rouen Cathedral, West Façade, 1894 (fig. 61), is one of the clearest of the series. Jacques-Emile Blanche speaks of its "atmospheric drama." But the more general critical opinion is that the cathedrals are the most evident indication of Monet's creative decadence; in the haystacks there was no question of form, but the Rouen cathedral possesses a very definite form, and Monet's painting tries to preserve it and fails.

At Giverny Monet made himself a flower garden for painting purposes, and in his garden pool he found the motif for his project of so painting solid objects, water, and the atmosphere that they should all merge and be one. This is the long series of water lilies, among them *Pool with Water Lilies, Harmony in Pink* (fig. 62). This picture can almost be considered a kind of wish for artistic annihilation. It contains no tragic overtone but is rather a display of artifice whose frivolous character is not mitigated by the exceptional ability displayed.

Meanwhile his public success became enormous; everyone clamoured to buy paintings by Monet, no longer single paintings but series. But the young artists were already drawing away from him, and a few critics told him truths that hurt. Nevertheless he looked at his own work dispassionately. "Today more than ever I am well aware of how false is this unmerited success which has come to me. . . . I know in advance that you will find my pictures perfect. I know that when I exhibit them they will enjoy a great success, but to that I am indifferent since I know they are bad." [9] So he wrote to Durand-Ruel on May 10, 1912. It is sad to think that in such moments of discouragement he did not remember that his pictures of Argenteuil assured him an eternal place in the history of art.

The reaction against impressionism, which followed closely on his great success, was directed especially against Monet—for he was considered the typical impressionist, and the enemies of impressionism overlooked his later tendencies. But he lived until 1926 when impressionism, no longer a matter of controversy, was everywhere considered one of the glories in the annals of painting and of France, belonging to history rather than to life. Thus, when he died Monet was mourned less as an artist than as the last representative of a legendary past, as a national hero.

[9] L. Venturi, *Les Archives de l'Impressionnisme,* I, p. 346.

Chapter Four

CAMILLE PISSARRO

IN CONSIDERING the taste of Pissarro, it is well to remember that he was born about ten years before the other major impressionists, that he contributed to the formation of impressionism after having been inspired by the daring of Monet, that he influenced Cézanne and Seurat only to be affected by them in turn, that he developed Gauguin as an artist and then cut himself off from him, and that finally, despite the difficulty of making a living from the sale of his pictures and the black poverty that often oppressed him between 1870 and 1890, he continued faithfully, without compromises but with many self-doubts, to modify and, as he believed, to improve his style.

One of his remarks, "I felt my consciousness emancipate itself as my eyes emancipated themselves," well indicates the relation between his art and his spirit. Although a convinced naturalist, he soon understood that art was not a subjection to the data of nature but rather an autonomous reality which differed from nature. A man of great heart, he espoused the cause of the disinherited and considered himself one of them, and he had complete faith in that growing socialism which identified itself with liberty of thought and conscience and was sympathetic to anarchy. He was incapable of harming an insect; he was good-natured and without guile, patient, faithful to his friends even though they were not always kind to him, resigned to endure personal injustice; and he was a rebel against all social injustices, quick to point his finger at moral failings and to condemn them, to fight for the ideal of humanity. But he was faithful above all to art and never stooped to use it as an instrument for achieving his moral and social ideals; rather, he infused these into the forms of his trees and his houses, endowing them with humanity by means of countless suggestions.

It is well known that impressionism contributed in its own way to the recognition of human dignity in the disinherited classes: its preference was for the humble motif, for cabbages and huts rather than for roses and palaces, and it was outspoken in its aversion to any social elegance or ultra-refinement. But none of the other impressionists travelled as far along that road as Pissarro, and for this reason he was accused, from 1870 until after his death, of being a vulgar and prosaic painter by critics who did not understand that he had discovered the poetry of humble daily things. He was not a polemist, and it never occurred to him to reply that a prince might be prosaic and a peasant poetic.

Duret wrote him in 1873, "You have an intimate and profound feeling for nature, and the power of your brush is such that a fine picture by you is something that is perfectly solidly set down on the canvas." [1] This is in contrast with what the same Duret called Monet's "fantastic eye." Pissarro did indeed paint within naturalistic limits, after adopting Monet's technique of divided colours, and Monet, on the other hand, produced masterpieces when he was able to make his imagination

[1] L. R. Pissarro and L. Venturi, *Camille Pissarro*, I, p. 26.

68

in the realm of light coincide with spatial construction as suggested by Pissarro. Thus Pissarro not only brought to full realization his own power of impressionistic visualization but also contributed to the perfect harmony which exists in the pictures of all the impressionists in the golden period of their art.

After 1880 Pissarro's taste was led astray by Seurat's scientific aspirations, by the sentimental primitivism of the pre-Raphaelites, by the search for decorative values of the *art nouveau*. But in his last years he found himself again and created a few more masterpieces. In other words, his humility before the motif and his perennially poetic naiveté and youthful enthusiasm made it possible for him to overcome his inadequate critical awareness and to devote himself to what he always loved and dreamed of—the life of nature.

Camille Pissarro was born at St. Thomas in the Antilles in 1830 and at the age of twenty-two left his parents' home and a situation with a business house to devote himself to painting. In 1855 he arrived in Paris, where he developed an enthusiasm for Corot. Two Danish painters, the brothers Fritz and Anton Melbye, taught him painting technique, a love of precision, and also a certain pedantry. But soon his models were Corot and Courbet, especially the former. He was accepted by the Salon in 1859 and continued to exhibit there, with few interruptions, until 1870.

All this explains why *The Côte du Jallais at Pontoise* of about 1867 (fig. 63), which is contemporary with Monet's *Women in the Garden,* is the work of an experienced painter who is considerably more traditional than Monet. This picture contains none of those relations of light and colour which will later constitute Pissarro's greatness, but the other qualities of the painter are all there. Despite the large dimensions of the picture (it is two metres wide), the total effect is obtained by subordination of details; there is thus a homogeneity of form and colour which reveals a fully conscious art. The volume of the hill, even though it is inspired by Courbet, is realized in pictorial style with a certain atmospheric distance, and it is therefore not ponderous. The wall surfaces of the houses are firmly represented in the manner of Corot, by means of contrasts of colour: they emphasize the precision of the areas of the hill. In the foreground the lightness and variety of the brush strokes suggest the immersion of the masses in the atmosphere. The colours are dark and precious, conventional, and perfectly harmonious. This is not the work of a genius, but of an austere, skilful painter, faithful to nature, conscious of the necessity that his work be a harmony of form and colour.

About two years later Pissarro painted *The Locks at Bougival* (fig. 64). The entire composition is conditioned by the reflections in the water. For contrasts of colour are substituted continuous nuances, fusions of light and shadow. The effect of perspective still gives a certain solidity to the composition, but the surface effect is stronger than that of depth, so that masses, although they are still present, lose some of their solidity and tend to become fluid. Pissarro probably would never have painted in this manner had it not been for Monet's *La Grenouillère,* but of the two pictures his is the more organic and harmonious.

Thus we see that Pissarro does not have Monet's daring, is

not the inventor of the new style, and indeed comes to it slowly, but what he assimilates he introduces into his own tradition, into the well-thought-out, well-constructed organism of his art, with an assurance that is lacking in Monet, who was always discovering something new.

At the outbreak of the war of 1870 Pissarro went to London, and he returned to Louveciennes in 1871. At that time Duret and Degas, then the only known buyers of his pictures, preferred him to Monet and Sisley. Back in Louveciennes he found the sky, the streets, and the trees of the outskirts of Paris, which he knew and loved so well and which he painted with spontaneous devotion. Before 1870 he had produced large pictures; now he limited their size—not only because he worked more easily in the open air if his canvases were small, but also because he no longer felt the need of the heroic; he sensed more keenly the relation between his own humbleness and that of the motif. He took special pleasure in painting streets in perspective, which allowed him to construct the space of the picture in the most elementary fashion and to fill that space with his lights and shadows. There are effects of rain, in which the nuances of grey are very fine, attuned to the melancholy of the artist; there are effects of sunlight, in which contrasts of colour assume a precise form of their own. Slowly, colour values begin to bloom out of the grey: first blues and greens show themselves, and then, very shyly, pink.

An example of these motifs of streets in perspective is *Road Near Louveciennes* (fig. 65), dated 1871. Despite the freedom and fineness of the brush strokes, the colour and surface contrasts are still crude.

But already in *The Route d'Osny, Pontoise,* which was painted in 1872 (fig. 66), colour gradation prevails over colour contrast, the atmospheric effect is fully realized, and the vitality of nature appears more intense. The road itself is of a different type: the function of the earlier streets in perspective had been to create space; now the feature is the curve, which offers greater pictorial possibilities because it balances the empty and the full, space and mass. (Curving roads were subsequently to be given especially rich development in the art of Cézanne.) In this picture by Pissarro light already acts as nature's interpreter, but the tones remain low in scale.

In 1873, however, there is a veritable explosion of colour, accompanied by a greater freedom of fancy. *The Haystack* of 1873 (fig. 67) is a masterpiece. A simple pile of hay in the midst of flat fields—no motif could be simpler. The mass of the haystack is almost conical, although not geometrically so, and it contains most of the pictorial value. Colour is exceptionally jewel-like and varied: the entire sky is a nuance of pink, white, purple, and blue. The field is composed of areas of white, yellow, green, and pink; each colour has its function in giving life to the penumbra and harmony to the whole. Already the light assumes an imaginative artistic value, which reveals the state of mind of the painter, his ecstasy before the majesty of nature.

Also of 1873 is *Village Street, Auvers-sur-Oise* (fig. 68), in which the intensity of the colour does not hamper the free contrasts of lights and darks. Here the volume of the objects depicted is emphasized, the huts become monumental—an effect which is the result of the artist's stylistic clarity, his freedom, his creative energy, his tragic afflatus. At this time he was in frequent personal contact with Cézanne, from whom he derived an aggressiveness of fancy that he had hitherto not known.

By 1873 the "emancipation" of Pissarro's eye was complete, and during the next few years masterpieces followed one after the other. Something had happened to Pissarro that had happened to other artists before him, for example to Piero della Francesca and to Vermeer: when intensified colour is given a new form which is perfectly adapted to it, the result is sweetness, purity, incomparable poetry. The slowness of the evolution of Pissarro's style, his modesty, his devotion to his ideal—all those elements favoured his arriving at maturity and perfection.

The motif of *Peasant Woman Pushing a Wheelbarrow*, 1874 (fig. 70), is a simple and modest one, but the blues, greens, yellows, and whites are enough to enchant the spectator and transport him to a dream world. The substance is fatty and pulpy, and it contains a diffused light, which, permeating the masses and giving them their reality, at the same time exalts this reality to the realm of fancy.

In 1875 he painted *The Little Bridge, Pontoise* (fig. 69). Here he has not only gone beyond the picturesque but has subordinated pictorial effect itself to his need for an ideal construction, and this he has achieved by means of reflections and brush strokes. Pissarro has not abdicated his own personality in the slightest degree, and yet the happy effect of this picture is in the style of Cézanne. We are transported into a spiritual realm in which every chance occurrence, every detail of place, is engulfed in an overwhelming sense of the eternity of nature. Nothing could be more monumental and yet more

73

natural. The full and the empty, mass and atmosphere, are fused in a firm, perfectly stabilized composition. The colours are few but precious: the basic harmony is established by the shaded grey of the tree trunks against the yellow of the bridge.

These extraordinary successes encouraged Pissarro and made him even bolder. *The Côte des Boeufs, Pontoise,* 1877 (fig. 71), is justly famous. The motif of the bare trees, which allow a glimpse of houses and other trees beyond, he had already employed at an earlier date. But at that time he did not have at his command his intense colours or his all-enveloping light. Light and penumbras intermingle and become fused, vibrating and giving vitality to the images, without disturbing the precision of the planes; these appear real even in the fanciful world of the picture, a world that is exalted by luminous yellows, greens, and blues.

Vegetable Garden and Flowering Trees, Spring, Pontoise, also 1877 (fig. 72), succeeds in maintaining a well-ordered composition despite what amounts to being a veil of brush strokes in the thousands of flowers. Joy, freshness, exultation in nature's springtime rebirth are completely conveyed. The flowers are white with blue shadows, like the sky, which also seems to be in bloom. These two light tones are framed by the blue grey of the houses and by the blue-yellow green of the earth. The freedom of the brush strokes and the exultant colour betray the inspiration of Monet, behind which, however, stands the constructive solidity typical of Pissarro.

Up until about 1880 Pissarro's painting was felicitous, due to his creative energy and his evident serenity of spirit. The latter was all the more notable in that it did not correspond at all with the conditions of his life: his poverty was never more terrible than in 1878, and even the moral encouragement given Monet was at this time denied Pissarro.

But he found incentives to creativeness in the ideal which he held in common with the other impressionists and in the independent impressionist exhibitions. Of the entire group he was the only one who remained absolutely faithful until 1886: he was in full sympathy with these declarations of independence from official art because he thought of the impressionist movement as one of the many revolts against the evils of established society. Beyond the hoped-for material advantages (which were never obtained) Pissarro also saw in the impressionist exhibitions the declaration of an artistic doctrine in which he firmly believed. When the exhibition of 1877, certainly the most important of the series, failed to achieve financial success, Cézanne and Renoir withdrew, followed a year later by Monet and Sisley. Pissarro remained in the breach with Degas and new recruits. He was never jealous of the successes of his old friends; in 1879, for example, he wrote of Renoir, "Now he is a success, I think, and I am glad of it. Poverty is a hard thing to bear." [2] He was tolerant of the compromises of others, but permitted himself none.

In 1880 the newspaper *L'Artiste* wrote of him, "Pissarro is now fifty years old, and his head is that of an apostle. He is never seen without a portfolio under each arm, a trait which causes him to be greeted at the Café de la Nouvelle Athènes with the words 'Hail to Moses!'—for he is thought of as bearing the tables of the law." The impressionists had never put their doctrine down in writing or formulated it in any way,

[2] L. R. Pissaro and L. Venturi, *op. cit.,* p. 37.

and the formulations made by critics—by Duranty, Burty, and Mantz—did not constitute a true doctrine. This lack of doctrine made it easier for the group to disintegrate: after 1880, when impressionism seemed destined to fail, Monet went off on his own track, Renoir followed the academic tradition, and Cézanne isolated himself to create a doctrine of his own. Pissarro stumbled upon the doctrine of Seurat, the creator of divisionism, which attracted him because it was based on scientific principles of colour. The division of colours which the impressionists had invented intuitively, Seurat applied rigorously according to principles. Pissarro's faith in science as a force for human and social progress made it natural that he should become enthusiastic over the new doctrine.

Moreover, from 1881 he had been trying to give his compositions a greater formal regularity. *Sunken Road, View over Epluches,* 1881 (fig. 73), exemplifies Seurat's taste for a clear-cut distinction between foreground and background, for an almost geometric regularity of areas, and for a reflective, static quality. Thus it was due to certain affinities of taste, as well as to his admiration of scientific principles, that Pissarro became a follower of the young Seurat. He gave not a moment's thought to the damage that would be done his authority as a celebrated, mature painter, and he took up his position in the opposition of the scientific impressionists to the romantic impressionists (Monet and Renoir). But he quickly realized that Seurat's pointillist technique did not suit his temperament or his vivacity of feeling—indeed, that it prevented him from doing successful work. Therefore, after committing several errors of taste in 1886 and slowing down in his production in the years immediately following, he once again sought spontaneous expression for his feelings, and he substituted the comma brush stroke for the pointillist dot and abandoned the clear-cut separation of dots in favor of intermediate passages. And on Seurat's death in 1891 he declined the proffered role of leader of the neo-impressionists.

His experience with divisionism was not in vain, however. It gave him a new conception of form and light, a conception in which they have a greater autonomy than before, both from nature and from accidental impression. Perhaps the difference between his two manners, before and after divisionism, can best be felt in comparing *Mère Larchevêque,* 1880 (fig. 74), and *Bathing Women,* 1894 (fig. 75). *Mère Larchevêque* is powerful in its portrayal of character, in its modelling, in its light. It is one of the artist's most vital images: an energetic, vulgar, crafty peasant woman, who is yet not entirely without good nature. The realistic portrait is subordinated to the pictorial effect, but its value consists only in its vitality.

In *Bathing Women,* on the other hand, the shower of light which gives form to the bodies, the water, and the trees indicates that the artist's sensibility has found an ideal order of its own which goes beyond realism, beyond the contingencies of nature, and attains a cosmic harmony which is grace itself.

The views of Rouen of 1896 and 1898 are certainly the masterpieces of Pissarro's last period. *The Grand Pont, Rouen,* 1896 (fig. 76), is a grandiose, distant vision, an exaltation of human activity, not without a touch of rhetoric. But the picture has a marvellous balance of atmospheric vibrancy and well-stabilized forms. The composition goes back to the stability, the assurance, of Pissarro's pre-impressionistic pictures, but the colour has a variety, an intensity, and a vitality inconceivable without impressionism and neo-impressionism. The purples, the reds, the greens, the yellows, the blues themselves create the effect of light and shadow, and hence the form.

The *Rue de l'Epicerie, Rouen, Morning, Grey Weather,* 1898 (fig. 77), and other similar pictures are Pissarro's "cathedrals." When he painted them, he realized the danger of their being compared with Monet's, which were enjoying considerable success and which Pissarro was doing his best to admire. Clearly the two artists had never been more different than they were in these years from 1895 to 1898. Monet was concentrating on the effect of light, and in the triumph of his subjectivity his motif counted for little. Pissarro, on the contrary, continued to pay close attention to the object represented; from it he derived a balance of form and colour and with imposing artistic effect communicated all its monumental value, all its constructive vitality.

Pissarro's urge to paint many pictures, to perform brilliant brush-work, to delineate movement, to excel in virtuosity, increased with the years. Views of Parisian streets, squares, houses, and bridges became the favorite motif of the last period. *The Place du Théâtre Français, Sunshine,* 1898 (fig. 78), is one of the most brilliant of these scenes. The impressionist brush stroke is used here with a vivacity that seems urgent and eager, and the total effect, which the artist would like to make grandiose, is chiefly one of complexity.

Pissarro died at the end of 1903, just after returning from Le Havre, where he had completed a series of quite successful views of the harbour.

Public success, which had begun somewhat earlier to smile on Monet and Renoir, did not come to Pissarro until 1892. The pleasure of achieving recognition and the enjoyment of material well-being after so many years of privation gave him new energy, and they were responsible, although his artistic strength was now declining, for his painting a few successful works. On the other hand, they caused him to produce at a frenzied rate and to display his qualities as virtuoso. With few exceptions, Pissarro's absolute value as an artist is to be found in his works of before 1880.

Chapter Five

ALFRED SISLEY

ANY pictures by Alfred Sisley, often delightful in their colour and their feeling, are familiar to us, but very little is known about his life and ideas. As a man he is the palest figure among the group of impressionists. Dying without achieving recognition of his worth as a painter and as a poet in painting, he was "discovered" immediately thereafter, to the accompaniment of much enthusiasm and speculation. Then he entered a kind of limbo: his excellence was indisputable, but he was to a large extent neglected because he was not a man of the moment nor connected with problems of taste. Sisley invented nothing, but he created works of art. Corot, Courbet, Pissarro, Renoir, and especially Monet taught him many things; he, Sisley, never taught anyone anything; he is characterized by a detachment from the problems of the day, by a certain timidity in accepting the innovations of others, by a certain reserve that admits no extremes, not even that of the highest quality. But reserve, discretion, refinement, accompanied by an intangible air of gentlemanliness and culture, are excellent conditions for the creation of art. The exact opposite of Monet, whose monumental accomplishment in the history of taste is rather overwhelmingly greater than his free creativity, Sisley's only interest consists in his ability to caress, enjoy, and contemplate tones of colour. He is certainly a minor master, but smallness in connection with mastery in painting does not exclude the absolute in art.

He was born in Paris in 1839. His parents were British, but there were many Frenchwomen among his forebears, who had lived partly in England and partly in France. Alfred was educated in Paris.[1] In 1857 he was sent to work in a commercial house in London, but his interests lay in literature and painting, and he studied Shakespeare, Turner, and Constable. Returning to Paris in 1862, he attended Gleyre's academy, where he met Monet, Renoir, and Bazille, and in 1864 he accompanied them to Chailly, near Fontainebleau. In 1866 he went to Marlotte with Renoir, in 1867 to Honfleur with Bazille. In 1866 he was accepted at the Salon, but his picture went unnoticed by Zola, Thoré, and Castagnary. Being a British subject, he went to London during the Franco-Prussian War, and there he established contact with Durand-Ruel, who in 1871 exhibited two of his pictures in London and in 1873 published three in his catalogue.

From this same year date the first critical judgements of Sisley's art as compared with Monet and Pissarro: Armand Silvestre says that of the three Sisley is "the most harmonious and the most timid," and Théodore Duret speaks of his "decorative feeling," which is lacking in Pissarro.

During the following years Sisley's fate was bound up with those of Monet, Pissarro, and Renoir. He had only the proceeds of his painting to live on, and he endured poverty with a dignity that kept him largely in retirement. In 1874 he

[1] Claude Sisley, "The Ancestry of Alfred Sisley," *The Burlington Magazine,* September, 1949.

exhibited with his companions in the first of those independent exhibitions that were later called the exhibitions of the impressionists, and he also showed there in 1876, 1877, and 1882.

These few facts are all that is known of Sisley from his beginnings until after the close of his happiest period of creativity, but many of his pictures speak clearly for him.

The picture accepted by the Salon in 1865 was *The Edge of the Forest of Fontainebleau,* painted the previous year (fig. 79). It is a large picture (over two metres wide), of the type which Pissarro, Monet, and Renoir were painting about the same time, that is, realistic in character, inspired especially by Courbet, all in grey, brown, green, blue, and black, heavy, serious, well executed. Only a certain nervousness in the brush strokes gives a foretaste of the future impressionist.

We must wait until 1870 to find a work of Sisley's which, although still pre-impressionist, is a miracle of colour, *The Canal St. Martin, Paris* (fig. 80). The manner of painting is that which Monet was employing in the same years, but the art is entirely personal, calmer than Monet, with less energy and with a more natural, ingenuous, and pure colour harmony. The green, blue, and violet of the foreground are harmonized with and darker than the sky-blue houses and the sky-blue white of the sky, causing the picture to achieve perfect chromatic unity.

The production dating from 1872 to 1876 is very copious and of a quality to which Sisley never again attained.

If we compare *Little Square, Argenteuil,* 1872 (fig. 81), with the work of Monet and Pissarro which had preceded it, we see not only the greater calm and naturalness of Sisley, but his continuation of the style of Corot, whose pupil he had declared himself when he exhibited at the Salon. A village square is for Sisley not a motif of contrasting light and shade or of pulsating human life, but rather a relationship of colours. And these colours are much more varied, intense, and rich than those of Corot. The yellow, pink, and green enhance the grey tones of the houses and the browns of the earth; the roofs are now brown, now dark blue, against a light sky of pinkish blue.

More completely original is the *Port-Marly* of 1873 (fig. 82). The composition is very happy, even though simple and traditional. The shore in the foreground, delineated with strong brush strokes, extends into an infinite distance the placid, mirrorlike surface of the water, which narrows in perspective between the shores up to the background of sky. The trees are reddish yellow, the water sky blue, the sky pinkish blue. The infinite delicacy of the brush strokes gives the water, the shores, and the trees just that degree of vibrancy which their life requires, as if the artist were careful not to disturb the calm and the grace of contemplation. The discreet tonal harmony, the decorative grace of the whole, the light melancholy which is infused into the charm of autumn —all are expressed with natural fancy. No one who demands plastic values and well-defined images should look at Sisley: his fancy loves things that are light and delicate; it loves the atmosphere which gives nuances to colour tones and reveals one aspect of eternal art.

In *Louveciennes, Heights of Marly,* probably of 1873 (fig. 83), Sisley shows another aspect of his art, its participation in the shimmering of light on the leaves of the trees on the outskirts of a village. The yellow of the light against the green of the shadow is the principal motif, accompanied by grey and brown tones, terminating in the blue of the distant mountains and sky.

In *Port-Marly* the distant view permits a summary treatment, which gives the canvas its pictorial charm; in *Louveciennes, Heights of Marly,* the near view demands the rendering of details, which might have resulted in descriptive realism were it not for that gift which is supreme in Sisley—his discretion, thanks to which every object comes under the influence of the vibrancy of the light, which is nevertheless calm and gentle, beautifying everything.

Snow effects often interested the impressionists, and it is understandable that they should have: it was an appealing task to bring out a harmony of intense colours from the greyish white. Monet, Pissarro, Renoir achieved happy effects. But perhaps no one has equalled the snows of Sisley, for the reason that delicacy of tonal gradations impressed itself on his eye in an incomparable manner. *Snow at Louveciennes,* dated 1874 (fig. 84), has pink tones that suggest feelings of sympathy and joy in the presence of the white mantle covering the houses and the earth, and the composition has an introspective, closed character revelatory of the artist's intimacy with his subject.

The Route de la Princesse, Louveciennes, Evening, dated 1875 (fig. 85), is a miracle of artistic transformation of a motif which in itself would be common and ugly: the name of the road seems a mockery. The chromatic boldness is more accentuated; the houses become pink, green, sky blue, and the road and the hills are the same colours but in a different tone.

84

The colours are gleaming and jewel-like and tell us of the artist's ecstasy in the sunset light even though he is not facing the sun itself, and they reveal to us the serenity of eternal youth and the artist's purity of spirit.

The flooding of the Seine at Port-Marly attracted Sisley's attention in many pictures: the shimmering of light in a body of all-enveloping water was a typical impressionist motif. In the Museum of Impressionism in Paris are two examples, both dated 1876: the *Flood at Port-Marly* and, better composed, *The Boat during the Flood* (fig. 87). Both are pictorially well fused, consisting of nuances of grey and sky blue with some brown tones. The natural sensation of encroaching wetness becomes by means of Sisley's brush an enchantment, a fairy-tale. The house that Sisley painted can still be seen, unchanged, on the road to Port-Marly, and it is revealing to look at the ordinary, vulgar little dwelling and to sense all the poetic transformation that Sisley achieved.

In the same year, 1876, he painted a picture of altogether different character—*Landscape* (fig. 86). In this he was inspired by the agitation of Monet; he wished to be strong and determined like his comrades, to depict earth, water, and especially trees and shrubs bursting with exultant life; and to this end he interrupted his composition and limited the variety of his colours, emphasizing the dark shades. The picture is convincing and effective because the artist has received a natural impression that remains the basis of his fanciful elaboration. He can do what he pleases, and he does it well. Yet one feels that the true quality of his contemplation is something else, that the more constant element of his art is found in *The Boat during the Flood,* and that his moment of restlessness, even though it is well expressed, should remain an exception.

Instead, this became the new direction of his taste, as seen in *The Seine at Suresne* of 1877 (fig. 88). Here the sky is covered with white and purple-grey clouds, forebodings of a storm, but to make them more agitated he paints them thick and deep, like a glacier, making his picture too heavy and throwing it off balance. On the land and on the river, too, everything becomes heavy, even though the tone is agitated to lighten the forms; the dark colours are too dark, the light colours too light and lacking in luminosity. The agitation does not succeed in expressing the motion of things. The effect is grandiose, to be sure, because of the painter's determination, but his artifice is apparent.

In 1878 Sisley felt that the public was becoming favourable to him, and he decided to abandon the impressionist exhibitions and to send his paintings to the Salon, as Renoir had done. But he was refused, and he felt more than ever isolated and was more than ever in need of money. From 1880 to 1883 his financial circumstances were improved by purchases by Durand-Ruel, in whose gallery he had his first one-man show. But he had less success than his companions. Durand-Ruel's purchases became infrequent, and there was a new desperate struggle against financial catastrophe.

Meanwhile Seurat and divisionism had burst explosively upon the pictorial taste of Paris. Pissarro had followed Seurat. Monet and Renoir had opposed divisionism and represented the romantic impressionists as against the scientific: nevertheless, they both renewed themselves, Monet going in the direction of the future fauvism and Renoir trying to return to tradition. Sisley desired to follow Monet, but his new experiments were increasingly contrary to his nature. In 1887 Pissarro said that Sisley's painting had not changed at all, that it was skilful and quite delicate but absolutely false.

Sisley did not give up and made attempts in all directions, at times not without success.

A Cottage at Les Sablons, 1885 (fig. 89), presents an intensity of light concentrated in simple forms, showing the artist to be interested in researches into divisionist light-effects, although his brush stroke remains the comma rather than the point. The picture as a whole preserves an attractive grace. On the other hand *Sunset on the River Loing, St. Michel, Moret*, 1889 (fig. 90), shows a rigorous synthesis of contrasts, parallel to that of Monet in his pre-fauvist moments. Yet Sisley's composition remains traditional, in fact pre-impressionistic, and from this results a lack of balance which shows that Sisley had not understood the reasons for the renewal in painting that followed the crisis of impressionism. Nevertheless, this canvas still contains the pictorial vitality of a master.

On other occasions, as in the *September Morning* of 1888 (acquired by the state—its first purchase from Sisley—for the museum of Agen), all the painter's skill does not suffice to conceal the lack of soul.

His colours become more and more garish, his forms take on volume; in his anxiety to realize effects he seems to return, after so many experiments, to his primitive realism—that is, to emphasize the representation of the physical nature of things, to the great detriment of his poetry.

This is the case in *The Bridge at Moret, c.* 1894 (fig. 91), in which the impressionist brush stroke and the reflections in the water are not enough to prevent the colours from clashing, the forms from appearing photographic, and the materialism of the representation from losing all its artistic strength.

As early as 1890 Sisley's health was undermined, and he steadily failed to achieve the success which was by this time smiling on Monet, Renoir, and Pissarro. From 1890 until shortly before his death he exhibited many paintings at the Salon de la Société Nationale. In 1892 Octave Mirbeau pointed out in the *Figaro* the difference between Sisley's earlier work and his more recent productions.

> His very fine, very vibrant sensibility was quite at ease among all the spectacles of nature; from them it received impressions which were not particularly sharp, but multiple and lively. . . . His painting contained more charm than strength, an innate grace, something that was alert, bright, and easy, a delightful air of devil-may-care; he infused the unfinished with a poetry that was often exquisite. . . . M. Sisley's recent exhibitions have perhaps disappointed these hopes, although this is not to say that he has lost all his qualities. He retains an elegance, a grace, a distinguished way of seeing things. But fatigue and lassitude seem to have come upon him. His brush is softer, his drawing relaxed. . . . The canvases that he offers us today are but a distant, weak echo of those paintings, so pretty, so youthful, so living, which I see in the depths of my enthusiastic memories, already old.

Sisley wrote him in protest, "You have become the champion of a coterie which would be all too pleased to see my downfall. It will not have that pleasure, and you will have accomplished nothing by your unjust and perfidious criticism." [2] What Sisley believed to be a commercial manœuvre seems to have been simply Durand-Ruel's negative judgement concerning his most recent works, and indeed after 1892 there was apparently no further communication between the painter and the dealer. When the latter again exhibited Sisley's works immediately after his death, none of the canvases was later than 1885.

Sisley's defender at the moment when he was abandoned by his friends was the critic Adolphe Tavernier, who asked the painter for his "aesthetic" and published it. This is the only occasion on which Sisley expressed his thoughts, and for that reason it is well to transcribe the most important points:

> The subject, the motif, must always be rendered in a simple, comprehensible fashion, which grips the spectator.
>
> The latter must be led—by the elimination of superfluous details—to follow the path indicated for him by the painter, and to see what has caught the painter's eye.
>
> Every canvas contains one corner that is particularly beloved.
>
> This is one of the charms of Corot and also of Jongkind.
>
> After the subject, one of the most interesting qualities of landscape is movement, life.
>
> It is also one of the most difficult to render. To give

[2] L. Venturi, *Les Archives de l'Impressionnisme*, I, 97–98.

life to a work of art is certainly an indispensable condition for any artist worthy of the name. Everything must contribute to it; form, colour, workmanship. It is the painter's emotion which gives life and which awakens the emotion of the spectator.

And although the landscape painter must remain in full control of his craft, his work, more animated at certain moments, must communicate to the spectator the emotion which the painter has felt.

You see that I am in favour of different kinds of workmanship in the same picture. It is not altogether the current opinion, but I think I am right, especially when it is a question of rendering an effect of light. For sunlight, although it softens certain parts of the landscape, exalts others, and these different effects of light, which express themselves almost materially in nature, must be rendered materially on the canvas.

Objects must be rendered with the proper texture, and above all they must be enveloped in light, as they are in nature. That is what we have to achieve.

For this, the sky must be the means. The sky cannot be only a background. On the contrary, not only does it give depth by its planes (for the sky has planes like the earth); it also gives movement by its form, by its arrangement in relation to the effect or composition of the picture.

Is there anything more magnificent, fuller of movement, than the sky that is so frequently seen in summer— I mean the blue sky with beautiful, shifting white clouds? Such movement! Such *allure!* The effect is the same as that of waves at sea—exalting, inspiring. And then, another sky—the sky at evening. Its clouds draw themselves out, often take on the form of a ship's wake, of swirls which seem to be immobilized in the middle of the atmosphere and then gradually disappear, absorbed by the setting sun. This sky is more tender, more melancholy; it has the charm of things which disappear. And I love it particularly. But I do not wish to speak of all these skies so dear to painters; I speak to you only of those which I prefer above all.

I insist upon this part of the landscape, because I should like you to understand fully the importance that I attach to it. . . .

Which are the painters that I love? To speak only of moderns, Delacroix, Corot, Millet, Rousseau, Courbet, our masters; all, in fact, who have loved nature and felt deeply.[3]

The function of feeling is thus of primary importance in Sisley's art, and he well knows, despite his love of the sky, the necessity of autonomy in art. Nevertheless, his deliberate renunciation of unity of style in a picture in order the better to follow the different effects of nature indicates his character as a realist and his failure to emphasize the importance of the impressionist renewal. Also, among painters he loves the masters, and does not speak of his comrades, and this is a confirmation of his lack of enthusiasm for the new taste—a lack already noted in his paintings.

[3] Published by Tavernier in the preface to the exhibition entitled *L'Atelier de Sisley,* Bernheim-Jeune, 1907.

Even Tavernier, who in 1892 had defended Sisley against Mirbeau's judgement, admitted in 1907 that the painter's masterpieces were created between 1872 and 1876. As J. C. Holl has said,[4] "In him two men were at odds, the dreamer and the technician: his work retained the imprint of this inner struggle." Between 1870 and 1877 he was not greatly pre-occupied with technique, and the dreamer created his own technique; but in subsequent years the technician was unable to create his own dream.

Gustave Geffroy visited Sisley at Moret about 1894 and received the impression of a man of great culture and dignity, but very sad, resigned to growing old with the presentiment that "during his lifetime no ray of glory would shine upon his art."

In 1897 there was a large exhibition of Sisley's work at the Georges Petit Gallery; numerous collectors sent their pictures. But with few exceptions the critics stayed away, and their silence was a crushing blow to Sisley. One year later he developed cancer of the throat. When he felt his end near, he called Monet to give him his last greeting, and he died a week later, on January 29, 1899.

[4] *Après l'Impressionnisme,* 1910.

Chapter Six

PIERRE-AUGUSTE RENOIR

WHEN he painted the *Portrait of Mlle. Romaine Lacaux,* 1864 (fig. 92), Renoir was twenty-three years old. Born in Limoges in 1841, the son of a tailor, he came to Paris with his family at the age of four or five. At thirteen he already had a trade—that of a painter on china—and later he decorated window-shades. Between 1862 and 1864 he studied at the School of Fine Arts, following at the same time the course at Gleyre's academy, where he met Monet, Bazille, and Sisley. In 1864 he went with them to Chailly near Fontainebleau, to study out of doors; and in the same year the Salon accepted his *Esmeralda,* an academic composition which he subsquently destroyed.

In the *Portrait of Mlle. Romaine Lacaux,* therefore, are to be seen both Renoir's budding temperament and the fruits of his studies. It is a portrait, but above all it is a beautiful child, dressed in her best, posed as for a careful photograph, against a backdrop of sky blue and pink that is like a fitting accompaniment to some innocent childish dream. The painting is timidly realistic, and it offends against none of the canons of grace. For all that has been said to the contrary, it belongs to no school. Thus as far as technique is concerned this is an academic picture, very much in the style of the time, not very dissimilar from the work of Winterhalter, the painter of the

93

Empress Eugénie. Nevertheless, it is a fascinating work of art because it displays Renoir's poetry. If we compare *Mlle. Lacaux* with the *Child with a Watering-Pot* (fig. 98), painted twelve years later, when Renoir had already created his personal style, we see that in 1864 the conventional representation of reality permits the painter's style to appear only sporadically, while in 1876 all reality is transformed into style. Yet in both paintings we see the same fancy, blooming in a vision of grace. It is astonishing that this should be so. For in 1864 Renoir was, so to speak, wearing borrowed clothes— the clothes of the Academy, which hampered him and which he later discarded in favor of his own—and yet his spontaneous force as an artist was such that even under such conditions it manifested itself in a manner that cannot be defined but rather felt, a manner that enchants us and that is a mode of art.

This astonishing achievement is symbolic of all of Renoir. During his long life he followed various stylistic tendencies, more or less suitable to his temperament, and he committed numerous errors of taste. But he always found himself again, and he succeeded not only in escaping from his errors, thanks to his ever-fresh vein of invention, but in making use of these very errors to produce something that was art. Anyone who attempts to judge Renoir according to criteria of style, which serve so well for an understanding of Degas, Monet, or Pissarro, quickly feels himself at sea. Renoir's art is indeed the culmination of two styles, but it is also an escape from still other styles which at one time or another he found acceptable. The coherence of his art from 1864 to 1919 is the result of something different from what is usually meant by pictorial style, and to this fact is due both the surprise continually caused by his huge number of pictures and the disappointment frequently experienced by persons looking at his pictures for the first time—a disappointment which always ends, however, in a victory for the painter.

These features of Renoir's art were, of course, related to his way of life. In 1866 the sister of his friend Jules Lecoeur said of him, "The poor fellow is like a body without a soul when he is not working at something," and she recounted an anecdote about his indecision and his submission to the whims of his friends.[1] In 1900 Renoir himself wrote to Monet, "You follow an admirable line of conduct; as for me, I am never able to know the day before what I am going to do the day after."[2] And there is the probably authentic remark attributed to Renoir by Vollard, "I am like a little cork thrown on the water and carried by the current. In painting I simply let myself go."[3]

He denied the accusation that he was a revolutionary in art, and yet without knowing it he revealed a taste which was fundamentally new, and which sprang from his spontaneous artistic force. He spoke against realism, against programs in art, against the idea of a small, closed group (*petite chapelle*), against the intrusion of politics into art. He had his own ideas on art and he liked to speak of them—indeed he seems to have spoken of nothing else—and he avoided arguments, expressing himself not in dialectic but in aphorisms, sometimes brilliant. He wrote more about art than has come down to us. But one of his theories which has been preserved is nothing less than

[1] L. Venturi, *Les Archives de l'Impressionnisme,* I, p. 30.
[2] Letter to Monet, August 23, 1900. Cf. Geffroy, *Monet,* 1922, p. 173.
[3] A. Vollard, *Renoir,* Crès, 1920, p. 37.

a project for a society to cure defects of taste—a project, it need scarcely be said, of extremely brief duration. It reads as follows:

In all the controversies that are daily caused by questions of art, the principal point, to which we propose to call attention, is generally forgotten: we refer to irregularity.

Nature abhors a vacuum, say the physicists; they might complete their axiom by adding that nature also abhors regularity.

Observers know that despite the simplicity of the laws which preside over their formation, the works of nature are infinitely varied, from the most important to the least, whatever the family to which they may belong. The two eyes of the most beautiful face will always be slightly dissimilar; no nose will be found placed exactly above the middle of the mouth; the sections of an orange, the leaves of a tree, the petals of a flower, are never identical; indeed, beauties of all kinds seem to derive their charm from this diversity.

If we examine the most famous plastic or architectural productions from this point of view, we easily see that the great artists who created them, anxious to proceed in the same way as nature, whose respectful pupils they always are, have taken great care not to transgress its fundamental law of irregularity.

We may thus, without fear of error, affirm that all truly artistic production has been conceived and executed according to the principle of irregularity; in a word, to use a neologism which expresses our thought more completely, it is always the work of an irregularist.

At a time when our French art, up until the beginning of this century so full of penetrating charm and exquisite fancy, is about to perish from regularity, from aridity, from the mania for false perfection whose ideal is the engineer's blueprint, we think that it is useful to react promptly against the deadly doctrines which threaten to destroy it, and that the duty of all persons of delicate feeling, of all men of taste, is to organize without delay, whatever their repugnance for controversy and protest.

A society is therefore necessary.[4]

It is a naive theory, valid as an artist's dream and with the merit of opposing two false principles: that of order, which is characteristic of all neo-classicism, and that of perfection, which is non-existent in life as in art. And it is an improvised theory, like a painting by Renoir minus its creative fancy.

Renoir's origins and character were those of the people, and his manner of speech was that of a day laborer, with rolled r's and a drawl, and he was so lacking in any "side" that the servants in the house of his friend Bérard treated him like one of themselves.[5] He was not difficult in his choice of models as long as he found a skin which did not "reject the light" and which was not *faisandée*—over-ripe—like that of society ladies. His taste was wholesome, elemental. In gather-

[4] L. Venturi, *Les Archives de l'Impressionnisme*, I, pp. 127–129.
[5] J.-E. Blanche, *Les Arts Plastiques*, Paris, 1931, p. 70.

ings he looked "thoughtful, dreamy, sombre," as his brother described him in 1879,[6] but when he painted his face brightened and he sang delightfully.

Voluptuousness was his essential artistic impulse. There was never any question of his feeling that his sensuality limited his art; on the contrary, he boasted of it. "A breast is round, warm. If God had not created a woman's breast, I do not know that I should have been a painter." [7] And he was not at all conscious of his quality of grace, which enveloped his every desire and transformed into free fancy everything in nature. He painted flowers while looking at a nude model or studied flesh tones in a bunch of roses. Even in his last years the warm sun of Cagnes and the intoxication caused him by shades of red exalted his sensuality to the plane of art. So that Katherine Mansfield is moralizing when she writes of him, "His feeling for flesh is a kind of super-intense feeling about a lovely little cut of lamb." [8]

His culture was decidedly elementary. He detested sentimentality and naturalism in literature as in painting, had an antipathy for Hugo and Baudelaire, for Flaubert and Zola (who, he said, "painted with bitumen"), and liked to read LaFontaine, Musset—"so pretty"—the elder Dumas and Daudet. The supposed affinities of Renoir with Verlaine or Mallarmé seem not to have existed. Rather, certain aspects of the art of Maupassant, the gay and carefree moments of his muse, the moments of illusion, recall certain attitudes of Renoir between 1874 and 1877.

[6] Edmond Renoir, in *La Vie Moderne;* cf. L. Venturi, *Les Archives de l'Impressionnisme,* II, p. 335.
[7] J.-E. Blanche, *op. cit.,* p. 71.
[8] *The Letters of Katherine Mansfield,* London, 1928, II, p. 131.

In 1867 he painted *Lise* (fig. 93). He was inspired by Courbet, more precisely by the central figure in the latter's *Village Girls,* 1851, of which he took over the aplomb, the assurance, the monumentality, the sober colour. If we compare it with *Mlle. Lacaux,* we see that Renoir's muse has become severe. And yet only the inspiration is external; the vision and the enchantment are Renoir's own. Renoir painted this picture not to draw a body, but to bring out the white of the dress, with its shadows that are now grey, now blue, and are broken into by the black of the ribbon, and the grey shadow on the pink-yellow face, and the grey of the parasol against the yellow-green background. The soft, overlapping shades of grey, which at once reveal and conceal, have a delicacy unknown to Courbet and a tone different from the greys of Corot. Therefore the image, despite its aplomb, is light, phantomlike, a revelation. *Lise* was a success in the Salon of 1868. Its sober colour found general approval, and it inspired a popular quatrain:

> *Où vas-tu, fille aux blondes tresses,*
> *A l'oeil provoquant et vainqueur?*
> *Ton courage est plein de promesses*
> *Comme le talent de l'auteur.*[9]

In September, 1867, in company with Monet, Renoir painted *La Grenouillère.* Three versions exist: those of the Oskar Reinhart collection at Winterthur and of the National Museum in Stockholm are close to Monet's composition (fig.

[9] Tintamarre, *Salon-Exposition des Beaux Arts de 1868,* Paris, chez Armand Léon, No. 2112.

51). But in the third, in the Museum of Modern Western Art in Moscow (fig. 94), the disposition of light and forms is more traditional and felicitous. Although the figures are brought forward, they are nevertheless not finished, and thus they increase the unity of style derived from the broken brush strokes in the reflections in the water. The trees of the background also participate in the variations of the light. The vibrancy of objects and persons gives the painting life—a life in the realm of fancy. And the vivacity of the brush stroke enhances the harmony of grey blue and green.

Thus, whether inspired by Courbet or by Monet, Renoir finds peerless poetry in lightness of brush stroke and delicacy of tone.

At the outbreak of the war of 1870 he enlisted in the light cavalry at Bordeaux but spent his time painting the portraits of his captain and of the latter's wife. Returning to Paris during the Commune, he painted, in addition to portraits, a "program painting" in which he combined elements of Velasquez, Manet, and Japanese prints. The year after he painted two revealing pictures: *Parisian Girls Dressed in Algerian Costume,* a pastiche derived from Delacroix, Courbet, and Diaz, and *The Pont Neuf* (fig. 95), a masterpiece. That is, in 1872 he found his true self in an outdoor motif and not in a painting of figures—an important fact in any attempt to understand what impressionism meant to Renoir. In *The Pont Neuf* blue dominates and harmonizes the whites, greys, greens, and low-toned yellows. Everything, the sky, the houses, the figures, the shadows, is seen in blue, and it is the nuances of blue which cause light to spring from the objects—a discreet light, contrasting with the large area of grey yellow on the bridge. This contrast, the fullness of the vision, and the virtuosity of the small but individualized human figures, are perhaps a vestige of his pre-impressionist training, but they are also the spontaneous manner of expression of a young man who is seizing control of his style and who is happy in his creative freedom and shouts his happiness aloud.

In figures the development of Renoir's style was slower. The famous *Theatre Box* in the Courtauld Collection, London, which was painted in 1874 and exhibited at the first impressionist show the same year, is certainly a marvel; and yet in it we feel the painter's defiant, triumphant virtuosity rather than spontaneous art. In 1876, however, there was a miraculous series of masterpieces.

The *Bathing Woman* (fig. 96) and *The Moulin de la Galette* (fig. 97) are perhaps the two most surprising creations of this year.

The *Bathing Woman* has a formal amplitude which belongs to tradition and which nevertheless glorifies the impressionistic colours; this is a foretaste of the monumentality which Renoir was so to love in his old age (*cf.* fig. 114). But the formal amplitude does not detract in the slightest from the grace, the joy, the vitality of colour and light. The pink flesh tones are transparent over green, the whites of the scarfs and draperies equally transparent over sky blue. The green of the armchair is shaded with purple; the blue of the background changes to purple; the black of the hair has blue reflections. It is an image of beauty, and it is something more: beauty become grace under the caress of colour and light.

In *The Moulin de la Galette* the images have the same

colour rhythm. The evanescent blues, greens, pinks, and yellows form an ever-changing unity, which has a reality beyond that which would have been achieved by means of outlines, and the colours sing of joy, grace, the smile of youth. It is a rapid, leaping dance rhythm which extends even to the seated figures. The vitality is intense, free, and yet light as a caress. Gradually, in the canvas, we become aware of numerous graceful girls (their faces divine in the half shadows) in relaxed poses, as befitting a popular outdoor dance hall in Montmartre. And we realize that the composition is of a rare kind, that it does not follow one line on the plane, one direction in depth, but is a simultaneous appearance of masses on the surface, despite a correct indication of perspective. If we have the patience to analyse still further, we see that this strange manner of composing is all one with the succession of the lights and darks and of the varied colours, that is, the entire composition, and not only the figures, is dependent on light. That this composition is entirely a creation of fancy and obeys no rules extraneous to its own unique existence has never been understood—not even by Renoir himself when in his old age he was seeking a more classic method. "Even today," he said at that time, "I am obliged to do violence to myself, to shake off my laziness, in order to create compositions and not paint only torsos or heads." [10] *The Moulin de la Galette* had done him no violence; it had been created with the same carefree happiness with which he had created the faces of his young girls.

By 1876, external influences, gropings, and programs had ceased to interfere with his work. In his scenes with figures

[10] André, *Renoir,* p. 55.

he had created an impressionism of his own, which was a perfect style because it was perfectly suited to his creative fancy.

The Moulin de la Galette illustrates the character of his impressionism. Vibrancy and discontinuity of brush stroke, division of tones for the purpose of achieving optical synthesis —that is, the style which extended to everything in the universe the principle of reflections of light in water—was more capable of achievement in landscapes than in figures, because the form of a tree, of a river, or of a hill is more susceptible of transformation according to the artist's fancy. The human form, on the other hand, is too familiar to the observer's eye, too closely bound up with our pride as human beings, for us to be able to be indifferent to its transformation. Renoir painted landscapes, flowers, and still lifes, but he preferred to paint figures. Indeed, his love of feminine grace was so great that it conditioned the transformation of images by his fancy. Monet loved nature for the purpose of interpreting it by means of his fancy according to the principle of light; Pissarro loved it for the purpose of recreating its constructive truth; Renoir loved it for the purpose of capturing in colour the grace which he felt in it. A too frequent discontinuity of brush stroke would have lessened the synthesis of grace which he derived from a face. Therefore the stroke is vibrant in clothing, in objects, in trees, in clusters of artificial lights, but it slackens in the faces, where gradations and nuances of tone are substituted for brush strokes. This was not a compromise but rather an ideal solution for obtaining from light and colour that grace which for centuries had been realized by plastic form.

A few examples of his many happy creations of these years confirm these observations.

The *Child with a Watering-Pot,* dated 1876 (fig. 98), is an unprecedented work of fancy, a moment of pure creation.

The *Woman with a Parasol, c.* 1876 (fig. 99), a fascinating harmony of greens and blues with a few touches of pink and yellow, fuses the figure and the landscape with small, broken strokes; in the face, however, these are so quiet as to be all but imperceptible. On one side of the picture space is vaguely hinted at, but the whole of the composition is seen on the surface, because the phantomlike lightness of the figure does not have to occupy space nor does the light itself have any weight. The identity of image and light is perfectly achieved.

The First Time at the Theatre, c. 1876 (fig. 100), repre-sents a theatre box, not closed as in the *Theatre Box* of 1874 but opening into the pit; the whole thing is a sparkle of light framing an enchanting profile.

That Renoir's impressionist style allowed him to penetrate the human soul, that the grace of his spirit did not exclude psychological complexities is well seen in the *Portrait of M. Chocquet,* 1876 (fig. 101). This patron of the impression-ists and especially of Renoir and Cézanne is sympathetically portrayed, with full justice done his sensibility. Years later Renoir said of this portrait that it was the "portrait of a mad-man by a madman." We can only sing the praises of such madness.

Social refinement was accentuated during the following years, and yet always present was the same fairylike enchant-ment—an enchantment of harmonies of blues and greens, or of yellows, pinks, and greens, of sparkling lights. These are seen in *At La Grenouillère*, dated 1879 (fig. 102), or in the *Woman in a Straw Hat*, of about the same time (fig. 103), in which the delicacy of the tones (all of which are light) recalls pastel, and even the reflections are tinted with pink.

Renoir had exhibited with the other impressionists in 1874, 1876, and 1877, but following the persistent hostility of the public and the disastrous financial results he was the first to withdraw from the group. In 1878 he exhibited at the official Salon, and the next year obtained a notable success there with *Madame Charpentier and Her Children*, 1878 (fig. 104). Madame Charpentier was the wife of the publisher of Flaubert, Zola, and Daudet and presided over a salon that was frequented by intellectuals and politicians; she was Renoir's patroness, and she saw to it that her portrait received proper official attention. Thus, that success which he had not achieved by means of his art alone Renoir did achieve through social connections. And when he was once launched, many realized that this so-called revolutionary was a tractable painter, quite capable of flattering a bourgeois model.

Madame Charpentier and Her Children is a large picture (1.90 metres by 1.54), and its size is an indication of the importance Renoir accorded it. The images are charming; the composition is nobly arranged; the woman, with her air of protective dignity, is dressed in black; the little girls, in white and sky blue, have a well-brought-up grace; the large dog, the table, the rug contribute to the impression of richness. What is lacking is the artist's spontaneity, his capacity to create outside of every convention, his ability to model his forms with light, the full body of his colour. The black and the sky-blue white of the images, the reds, yellows, and greens of the room are materials for the representation of a social convention; they are not a creative necessity. The picture is a social but not an artistic masterpiece.

As seen in the paintings reproduced as figures 102 and 103 and in many others, even after 1878 Renoir painted according to his impressionistic, personal, autonomous style whenever he was able to do so—that is, when he was free from social obligations. It is clear, however, that he was undergoing a spiritual crisis. In the memoirs of his friend Georges Rivière we read that Renoir did not want his wife and child to endure the privations that he had suffered before his marriage. "He was haunted by the necessity of assuring their existence, of making it as easy as he could. From then on he strove to find a formula which would satisfy at the same time his conscience as an artist and the taste of buyers of pictures. This moral crisis did not last very long, but long enough to be recorded in a certain number of important pictures which I can never look at without experiencing a feeling of pain." [11] Actually this crisis began in 1878, even before Renoir's marriage.

Certainly for some time Renoir himself was not aware of it —a fact which confirms the view of his character indicated above and at the same time explains the moral if not the artistic aspect of his conduct. His spontaneous naive acceptance of different kinds of reality prevented him from distinguishing those motifs which were suited to his fancy and style from others which were alien to them.

Following his success at the Salon of 1879 he was so pros-

[11] G. Rivière, *Renoir et ses amis*, 1921, p. 199.

perous that he was able to decline an offer of money made him by Durand-Ruel, and he felt that France was too small for him. In March, 1881, he went to Algiers and from there wrote to Durand-Ruel to justify his sending of pictures to the official Salon and his withdrawal from the group of impressionists. "I must simply paint as well as possible. If people accused me of neglecting my art, or of sacrificing my convictions out of foolish ambition, I would understand the critics. But since nothing of that kind is involved, there is no basis for criticism. On the contrary . . . I am keeping away from all painters, living here in the sun, in order to think. I believe I have found what I need. I beg you, therefore, to plead my cause with my friends. My sending pictures to the Salon is a purely commercial matter." [12] From Algiers he went to London, where he visited his friend Théodore Duret and even studied English, but he soon returned to Paris and wrote Duret, "I am struggling with flowering trees, with women and children, and that is all I care about." [13] Aline Charigot, his future wife, entered his life at this time, and she is shown playing with a little dog in the foreground of *The Boating Party at Lunch* (fig. 105), which he painted in the summer of 1881.

The restaurant of Mère Fournaise at Bougival on the Seine had been frequented by Renoir and his friends since the time of the painting of *La Grenouillère*. There he once again found himself in an atmosphere similar to that which had inspired *The Moulin de la Galette,* but now there was added his new enjoyment of the pleasures afforded by gracious women, good wine, flowering trees, reflections of water and light, and by the

[12] L. Venturi, *Les Archives de l'Impressionnisme,* I, p. 115.
[13] Michel Florisoone in *L'Amour de l'Art,* February, 1938.

refined intelligence, subtle gaiety, and witty conversation that are among the greatest charms of Parisian life. It was natural that here Renoir should not feel hampered by demands imposed by social convention and that he should create freely according to his impressionistic style, once again inventing a composition that was beyond all rules, alive and fantastic, with certain forms more clearly delineated than previously and with stronger, full-singing colours, red predominating over the blue-green harmony of 1876.

This work, the last of Renoir's impressionist period, can be considered the glorious close of his youth.

In the autumn of 1881 he went to Italy, where he visited Venice, Florence, Rome, Naples, Palermo. From Naples he wrote to Durand-Ruel on November 21, "I am still in the agony of search. I am not happy, and I rub out and rub out again. . . . I went to see the Raphaels in Rome. They are wonderfully beautiful, and I should have seen them earlier. They are full of knowledge and good sense. Unlike me, he did not seek impossible things. But they are beautiful. I prefer Ingres in oil painting. But Raphael's frescos are admirable in their simplicity and grandeur." [14]

Thus his crisis had been transferred from the social sphere to that of his art. In Paris and Algiers his search for a form outside impressionism had been a social necessity and his exhibiting in the Salon had been a commercial move; in Rome, the study of Raphael seems to have made him suspect that with impressionism he had sought the impossible. Indeed he saw Raphael with the eyes of Ingres; he wished to turn

[14] L. Venturi, *op. cit.*, pp. 116–117.

backward, leaving impressionism, Courbet, and Delacroix behind, to regain the pure form of neo-classicist romanticism.

As we have already seen, the crisis of those years was common to all the impressionists. But Renoir's crisis was unique in that he sought to ally himself to the tradition of plastic and drawing against which impressionism had rebelled, a trend that was all too likely to fall into academism. He is indeed the "cork carried by the current," unable to distinguish the various currents which are carrying him.

For several years the figures painted by Renoir bore the mark of the crisis caused by Raphael and Ingres. His landscapes, however, did not. Returning from Italy, he met Cézanne in Marseilles, and worked with him at L'Estaque. Cézanne was at that very moment laying the foundations of his constructive style, which without opposing or denying the light-colour feelings of impressionism was to give them an architecture of space. From him, Renoir derived an understanding of the value of volumes and planes in depth, and in one picture, *Rocks at L'Estaque,* he imitated him. But elsewhere he absorbed into his impressionistic style certain of the demands which Cézanne made of his own art, and in these cases the results were excellent. For example, in *L'Estaque* of 1882 (fig. 106) the brush stroke, the light, the rapidity and lightness of the vibration are typical of Renoir and of his best impressionistic style, but the closed composition and the volumes and planes in depth representing the bay of Marseilles are a new contribution which, although in perfect accord with his style, have an evident Cézanne-esque character.

It was thanks to landscape, to outdoor painting, that Renoir was able to continue his impressionistic spirit even during the years of crisis. The importance of landscape in his work, which is apparent in the manifesto of the "Society of Irregularists" mentioned before, is explicitly confirmed in a letter written to Durand-Ruel from La Rochelle in the summer of 1884: "I have lost a great deal, working in four square metres of studio. I would have gained ten years had I followed Monet's example a little." [15] (Monet was at this time painting at Bordighera.)

However, Renoir struggled to find a new style for his figures.

In the autumn of 1885 he wrote to Durand-Ruel, "Once again I have taken up my old soft, light style of painting, and will never again abandon it. It is a continuation of 18th century painting . . . (a kind of lesser Fragonard). I have just finished a young girl sitting on a seashore, which I think will satisfy you." [16]

Renoir does not say in his letter whether the young girl is clothed or nude, but if nude the picture is probably the *Bathing Woman* (fig. 107). Of all his works this is perhaps the closest to Fragonard. All experimentation with light is omitted, but the figure is caressed so lovingly by the brush, and is so sensitive even though its forms are modelled and plastically abstracted from the atmosphere, that in it Renoir's spirit is fully realized. Thus out of an older beauty a new one was born, thanks to that intangible which can only be called the ardour of creation.

At this time Renoir became obsessed by the accusation that he could not draw as well as Degas. Over a long period he executed drawings and sketches for a composition which

[15] L. Venturi, *op. cit.*, p. 130.   [16] L. Venturi, *op. cit.*, p. 132.

became *The Grandes Baigneuses,* 1887 (fig. 108), exhibited at the International Exhibition at the Georges Petit Gallery, which opened May 7, 1887. Monet spoke of it as "a superb picture, understood not by all but by many." Renoir said of it, "I think that I have taken a step forward, a little step, in the public's esteem. The public seems to be coming . . . Why this time and not the others? I can't understand it." [17] More than sixty years later we are better able to understand; no picture that he had painted up to that time corresponded as well as *The Grandes Baigneuses* to the public's academic taste. Pissarro noted that Renoir was now concentrating on line and that therefore his figures were separate entities, detached from each other without regard to colour.[18] The composition was inspired by a relief by François Girardon in the park at Versailles: thus Renoir's desire to refresh himself at the eighteenth-century source becomes in this case direct imitation.

Outlines are pure, obviously inspired by Ingres; the masses are well balanced on the surface; but life itself is lacking, that life which since 1864 Renoir had always infused into his images. His preoccupation with purity of form petrified his creative force, and the colour does not succeed in giving life to the abstract forms. The flesh tones are warm purple browns, the stuffs are now sky-blue white, now light yellow and blue, and the whole is well harmonized with the marvellous landscape of blue, red, yellow, and nuances of green; nevertheless we feel that the colour does not constitute the forms but remains extraneous to them. The purity of the forms and the vitality of the colouring are two distinct acts of creation, never

[17] L. Venturi, *op. cit.,* pp. 325 and 138.   [18] *Letters,* pp. 107–108.

fused. At this moment of refinement of form, Renoir committed a grave error of taste.

He was guilty of numerous such errors until 1890, especially in compositions and portraits. He went wrong much less often in his heads of girls: in these the liveliness of his impression was so strong that it held in check his tendency to emphasize line. *Young Girl,* for example (fig. 109), probably about 1890, is very pure in form; but its outlines are nuanced and allow for a continual gradation of colours on the yellow-green background—from the reddish blond of the hair to the light flesh with its suggestion of full-blooded youth. Here refinement does not detract from the vitality of the image but renders it the more precious.

By 1889 Renoir was quite content with his own work; in 1890 he exhibited for the last time in the official Salon, and in 1892 a large one-man exhibition at Durand-Ruel definitely established his position: the state purchased one of his pictures. Now, after various fluctuations of fortune, his place was assured, and he was to have no further financial worries. About this same time his health began to deteriorate and caused him much suffering, but he fought back with courage. He continued to seek out his style and constantly modified it —not for the sake of others, as in 1878 and 1887, but for himself, to achieve full expression.

Bathing Girls Playing with a Crab, about 1897 (fig. 110), reveals that the crisis is definitely over. The figures in this composition are no longer coldly executed, meaningless exercises in line and virtuosity; they are young girls freely playing, darting between the reefs, their pink flesh silver in the light against the blue-green sea and violet-grey sky; the picture is like a cry of joy by the artist. Here the lines are really intertwined; the composition is taken not from the works of others but from nature. Renoir has rediscovered himself.

The first and most important effect of this new state of Renoir's art was that his style once more became unified, in figures as well as in landscapes. The clash between the two styles in the years 1880 to 1890 had resulted from a compromise with respect to the theme represented, from a shifting of interest away from the painting to the motif. After 1890 the landscapes are still executed out of doors, and light continues to be vibrant in the colour, but the separation from nature is increasingly evident in the intensity of the colour, in the attention given to volumes, and in the summariness of the outlines. The representation of reality becomes secondary to the presentation of a world of the painter's fancy, a world which he fills with his lyrical enthusiasm for light and life. Figures become a synthesis of abstract form and air; in them, Renoir's former grace is transformed into monumental values, very solid volumes are immersed in a cosmic vibrancy, and his sensual enthusiasm and exuberant fancy are objectivized in singing reds and massive forms.

There is an undeniable parallel between Renoir's new researches and those of Cézanne. In Renoir's impressionist period, volume was lightly, happily sacrificed; now it is an essential condition of his art. And beyond the volume and the vision there is a new consciousness of the autonomy of art, of its development by the fancy in an ideal world—a consciousness already given full pictorial realization by Cézanne about 1885.

One who loves the creative temperament of Renoir in his impressionist period, his identification with the graceful variation of light and colour, his "irregularity," is apt to feel that his new, later style is less well adapted to his temperament. And it is true that Renoir's temperament and his style now become divergent. Memoirs by his friends and acquaintances written at this time [19] show us that he had not essentially changed in personality from the gentle, easy-going lover of grace visible to us in his style of 1876. But from 1896 on, his style *has* changed. It has a new solemnity that goes beyond his character as a man. And yet this divergence between the man and the artist, far from resulting in creative weakness, becomes a creative force; it is as if Renoir's new art signified not only a withdrawal from the life of nature in favor of the production of his fancy but also a detachment from his own life as a man.

His physical suffering was atrocious. "I really think I am finished as far as painting is concerned," he wrote in 1904. "I can do nothing more." But at Cagnes, where he spent every winter and spring from 1903 on, he revived in the sun, amidst the abundance of money, which he accepted with a gently ironic smile, and the honours which meant so much to him. Paul Durand-Ruel, who visited him in December, 1912, wrote, "Renoir is in the same sad state, but always astonishing in his force of character. He cannot walk or even get up from his armchair. Two people have to carry him everywhere. What agony! And still he shows the same good humour, the same contentment when he can paint. He has already done several things, and yesterday he completed an entire torso,

[19] For example, Thadée Natanson in the *Revue Blanche,* 1896.

begun in the morning. It is not very finished, but superb." [20]
Monet, living far away at Giverny on the Seine, received on
one day the news that Renoir was dying and on the next the
news that he was fully active, and he rejoiced in the miracle.
There is something heroic in Renoir's triumph over hostile
nature, over death itself, for more than fifteen years, in order
that he might continue to enjoy the sun, flowers, and the nude
and to capture in his art his delight in colour. He was sincere
in 1876 when he painted in a manner that was contrary to all
heroism, but he was just as sincere after 1900 when he gave
every picture a heroic afflatus. He owed his new moral greatness to his struggle for life, and the greatness of his art was
the token of his every resurrection.

The production of these years is immense—perhaps because Renoir no longer had to search to find his way, perhaps
because the execution is summary and rapid. His portraits, in
general, are not among his best things; except when he
painted children, the impulse of his fancy was too free to find
complete realization in an objective image. But as in 1876 he
achieved full expression in the portrait of Chocquet, now in
1910 he triumphed again in that of *Paul Durand-Ruel* (fig.
111), with whom Renoir more than anyone else in the impressionist circle maintained relations of affectionate friend-
ship. The refinement of the face and expression is worthy of
the portrait of Chocquet, and if the latter has more grace and
is a more exceptional work of art, the 1910 portrait is more
surely composed and richer in humanity.

Similarly we may compare *L'Estaque* of 1882 (fig. 106)
with a landscape of the last years, for example that reproduced

[20] L. Venturi, *Les Archives de l'Impressionnisme,* I, p. 107.

in figure 112. The summariness of the execution harmonizes with the synthesis, the vitality of the effect, the artist's freedom of fancy.

Certainly the style of the last years is revealed in all its power in the more or less completed nudes painted from his models (among whom Gabrielle and Dédée have remained famous). The *Woman's Torso* of about 1905 (fig. 113), *After the Bath* of 1913 (fig. 114), *Gabrielle at the Mirror* of about 1910 (fig. 115) are typical examples of a very long series. Monumentality, vitality, power have amply compensated for grace, and it should be remembered that at this time Renoir dedicated himself to sculpture, feeling a need to emphasize full relief. And his emphasis upon the rotundity of his models is, as in the case of Rubens, an incentive to pictorial volume.

In the *Woman's Torso* the contrast of light and shadow has a romantic character and an effect of mystery; in *After the Bath* every extra-pictorial allusion is lacking, and the beauty of the work depends upon the colouring and more especially upon the harmony of the reddish pinks and greens and whites. The red hair and reddish pink flesh, the strips of red in the background, the red rug—all these varied reds have a life of their own, catch fire together, and are limited by the greens and the whites. Their vitality is exceptional in the art of all time; they are the product of pure fancy, representing detachment from physical reality and mirroring an exalted emotion.

The colour of the late Renoir becomes, so to speak, cursive —that is, as the product of a constant manner of feeling, it takes into account neither the motif nor the natural impression and can serve every requirement of the artist's fancy.

Renoir's pretexts were many: scenes from Greek plays, caryatids, judgements of Paris, compositions of bathers—any pretext served for the continual flow of his harmony of reds.

Bathing Women (fig. 116) is one of the most felicitous. Here, as in *The Grandes Baigneuses* of 1887, the poses of the images mean nothing; they exist for the simple purpose of balancing the composition and for nothing else. But of the pure line and formal effort of 1887 nothing remains; there is only a continuous flow of reddened masses, which acquires a naturalness and spontaneity of its own thanks to the vitality of the colour harmony.

Renoir's last style is not a synthesis of his former manners. He did not look behind him, towards his glorious past, but, profiting by all his experiences, he launched headlong towards a new style, which in its autonomy, in the daring of its form and colour was a door opening into the future.

Chapter Seven

PAUL CEZANNE

IF ONE were to pretend to converse with an artist by looking at his pictures, one could imagine the delight of a meeting with Renoir, the benevolent, lavish welcome of Pissarro, the acute interest which would be aroused by a meeting with Monet. But one would feel a certain fear before the greatness of Cézanne, as if one were entering an unknown world—a world vast, rich, severe, studded with peaks of such great height as to seem—or perhaps to be—inaccessible. And after wandering about in that world, say for twenty years, and admiring all its wonders to the accompaniment of a chorus of voices singing hosannas to the master, one would pause to reflect on all the obstacles which the critics and the artist himself have placed in the way of an understanding of that world, and one would come to pessimistic conclusions concerning the theoretical bases of the critics and concerning the artist's own lack of consciousness of his greatness.

Indeed the critics' prejudices still continue although today they assume different forms from in the past. "Incomplete art," "genius without talent," "failure"—all those legends invented by Zola, Duranty, and their circle were long an obstacle to an understanding of the artist Cézanne. And even the best critics of today, who have destroyed those legends and proclaim Cézanne's perfection, feel it necessary to measure him by classic standards instead of recognizing that his fancy is neither classic nor romantic but simply his own.

Cézanne himself, after suffering atrocious discouragements (very understandable considering the general obtuse hostility which his art aroused) and after being driven into isolation by his own exacerbation, continued to the last to proclaim his own dissatisfaction at his inability to "realize"—a dissatisfaction with which those who listened to him were only too glad to agree. True, from time to time Cézanne rebelled against the judgement of others and against his own depressions: "I am beginning to find myself stronger than those around me" (1874); [1] "There is only one painter alive at the present time, myself"; "There are two thousand politicians in every legislature, but there is only one Cézanne every two hundred years." [2] Those were sudden flares, quickly extinguished. The admiration of young painters was a balm to his spirit in his last years, and dogged, desperate work was his means of defying his own and others' lack of understanding.

Cézanne was born at Aix-en-Provence in 1839 and died there in 1906. The son of a hatter who prospered and became a banker, he had the advantages of a fairly complete humanistic education in his native city and of being able to go to Paris to study painting and to continue to paint in his own way without worrying about the necessities of life.

In Paris he assimilated the pictorial experiments of romanticism, realism, and nascent impressionism; Aix held the possibility of solitude, of meditation, of love for the vastness and solemnity of nature, for the sun of the Midi. The two cities were the two poles of his life: the one was the scene of his

---

[1] L. Venturi, *Cézanne*, p. 26.   [2] Rewald, *Cézanne*, p. 416.

intellectual torments; the other saw the free expansion of his personality.

His humanistic education, his love of literature, which caused him as a youth to hesitate between poetry and painting, his romantic enthusiasm, his life-long admiration for Delacroix and his interest in the realism of Courbet—all these kept Cézanne from participating in the first impressionist attempts of Monet, Renoir, and Pissarro, although he was acquainted with all three of those artists. As early as 1866 Cézanne wrote to Zola, "Pictures painted indoors, in the studio, will never equal those done in the open air . . . I must resolve to work only out of doors." [3] And it is well known that Zola's ideas expressed in defence of Manet, Monet, and Pissarro were suggested to him by Cézanne.

Nevertheless in his production from 1865 to 1871 there is to be found no outdoor painting, no approach to impressionism.

The *Portrait of a Monk,* 1865–67 (fig. 117), *Pastoral,* 1870 (fig. 118), and *Melting Snow at L'Estaque, c.* 1870 (fig. 119), are three typical examples of Cézanne's work when he had barely finished his schooling.

In the *Portrait of a Monk* he painted, in the habit of the member of a religious society, an individual of whom during these years he made no less than five other portraits and who has entered history as Uncle Dominic. The monk's costume allowed Cézanne a strong contrast of colour between the light yellow white of the habit and the purple grey of the background, a colour relation broken into by the reddish pink flesh, by the brown-black hair, and in general by the black

[3] Cézanne, *Correspondance,* pp. 98–99.

120

shadows. The painter's aim was to achieve a richness of substance *per se*, independent of what it represented and independent of any effect of light and atmosphere. And since a thick colour is more intense as to chromatic quality than a colour which is thin and transparent, Cézanne used the palette knife rather than the brush. In the use of the knife he followed Courbet, but the richness of his substance is greater than that of the latter. And the brutality of the effect, too, is greater than Courbet's because of the absolute lack of chiaroscuro or of nuances of colour. The image is not modelled, but stands out, that is, it detaches itself from the background by force of contrast rather than by chiaroscuro. The form is presented as a mass, powerfully framed, a summary mass intended to be seen from a distance but executed as though it were sensed materially at close range. In this picture Cézanne takes possession of pictorial substance: he does not represent a human image. The model does not interest him *per se* but only for his own reaction. Looking at this image, no one can deny that the painter has mastered the means of his art with youthful fury, one might even say with rage; but as happened in the youth of other great artists, for example Titian and Velasquez, he is vigorous in his execution before he has discovered the relationship between execution and conception which is fundamental to art. Antony Valabrèque, a friend who posed for Cézanne, wrote Zola on October 2, 1866, "Every time Cézanne paints one of his friends, he seems to avenge himself for some hidden injury." [4] There could be no better comment on the unleashed energy and the artistic limitations of the *Portrait of a Monk*.

[4] Rewald, *Cézanne*, p. 168.

His unsatisfied sexual longing, complicated by his timidity in the presence of women, explains certain compositions of these years which seem like obsessive dreams, for example *The Temptation of St. Anthony* and *Pastoral* (fig. 118). Cézanne does not contemplate his passion, he lives in it; thus he does not represent it but imposes it on the observer. The colours are of a magnificent intensity, not only in the blue of the sky and the yellow white or orange pink of the clouds but also in the greys, blacks, and browns (with an occasional touch of pink) of the foreground. The forms are seen without outlines or chiaroscuro, as masses which appear or disappear according to the caprices of the painter's sensuality, and which would have artistic value only if immersed in atmosphere by means of vibrancy of light and shadow. But his insistence on thick, rich substance allows for neither atmosphere nor light, and for this reason the effect is arbitrary, valuable only as the affirmation of a romantic dream, as the need to go beyond the representation of reality. What seemed to the critics a weakness of drawing was thus only an effort to escape from the current tradition of drawing, to make the human image equivalent to the form of a cloud or of a boat. And if the result is not happy, this is because of the excessive passion, not yet dominated by art.

Cézanne achieved stylistic coherence more easily when he painted a landscape, as in *Melting Snow at L'Estaque* (fig. 119). His passion is strong: the snow, the trees, the very earth seem swept away by the fury of the elements, and the entire composition keeps precipitous pace with the impetus of passion. The colours, however, become lighter: orange in the sky, yellow and black in the trees, red in the roofs, and the greys are nuanced. Thus, despite the passion the painting as a whole reveals the detachment of an observer.

It is not by chance that the fullness of Cézanne's art was first achieved in a still life, *The Black Clock,* 1869–71 (fig. 121). Previously he had imagined hallucinatory scenes, but their subjects were of considerably less importance to him than their colour harmonies, and for this reason he felt himself at his ease when subject interest did not exist. In *The Black Clock* substance is still thick, but now he uses the brush rather than the knife and spreads the layers of colour with greater lightness and delicacy. Whites and blacks still dominate but are varied with reds, yellows, blues. Above all, the form harmonizes with the colouring; planes become well defined; volumes appear. Passion remains, but it is totally inherent in forms and colours; it is the passion of art rather than of sensuality.

In his achievement of this result Cézanne had been favourably influenced by Manet, with his beautiful lightness, his refinement, his civilization; but when Cézanne took over elements from the art of others, he so radically transformed them and filled them with passion that it becomes difficult to sense their presence.

It was natural that a production of this kind, which was without direct precedent, should frighten both friends and enemies. They did, of course, vaguely sense the genius of the artist, the "freak of nature" as Duret and Pissarro called him, but they were so confused that to justify themselves they improvised the theory of Cézanne's inability to "realize." At that time there had been limited experience with the secrets of mystery in art, and the principle of the necessity of fidelity to nature was unquestioned, even though temporary infidelities were permitted. Today our familiarity with abstractions in art makes it easy for us to understand that in his passionate fancy of the years 1865–71, Cézanne, using realism as a point of departure, had sketched a style which anticipated fauvism and expressionism.

After painting at L'Estaque, near Marseilles, during the war of 1870–71, Cézanne returned to Paris and to Auvers-sur-Oise, and following Pissarro's advice and example, he turned towards impressionism. In his works previous to 1872 he had looked not outward but within himself, and even if he had not evidenced a sense of structure in his compositions, he had emphasized the weight, volume, solidity, and largeness of his images—a premise, even though slight and as yet evident chiefly in feeling, of formal structure. Pissarro taught Cézanne above all to look at the world outside, to study external reality rather than merely to love or hate his model, and to find in light and shadow the reason for every form; and furthermore, since it was Pissarro himself who had brought to impressionism a structural consciousness of vision, he taught him to extend the solidity and volume of the image, inborn in Cézanne, to an architecture of the picture.

The House of the Hanged Man, 1873 (fig. 120), shows us Cézanne at the height of his renewal. He still employs the thick substance of his earlier years but adapts it to the rather summary nuances with which he seeks to show objects as a function of light and shadow. The sense of volume takes possession of the space in depth, and is thus affirmed and intensified, while at the same time it achieves full artistic value and naturalness. That is, Cézanne fully realizes the relation between volume and space, carrying to an extreme what he had assimilated from Pissarro and giving it a sense of firmness, of synthesis, a sense of things seen in an eternal and universal light, with a new effect quite different from any achieved by Pissarro. If the light is still summary, it is so because of the need he felt for synthesis and largeness.

Thus in a little more than a year Cézanne made himself over completely. He put behind him his romantic rhetoric, his painting of the impossible, his pride in painting things that had never been seen but that had troubled his restless fancy. And for these he substituted the humility of the artist who worships his motif because it is created by nature, the complete balance of the man who feels everything in the universe as sharing his own intimate life.

The Boundary Wall, c. 1876 (fig. 122), shows that Cézanne has not only assimilated the motif and the manner of seeing things characteristic of the impressionists but also their manner of execution. The colours are applied with strokes that are discontinuous, short, and slanted in all directions, in order to allow reflections to fuse light and colours in the brush stroke. The wall is purple with reflections of the trees in blue, the field is green, the earth green yellow, the trunks are grey or grey brown, the foliage green with one yellow branch, the roofs red, and the sky grey. Deep space is obtained almost entirely by means of the colours, which are more or less enveloped in atmosphere. In short, everything in this picture is in conformity with impressionism, and not even Cézanne's particular sense of largeness clashes with it.

The value of Cézanne's new vision is apparent in landscapes and in the *Still Life* of 1873 (fig. 123). Motif and background no longer clash but by their accord accentuate the synthesis of the vision, and there results from this the immersion of objects in atmosphere. The artist places in the background a tapestry to vary his planes continually, to solve the problem of space around the objects, to give them, as it were, a breath of luminosity. And the synthesis of the vision, which extends to both full and empty areas, makes it possible to define the planes and volumes of the objects. Although objects are firm, lightness results from the vibrancy of the reflections. On the base of whites and greens, the blues of the vase and the reds of the tomato and of the wine are of a brilliant intensity. As in *The House of the Hanged Man* the substance is still thick, but the fusion of light and form is complete.

We can well understand the new human inspiration which impressionism suggested to Cézanne in his *Portrait of Victor Chocquet*, 1876–77 (fig. 124). The hair, the beard, the blue-grey coat, the blue-white shirt, the reddish flesh tones stand out against a light green background: the effect is thus one of dark on light. Brush strokes, although thick in colour, vary in order that the light may be vibrant, indeed that the light itself may form the image. From this perfect unity of form and colour springs the image of a man, the patron dear to Cézanne and to Renoir, sensitive, serious, melancholy, strong willed, with a profound moral sense. Here the object of art and the representation of a human life become identical because of the interest which the man Chocquet arouses in Cézanne and because of the artist's ability to see not only objects in nature but also spiritual values. If this picture is compared with the *Portrait of a Monk,* we can measure the road travelled by the artist in about ten years and the infinite vastness of his new horizon.

In 1874 and 1877 Cézanne had exhibited with the impressionists. He had been attacked even more violently than the others, and although he was loyal to them, he was depressed by the failure of the exhibitions to achieve any financial success, and he withdrew from the group, as Monet and Renoir had also done, and gradually isolated himself and lived for longer and longer periods at Aix.

This is the reason which he gave in 1889 for his isolation: "I had resolved to work in silence until the day when I could defend theoretically the result of my efforts." [5]

The theory which Cézanne wished to formulate in words, and even more in his works, is today well known.

Painting is for Cézanne a "means of expressing sensations." They are sensations of colour: "Pure drawing is an abstraction. Drawing and colour are not at all distinct, everything in nature being coloured. One draws as one paints. Rightness of tone produces both light and the modelling of the object. The greater the colour harmony, the more precise the drawing. Contrasts and relationships of tone—that is the whole secret of drawing and modelling." "A strong feeling for nature— and certainly mine is very keen—is the necessary basis for every conception of art, the basis on which the grandeur and beauty of the art of the future must rest. And no less essential is the knowledge of the means of expressing our emotion." (1904.)

[5] L. Venturi, *Cézanne*, p. 42 *et seq.;* also for passages quoted below unless other references are given.

As Henri Matisse once said, "There were so many possibilities in Cézanne that more than another man he needed to put his brain in order." A famous letter of 1904 indicates what this order was: "See nature as cylinder, sphere, and cone, the whole placed in perspective, so that each side of an object or plane is directed toward a central point. Lines parallel to the horizon give breadth—that is, a section of nature, or, if you prefer, of the spectacle which God the Father, omnipotent and eternal, unfolds before our eyes. Lines perpendicular to the horizon give depth. Now nature is for us more a matter of depth than of surface—whence the necessity of introducing into our vibrations of light, represented by reds and yellows, a sufficient number of bluish tones to give a feeling of air." [6]

Cylinders, spheres, and cones are not to be seen in Cézanne's paintings; thus his statement expressed an ideal aspiration towards an organization of forms transcending nature—nothing more. And this statement can be completed by others:

"The method emerges on contact with nature. It is developed by circumstances. It consists in seeking the expression of what one feels, in organizing sensations into a personal aesthetic." [7]

Or, as Emile Bernard quotes him as saying, "The transposition made by the painter according to his personal optics gives a new interest to the nature which he has reproduced. He puts down as a painter what was never before painted; this makes him a painter absolutely. That is to say, something other than reality. This is no longer banal imitation." [8]

Cézanne expressed the wish to "make impressionism some-

[6] Cézanne, *Correspondance*, p. 259.
[7] Rewald, *Cézanne*, p. 348.
[8] Emile Bernard, *Souvenirs sur Paul Cézanne*, Paris, n.d., p. 114.

thing solid and lasting like the art of the museums," a wish which he confirmed by saying, "In my thought, one does not substitute one's self for the past; one merely adds a new link to the chain." [9]

All this gives a summary idea of the kind of aphorism that with Cézanne passes under the name of theory.

From it we can deduce especially his need to find a relationship or rather a fusion between the sensation of colour and light and formal order, and between spatial composition in depth and the laying of tones on the surface, in order that he might go beyond any imitation of nature and create for himself a personal optics and a personal aesthetic. Now it is obvious that Cézanne brought his painting to realization but not his theory. An optics, an aesthetic are realized in volumes of philosophy, not in works of fancy. His *aspiration* to his own optics and his own aesthetic was realized as he went along— but precisely *as aspiration*, as desire, not as formulated thought. And his painting is art precisely because in it thought is present only as aspiration. Cézanne's complaint that he was unable to "realize" was valid only as regards his thought, not his art.

The landscapes reproduced in figures 125 to 131, all painted between 1882 and the end of the century, are typical examples of Cézanne's happy creations in the period during which he was concentrating particularly on his search for formal order. A gradual transition from search to certainty is evident if we compare *The Little Bridge,* 1882–85 (fig. 125), with *The Bridge over the Marne at Créteil, c.* 1888 (fig. 126). The impressionists had found the essential principle of their art

[9] *Correspondance,* January 23, 1905, p. 273.

in reflections in water: Cézanne derived from these the motif for reconstructing his elementary forms. In *The Little Bridge* this is emphasized by the circle resulting from the reflection of an arch of a bridge. But he retained his sensitivity to the irregularity of nature, and therefore he distorted the circle and thus succeeded in harmonizing vision in depth and vision on the surface. The effect is precisely a vision on the surface with continual suggestions of deep space. By means of a complicated study of reflections and by means of corrections in key with these, he regains ingenuousness of vision. The brush stroke is broken but regular, with a constant rhythm, and the dominating green becomes yellow when representing light and blue when it enters into shadow.

The Bridge over the Marne at Créteil develops space in depth and emphasizes the synthetic character, thus giving an effect of monumentality. The balance is perfect between the empty areas (the sky and that part of the water untouched by reflections) and the full areas, consisting in part of the reflections, which have the necessary transparency and yet are ordered in such a fashion as to acquire a quality of volume. The colours, too, varied yellows, reds, and greens, form part of a general harmony of contrasts and of nuances of blue. Despite the variety of the elements, unity of vision is perfectly achieved, and it is a vision of the absolute, of firmness, certainty, largeness.

Similarly *Houses at L'Estaque*, 1882–85 (fig. 127), is a delicate, tremulous vision of rock strata and of houses with but few doors and windows, these being omitted to draw attention to plain surfaces in sunlight or in penumbra. All this is spontaneously created, not pre-ordained or deliberate.

Cézanne seems to discover his abstract form as he goes and to be surprised at his own discoveries. This is the moment in which he succeeds in giving order to his feeling, and in which his feeling, in turn, acquires a self-evident existence thanks to this newly discovered order. The result is a particular charm which recalls that produced by the works of the Italian primitives.

The Montagne Sainte-Victoire, near Gardanne, 1885–86 (fig. 128), shows Cézanne already in full control of his regular volumes and of their distribution in deep space. The tremulousness of the preceding picture is lacking; there is certainty and complexity of organization. Houses, rocks, everything is treated with the same distribution of light and shadow and of light blue and pink tones beyond the green field, to constitute the voluminous mass against the sky. Seen from Gardanne, the Montagne Sainte-Victoire is nothing but a rocky slope, and Cézanne takes advantage of the very barrenness of the motif for the simplification and regularization which makes his picture monumental.

Seen from Aix-en-Provence, on the other hand, the Montagne Sainte-Victoire is an almost conical mountain. From youth to old age Cézanne portrayed his mountain with special affection, and in 1885–87 he represented it several times looming over the entire valley of the Arc to which it lends grandeur and poetry, as for example in *The Montagne Sainte-Victoire with Tall Pine* (fig. 129).

If we look at the Montagne Sainte-Victoire from the point at which Cézanne stood (Bellevue), we notice that he has brought the mountain forward, to give its volume a greater solidity and to adapt it to the concavity of the valley; this is another example of organized form distorting the natural vision, but for the purpose of giving it a salience which the natural vision does not possess. And this salience has the effect of bringing the more distant parts violently forward to the surface, as is emphasized by the pine tree framing the scene. Here the decorative intent is clear, but this is the decorative quality which characterizes any distribution of pictorial elements on the surface and yet does not hamper vision in depth but rather makes it clearer by contrast.

The energy of representation, the implicit passion, present in the decorative value of *The Montagne Sainte-Victoire with Tall Pine,* can be seen in another *Montagne Sainte-Victoire* painted between 1894 and 1900 (fig. 131). Here the mountain no longer closes the wide valley; it is felt by Cézanne in all its strength, all its largeness, and it becomes menacing. The summariness of the foreground brings the rocky mass forward, and the simple forms of the rocks have a potential of motion, or rather of struggle, of battle. Passion once more prevails over contemplation. Instead of feeling the serenity of a broad vision, we hear the cry of forces unleashed by the earth.

Cézanne had for some time been enchanted by the motif of *The Bay of Marseilles, seen from L'Estaque,* and he painted it several times, for example in the picture reproduced in figure 130, painted between 1883 and 1885. In reality, the mountains seen from L'Estaque are many miles farther away and hence can be seen but vaguely. To indicate their structure, Cézanne brought them forward. But he preserved the space-relationship between nearness and distance, choosing to change the foreground and make it more distant than in reality. That is, he abstracted both foreground and background from their real positions, and he excluded from the space of the picture the place where he was standing and hence every subjective reference. He treats the surface of the sea in similar fashion, seeing it from a considerable elevation (today we would say from the air), in order that it may appear to rise and give the impression of great volume. And it is the mass of the water which makes the distance of the background convincing, even though the mountains have a thickness of volume that in reality is theirs only when they are seen at close range. Cézanne thus organized an objective relationship between the village, the sea, and the mountain, objective not with respect to nature but with respect to the picture, to art. In nature "near" and "far" are the material terms of a finite world. Cézanne's work is thus coherent, self-sufficient, belonging to no particular world; it is a world in itself, which belongs to the infinite and to the universal and has the solemnity of things that live eternally.

In still lifes the unity of artistic vision as Cézanne understood it—that is, autonomous with respect to the vision of nature—often inspired him to compel the volumes, the forms in depth, to conform to the surface effect. A typical case is *The Kitchen Table,* 1888–90 (fig. 132). As Erle Loran has shown, the basket of fruit and the plane of the table are seen at different levels, and the left and right parts of the table cannot possibly meet under the table-cloth. That is, Cézanne consciously distorts objects to represent them from different points of view, to turn around them and emphasize their three-dimensional character, and to realize by means of distortion the vital energy of the objects. This is a system which

133

he frequently employed, and he emphasized it in the production of his last years, both in landscapes and in portraits, always for the purpose of increasing vitality. Yet he always knew how to preserve the verisimilitude of his unified vision —that is, the parallel between artistic and natural vision, unlike the cubists, who made use of his distortions to break up their vision into fragments.

The celebrated beauty of Cézanne's still lifes depends precisely on the authority with which he succeeds in convincing us that his "distorted" vision is truer, more self-evident, and more vital than the common mortal's vision of real objects.

Whereas between 1882 and 1888 Cézanne's attention seems to have been concentrated chiefly on landscape for the purpose of finding in it the order of his sensations, from 1890 to the end of the century his greatest masterpieces were human figures.

The *Portrait of Paul Cézanne*, 1890–94 (fig. 133), is perhaps the most human image of himself that he produced. The meetings of the facial planes are as energetic as those of the planes of the rocks in *The Montagne Sainte-Victoire* (fig. 131), and yet they faithfully depict the impression made by Cézanne's face in reality, his moral nature and his sharp, penetrating glance. The image is perfectly framed in space, out of which its volume looms like a sudden, impressive apparition.

An expression of free, outdoor grace full of natural dignity is given by *Madame Cézanne in the Greenhouse, c.* 1890 (fig. 134). The unbroken line of the forehead, the way the oval of the face is fitted into the concave line of the hair, the formal regularity of the nose, mouth, and chin reveal the artist's geometric ideal. And the ideal is given life by the delicacy of

134

the tones and of the flesh tints, which are lighted with yellow, pink, and red and shadowed with green and blue. The tone is truly the breath, the serenity, the grace of this face, which rises like a flower from the dress and from the background blues and browns, touched with red, green, and yellow.

Woman with a Coffee-Pot, however, 1890–94 (fig. 135), is massive as a tower. She is seen full face, with a clarity of form that seems pitiless. But the position of the image in space and the prominence given to surrounding objects confer absolute unity on the entire picture. The intense blue of the dress, faceted about the volume of the body, contrasts with the delicate pink grey of the background and with the bright orange tone of the flesh.

Cézanne's most famous composition is perhaps *The Card Players,* 1890–92 (fig. 136). He painted this motif several times, with a greater or lesser number of players, but this is probably his definitive version. The colour effect is based on contrasts: between the purple blue of the coat of the player at the left and the yellow with blue shadows of the player at the right, and between all those tones and the reds of the background and flesh and the yellow of the table. With a thousand nuances, these tones give volume to the images. The firmness and the character of the figures, the vividness of their activity, the solidity of the well-knit composition show that the intensity of the colour does not detract from the whole but glorifies it. A continuous outline would have isolated the images; they form parts of the whole because, like the table and the background, they are made up of colour areas. For modelling Cézanne substituted modulation and thus set up a rhythm of areas. Each bit of the picture is linked to every other bit—by means not of a skeletal structure but of a relationship of planes. As Cézanne said to Larguier, "Painting is not a servile copying of objects, but the discovery of a harmony among numerous relationships." And the unity that is born of these relationships is not physical but spiritual; it gives us the character rather than the physical structure of the two peasants. "To study nature is to extract the character of one's model," Cézanne once said. A peasant of Cézanne is as individualized as a portrait and as universalized as an idea, solemn as a monument and firm as a moral conscience. "I love above all else the aspect of people who have grown old without violating custom, following the laws of their age. Look at that old man who owns this café, what style he has!" Cézanne said to Borély. Not in conventionality, but in the frank sincerity of the reality of the people, in life which conforms to truth, Cézanne felt the nobility of style.

After 1890 the artists' reaction against impressionism, which had already obtained a success with the public, and later their reaction against symbolism, caused Cézanne to receive the attention of young painters who, however, were unable to obtain an adequate knowledge of his work until 1895 when Vollard opened his first one-man exhibition. Despite the persistent opposition of the public and of the newspaper critics, Cézanne's fame spread. At first he was vexed by this, considering it merely an interruption of his solitude, but about 1900 he understood that the young men were of serious intent, and he was generous with benevolent welcome and advice when they made pilgrimages to Aix. In the meantime, Cézanne, who like Zola had been a convinced anti-clerical, felt the need of embracing the Christian religion as a protection against all the humiliations which he had suffered, and he achieves a new religious sense in his visions of nature. During his last years he formulated his thoughts on art in conversation and in writing, but his painting departed ever further from his theory and became more and more an effusion of his feeling, of his passion for all of creation. In 1904 his exhibition at the Salon d'Automne definitively established his success, and in this Cézanne took great joy. Then he returned to Aix and worked until his death.

In this period the unity of style achieved in the preceding years becomes increasingly synthetic and is full of the breath of passion. The autonomy of his style becomes more rigorous, both with respect to the motif, which he analyses continually and passionately, and with respect to the regular and abstract forms concerning which he had theorized.

Under his brush even a few apples on a table become a tragedy, as for example in the *Still Life* of 1895–1900 (fig. 137). The transformation of the fruit, the glass, the jug, and the rest in light and shadow, in purple blue, in reds, in orange yellow is so radical that instead of looking at the objects we feel the passion that transports the tones of colour and saturates them with intense and tumultuous life. Care of execution, small brush strokes which had previously distinguished light and shadow, now give way to wider, fused strokes which at times leave parts of the canvas uncovered. To go further with the execution would have meant losing the impulse of passion, and Cézanne knew when to stop.

In 1896 we went to Talloires, where he painted the *Lake of Annecy* (fig. 138). The unity of the vision becomes so

137

complete that the water of the lake is utterly fused with the trees, the houses, and the mountains; everything seems to become a function of the blue which forms both light and shadow, nuanced at times into pink and green. Here order is given to chaos not by God according to the laws of nature but by an artist according to the requirements of his picture.

In the last years of his life he looked again and again at his *Montagne Sainte-Victoire* (fig. 139), with an eye always ingenuous and creative as in his first youth. Now he sees it as distant, imposing, no longer by virtue of its volume but in its spiritual light as it rises skyward from the earth, an immense space in which the orange and the purple-blue-green tones symbolize the things of this world. With ever-freer brush stroke, as in his water colours, he creates a colour that is ever more intense. From the valley to the mountain leads the path from shadow to light, from the earth to the sky. Light becomes tenuous and distant. Cézanne seems to be reciting a low-voiced evening prayer.

Some of the greatest creations of his last years are water colours.

In portraying his gardener *Vallier* in 1906, the last year of his life, whether in oil or in water colour as in figure 140, Cézanne seems to be portraying himself, conversing with himself. The solidity of the image and the extreme vivacity of light and brush stroke reveal the old man's mortal despair in the face of approaching death. Precisely because the forms of the image are not clearly defined, it reveals the spirit more freely.

In his last years, as is well known, Cézanne painted many compositions of bathers. In a number of large oils he devoted himself to the architecture of the scene with an extraordinary sense of the grandiose. But in many water colours he represented the same motif in a lighter, more improvised, more intimate spirit. The water colour reproduced in figure 141 is a continual flow of atmospheric masses, of figures that are phantoms seen in a dream, closer to music than to architecture.

Thus in his last years Cézanne renewed the romantic impulses of his first youth, but he did not renounce the harmony, the balance between the drive of passion and the vision of forms and colours, which he had retained ever since the first years of his impressionism. His study of light and shadow, of planes and volumes, of space and its relationships with the image, and especially his need to imagine a whole which is the world of art distinct from that of nature enabled Cézanne to create a long series of works which are perfect in themselves and which at the same time inaugurate a new era in the history of art.

Chapter Eight

GEORGES SEURAT

G EORGES SEURAT was born in 1859, twenty years after
Cézanne, and he turned to art about 1880 when impressionism had ended its heroic period and already
entered its period of crisis. He thus belonged to the post-
impressionist generation, and since he was very precocious, at
the age of twenty-seven he was recognized as the leader of a
new school, that of neo-impressionism or scientific impressionism as opposed to romantic impressionism. He died
young, in 1891, but his work had wrought a change in the
taste of the world. Out of a pressing need for theory, he superimposed a doctrine on feeling and intuition. With him the
optical mixing of colours, which the impressionists had substituted for the mixing of pigments, became more rigorous
as a result of his following the scientific laws of Chevreul,
Rood, and others, and the spatial composition which Cézanne
had developed from his own sensations of colour, Seurat confined within geometric lines and figures, which took on the
quality of symbols.

Certainly he accepted several impressionistic principles:
subordination of subject to motif, representation of contemporary life, love of landscape, attention to effects of light and
shadow. But here the affinities end. Impressionism had liber-
ated feeling. Seurat, on the other hand, thought only of

method, based on mathematical and physical laws. He rejected his own poetic quality, which was quite lofty, saying, "Literary men and critics see poetry in what I do. No: I apply my method, and that is all." [1] The importance of Seurat in the history of taste is due to his conviction that the origin of art is in the laws of science; in him all the abstract painting of the twentieth century found its prophet.

Brought up in a devout, severe, reserved family, never on terms of familiarity even with his friends, a kind of latter-day Jansenist, he followed the courses at the Academy of Fine Arts under the guidance of Henri Lehmann, a disciple of Ingres. That is, he had the same artistic training as Degas, though more superficial and thus more easily discarded. Still, even in 1888 Pissarro could remark that "Seurat belongs to the School of Fine Arts." [2] Jacques-Emile Blanche recalls that at the Académie Julien, where Seurat's influence was strong, the students were inculcated with "the primary geometric principles . . . useful in the construction of a nude figure, but which Seurat knew how to stylize and which he applied even to the distribution of light in black and white." [3]

Thus the first revolution against impressionism had an academic origin. But since every revolution in painting is against the academy, Seurat fought on two fronts, and set his geometry against impressionism and his chromatic light against the Academy. His synthesis is the geometrization of light.

Until 1883 Seurat drew more than he painted, drew like Ingres with a fine subtlety, and like Holbein and Poussin; he

[1] Coquiot, *Seurat*, p. 41.
[2] Rewald, *Seurat*, p. 115.
[3] *Les Arts Plastiques*, 1931, pp. 267–8.

studied Delacroix and his theories, and he read Charles Blanc and Chevreul.

Suburb, 1883 (fig. 142), is timid, reserved, slight; still, it is a finished work of art, revelatory of a manner of contemplation which is Seurat's own, of his deep feeling, of his detachment from the theme, his ability to reduce a motif to its elementary simplicity, his calm which dominated every emotion, the melancholy with which he regarded life. That same year, Cézanne painted in *Houses at L'Estaque* (fig. 127) houses that were simplified with a rigour that was the synthesis of a thousand experiments; with an utterly different spirit, out of sheer need of fancy and with evident ingenuousness, the young Seurat achieves an even more extreme simplification. His colours are many, varied, and intense; the houses white with blue and black roofs, the fields and sky green, blue, red. There is not the slightest hint of an interpretation of reality; it is the creation of another world, in which pure crystals emerge out of a light mist. Even before creating his own technique, Seurat was already an accomplished, ingenuous artist with the soul of a primitive, from whom one would not expect a scientific method.

The problem of the interpretation of reality, however, is very keen in Seurat, as is shown in *Peasant with a Hoe, c.* 1884 (fig. 143). Here the influence of Pissarro and the broken brush stroke of impressionism is clear, and yet the volume of the image is felt rather more intensely, and the distinction between the areas of light and shadow is more decided and regular, that is, the tendency toward theoretical abstraction is spontaneous, purely intuitive, and of an evident artistic quality. The colours are intense—the orange of the field, the white of the shirt, the yellow of the haystack—and all have purple shadows.

The impressionists had stopped painting the very large pictures dear to the academic tradition. But Seurat, a product of the Academy, tended to give new order to his sensations in such a way as to achieve a monumental effect, and he liked to make an impression with works of imposing size. Therefore in the first exhibition of the Salon des Artistes Indépendants in 1884 Seurat exhibited *A Bathing Party, Asnières* (fig. 144), in preparation for which he had made various drawings and sketches from life during the preceding year. The architectonic ideal of composition is in this picture already quite evident, and it is achieved with complete coherence: the absolutely static quality of the images, their lack of individual expression the better to define their function in the whole, the clear-cut distinction between the areas of light and dark, the majestic calm of contemplation. In order the better to emphasize the architectonic function of the figures, Seurat paints them with large areas and coarse pigment, in contrast with the field and the river, which are done in small strokes of red, yellow, green, blue, and purple with delicate impressionistic gradations. There are thus two opposing visions— the architectonic and the impressionistic—and yet in their very contrast, between the eternal and the fleeting, between the solidity of form and the fluidity of light, they achieve a solemn poetry.

It was natural, however, that Seurat should feel the need of eliminating the contrast, of arriving at a perfect fusion of form and light, of creating architecture out of light itself. *The Seine at Courbevoie,* 1885 (fig. 145), is perhaps the first work in which the possibility of fusion appears to the artist, and this circumstance gives it a particular fascination.

First of all, he brought the motif forward by pulling it violently to the surface, and thus he emphasized the fragmentary character of the nature which he reproduced, in order the more freely to construct the architecture of the picture; then he applied to the houses, water, figure, and trees—all of which appear as shadows in the diffused light—touches of colour which are broken and of ever smaller size, almost like punctuation marks. The contrast between figures and landscape in *A Bathing Party* had enabled Seurat to construct his architecture by means of the figures alone, for which the landscape was only a background. In *The Seine at Courbevoie,* on the other hand, it is the landscape which is architectonic, and the figure is merely an element in it. The figure is made more rigid in an effort to control the vibrancy of the light, and the picture possesses a certain poetic irony which enlivens the ecstatic vision. The brush stroke, too, is made more rigid; it is no longer varied like the impressionist stroke; and thus in this picture we see for the first time that pointillisim is the method most suitable for crystallizing light architectonically.

This problem of the unity of figure and landscape in the architecture of light was Seurat's great preoccupation between 1884 and 1886, when he finished many drawings and sketches for a large picture which he finally exhibited in the last impressionist exhibition: *A Sunday Afternoon on the Island of the Grande Jatte* (fig. 148).

When he painted the field, the trees, and the water among which the figures were to take their places (fig. 146) the masterpiece emerged spontaneously. Far from diminishing the vibrancy, which is life, the crystallization of the light makes it tangible and eternal.

And in the definitive sketch of his composition (fig. 147) he maintained the same inclusion of images within vibrant atmosphere that we saw in *The Seine at Courbevoie*: the images appear like phantoms in an unreal world.

But in the definitive picture the forms are too precise, we are too conscious of the solidity of the images—we cannot help feeling the contrast between their reality and their unreality. The silhouettes are characterized by an air of disillusion, which irritated Seurat's contemporaries and seemed to them ridiculous. To us, it seems rather humorous and amusing. But in any case it has an effect of illustration, which does not harmonize too well with Seurat's ecstatic feeling for sunlight. In the small picture without human figures (fig. 146) this ecstasy in the presence of nature and light is unspoiled. In the definitive version it is as though a crowd from a night club had suddenly entered a church, and it is evident that the painter has no sympathy for this crowd and is profiting from his sense of regular forms to emphasize the ridiculousness of the fashion of the day. This is all done ingenuously or, rather, with a mixture of ingenuousness and intention which is disconcerting. The colours of the field are distributed in two very distinct areas: in the part of the canvas which is in light, the local colour, a warm green, is in large part covered with brush strokes in darker browns or cold greens; in the part which is in shade, the local colour, a cold green, is punctuated by lighter tones of orange and purple. From this superimposing of dark tones on light local colour, and vice versa, results

145

an extraordinary and vibrant complexity of colour and light. And yet we cannot help feeling that the picture is a trick, even though a very refined one played by a genius. This is not true of the background: here, in the water and the wall, the super-imposing of colours is less distinct, and the sweeps of the brush in blue, purple, yellow, white, red, and green constitute an even colour. Beneath an appearance of calm, the reflections in the water have a continuous vibrancy, and the white light on the wall takes on a fairy-tale quality. These are the lyrical, free touches in the picture. They are a miracle, disturbed by the everyday life which goes on in the foreground.

The picture scandalized the public and aroused the hostility of both traditional and impressionist painters, but this was balanced by the enthusiasm of a few young artists and of Pissarro, who defended the right of scientific impressionism to use colour in its own way, and of a few critics, the most perspicacious among whom was Félix Fénéon. The *Grande Jatte* made it impossible to continue the impressionist exhibitions: everyone felt that something new had been born and that whether one accepted it or rejected it, it would play a rôle in the evolution of taste. As for Seurat, he was convinced that in the *Grande Jatte* he had definitely found his method and that he had only to follow it rigorously to satisfy himself. He was fearless of the danger of method, which can destroy or sterilize sensation.

Seurat's large pictures with compositions of figures were painted in the studio, sometimes at night; his mental calculation of colour harmony was so precise that he thought he could avoid the changes in the perception of colour caused by artificial light. This ability to calculate has been admired as a sign of intellectual force; to us it seems rather a sign of fatal alienation from artistic feeling. But during the summer he abandoned his studio and studied the motif at the seashore: at Grandcamp in 1885, at Honfleur in 1886, at Port-en-Bessin in 1888, at Le Crotoy in 1889, at Gravelines in 1890. On June 25, 1886, he wrote from Honfleur to Signac, "It has been fine weather here for the last five days. I hope soon to be able to apply myself seriously to my canvases. Up to now I have done only sketches, to get used to the place. . . . I see the Seine . . . a grey sea, almost undefinable, even under the brightest sun and blue sky, at least during the past few days." Shortly thereafter he wrote, "The wind and the clouds have bothered me these last few days. I wish the calm of the first days would return." [4] Thus the landscapes to which Seurat devoted his summers were painted out of doors, and he met the same difficulties and made the same complaints concerning the weather that the impressionists had so often met and made before him. His vision is certainly original and different from that of the impressionists, pervaded as it is by a need for intensity and order, for re-elaboration of feeling by the mind. But feeling was there, and it was keen and vibrant even within the limits imposed on it by order. In other words, he found in his landscapes painted between 1885 and 1890 that balance between feeling and theory that was necessary for artistic creation. Therefore these landscapes are his greatest masterpieces, the absolute work of his genius, far superior to his compositions.

We reproduce *The Roadstead at Grandcamp*, 1885 (fig.

[4] Rewald, *Seurat*, p. 111.

149), *Sunset, Grandcamp,* 1885 (fig. 150), *Fort Samson at Grandcamp,* 1885 (fig. 151), *Fishing Boats at Port-en-Bessin,* 1888 (fig. 152), *Le Crotoy, Looking Downstream,* 1889 (fig. 153), *Le Crotoy, Looking Upstream,* 1889 (fig. 154), and *The Channel at Gravelines, Little Fort Philippe,* 1890 (fig. 155).

In the presence of nature, between 1885 and 1890, Seurat's style remains quite constant. The greater or lesser firmness of line depends more on the artist's reaction to a particular natural effect than on a deliberate principle of style. In figure 149 the vibrancy of the light absorbs all lines; in figure 150, painted the same year, line is definite; and line takes on the character of ingenuous creation, of intuitive necessity. There is no hint of irony. In the presence of the expanse of the sea, or of shrubs, houses, or white sails, Seurat responds with all the depth of his feeling.

At times, as in the *Sunset, Grandcamp* (fig. 150), colour is intense, light and varied: in the sunset the sky becomes green, yellow, pink, and purple; the water turns yellow and the beach purple pink. The painted frame (an idea of Seurat's, much scoffed at by his contemporaries) served, with its purple effect resulting from the optical synthesis of many colours, to thrust back the vision of the sea to an indeterminate distance.

In *Fishing Boats at Port-en-Bessin* (fig. 152), on the other hand, the artist's attention is concentrated on the way in which even intense colours, when they are complementary, are made white by diffused light. From the thousand colours juxtaposed by means of dots, there results a fused effect of grey containing white, green, and sky blue. It need scarcely be said that although the aim of divisionism and pointillism was to represent light with colours, Seurat's light is not at all natural and exists only in a world of fancy and dream.

Everything is clear, celestial; the effect seems timid, but what we see is Seurat's fervour protected by his order. But the order is not superimposed; it emerges from the colours themselves; it does not take the form of line but rather of nuances. It is an enchantment; never more than in this picture does one feel Seurat's purity of soul, his spiritual affinity with Fra Angelico.

Le Crotoy, Looking Upstream (fig. 154) has a curve of beach which is an obvious hint of the geometrical; it is at once an ideal form and a representation of nature; it glorifies the light colours—white, green, sky blue, purple. And the same is to be said of *Le Crotoy, Looking Downstream* (fig. 153), which is certainly more complex but no less natural; here the only hint of geometry is a shadow on the edge of the sand, as demarked by the wind.

Although *The Channel at Gravelines, Little Fort Philippe* (fig. 155) reveals an interest in the decorative which increased in Seurat during his last years, this is so intimately bound up with the vision that it appears spontaneous and convincing, and at the same time detached from the world, projected into an infinite distance, seen in a dream, pure poetry.

The guileless, childlike soul of Seurat is fully revealed in these landscapes, and we become aware that the armor of the scientist, the reserve of the youth who isolated himself even from his friends, the care with which he kept everything, even his success, to himself—all show his need to conceal the extreme sensitivity and the ingenuousness of which he was made.

Art criticism in France, which had reached a lofty level in Baudelaire, had subsequently limited its function to being concerned exclusively with ways of seeing and was oblivious of the relationship between these and the creative spirit. Thus those of the critics of 1886 who did not demolish Seurat vied with each other in praising his technique and interpreting his colour theory, which they declared were the two essentials of his art. It was natural, therefore, that he should feel confirmed in his theory and that he should use it disdainfully as a shield against those who knew nothing and understood nothing. He applied his theory in his painting and discussed it with his friends, but he gave a public exposition of it only in August, 1890, less than a year before his death. He added a theory of line to that of colour and emphasized the symbolic character of both.

This is what Seurat called his aesthetic:

Art is harmony. Harmony is the analogy of opposites, the analogy of things that resemble each other, of *tone,* of *colour,* of *line,* considered in terms of the dominant and under the influence of light in combinations that are gay, calm, or sad.

The opposites are:

For *tone,* one which is more $\left\{\begin{array}{l}\text{luminous}\\ \text{light}\end{array}\right\}$ for one which is more sombre.

For *colour,* the complementaries, that is a certain red opposed to its complementary, etc. (red green; orange blue; yellow purple).

For *line,* those making a right angle.

Gaiety of *tone* is the luminous dominant; of *colour*, the warm dominant; of *line*, the lines above the horizon.

Calmness of *tone* is the equality of dark and light; of *colour*, equality of warm and cold; and for *line*, the horizontal.

Sadness of *tone* is the dark dominant; of *colour*, the cold dominant; and of *line*, lines which slant downward.[5]

It is easy to show that such a theory belongs to the domain of imagination rather than to that of thought, that is, it is not a philosophical theory but a preference of taste, which can be judged only in relation to the artistic result. Harmony varies according to the fancy of the artist. A colour and a line in themselves never correspond to a state of mind that is fixed for all eternity; for their significance they depend not only on the individual but also on the fleeting moment in which the individual creates them. Their only universal character is that of being art.

Therefore, if we consider the elementary and ingenuous nature of his theory, we begin to suspect that Seurat's insistence on his method, on his science, was nothing but an illusion, a need to find an intellectual basis for his work. And it need scarcely be added that such a basis could not exist or existed only at the moment of creation.

It existed in his landscapes, which, it might be pointed out, were quickly and easily understood and admired by many people. But in his compositions after the *Grande Jatte* this basis, which he had so fervently sought, proved to be somewhat treacherous.

[5] Rewald, *Seurat*, p. 122.

The Models, 1887–88, *The Parade,* 1887–89, *The Chahut,* 1889–90, and *The Circus,* 1890–91, are compositions painted in the studio. The slowness and meticulous care of their execution are indicated in a letter of 1889 from Seurat to Octave Maus in which he says that he has been working an entire year on *The Models.* And the drawings, sketches, and preparatory studies became ever fewer. Fifty of them for the *Grande Jatte* were found in Seurat's studio after his death, but only one each for *The Chahut* and *The Circus.* Thus, in his last years, Seurat studied increasingly less from life and concentrated increasingly on his abstractions; he became progressively less interested in colour relationships (of which he was such a master that he was able to paint them from memory) and progressively more interested in the symbolic expression of lines.[6]

If we look at the studies of the three *Models* (figs. 156, 157, 158), we see that they have the same chromatic sensitivity, the same modelling achieved by means of light, the same architecture of light, the same forceful interpretation of the world that we noted in the *Grande Jatte.* In the definitive version of *The Models,* however, linear arabesque is emphasized and the colour effect is weak. Of the three studies, only the nude seen full face seems too definitely outlined to be completely immersed in the vibrancy of colour. The other two are masterpieces of sensibility.

To understand the tendency to linear decorativeness which characterized the compositions of 1888–91, it is enough to reproduce *The Circus* (fig. 159). Despite the two distinct

[6] For the interpretation of Seurat's style in his last years and for his relations with Gauguin and the *art nouveau,* I have made use of the essay by Robert Goldwater in the *Art Bulletin,* June, 1941.

planes, that of the bust of the clown and that of the spectators
in the background, spatial vision disappears, perspective is
deliberately avoided, and the images are superimposed on the
surface to draw attention to the expression of line. The whole
is a succession of arabesques. There is one linear rhythm in
the silhouette and hat of the clown in the foreground, another
in the fingers of the clowns and in the tail of the horse, another
in the legs of the somersaulting clown and in the clothing and
head of the equestrienne, and there is an insistent repetition
of immobility in all the figures of the spectators. These linear
rhythms communicate no sense of reality, and yet in this
picture even pointillism is insufficient to take us into a dream
world. Nor is there any general effect of light. All that
remains are a few jewel-like tones.

The tendency of taste which appears in *The Circus* parallels that of the *art nouveau,* as it was soon to be called, that is,
a decoration that arbitrarily exploits elements taken from
reality and makes them refined and decadent, and which is
also close to literary symbolism, to the surface composition
and "syntheticism" achieved by Gauguin during these same
years, and to that expressionistic decoration which was to be
the greatness of Toulouse-Lautrec.

Seurat had created divisionism and pointillism to express
his ecstasy in the presence of the light which gives life to the
world, and his fervour had reached such a degree of intensity
in its immersion in light that it had enabled him to create a
fairy-tale, eternal world. But now he leaves this lofty dream;
he finds himself among men, in the midst of a style which he
sees to be ridiculous, among followers who are profiting too
much from his discoveries and who arouse his jealousy; and

he cannot adapt himself to this commonplace life. He is disillusioned and reserved, and except during the portion of the year when he is contemplating the sea he frequents the café-concert and the circus in a vain search for enjoyment, and he expresses his frustration in caricature. But he is a man of the absolute. His transition from impressionism to pointillism, from feeling to science, was a striving after the absolute, transformed into art by the force of his ecstasy. Similarly, he now progresses from caricature to arabesque, from tri-dimensional space to the surface, from light to line, for he feels that he has to justify his irony as absolute art. But at the same time he is a man of ecstasy, a dweller in a world of dream, and irony avenges itself upon him because he cannot adapt himself to this sphere. Toulouse-Lautrec adapted himself to it with the utmost ease and created a unique synthesis of the decorative and the expressive. Seurat made the effort of a genius, but in this new undertaking, the creation of capricious arabesques, his pointillism was a stumbling block, and he was the victim of his own irony: although there is a refined humor in the details, the pictures as a whole are almost ridiculous.

Thus we must return to his landscapes to understand his greatness. The Belgian poet Emile Verhaeren memorialized him as follows: [7]

> I knew this painter. He gave me the impression of a timid and silent man. . . . To hear Seurat explain himself, make his confession, as it were, concerning the work which he produced each year, was to listen to someone who was sincere, and to be convinced by someone who

[7] *Sensations,* pp. 198, 200.

was persuasive. Calmly, with brief gestures, looking at you steadily, speaking rather professorially in his slow monotonous voice, he pointed out the results he had obtained, those things in his pictures which could not be questioned, what he called "the basis." Then he consulted you, called you to witness, waited for the word which would show him that you understood. He did all this very modestly, almost fearfully, although you felt his silent pride in himself. He depreciated no one, even expressed certain admirations which at heart he did not feel; but you felt that he was gracious, without envy."

Timid and modest though silently proud, generous, eager for absolute certainty, professorial, it is a psychological description of Seurat's style. When he forgets theory, when the smallness of his dots of colour is truly the expression of his timidity and modesty, not mere obedience to rule, when the light inundating his visions springs from his spontaneity and generosity, not from his calculation, at such times Seurat does not oppose reality or struggle against it, but stands before it in wonder—as a child might, who has not yet learned to understand it or to love it.

His method, so precise and certain, is the anchor of safety which his childlike soul needs, and so tightly does he cling to it that he is not aware that something else blossoms from his canvases—his poetry, the quality of his fancy. And perhaps we owe to his method, to the certainties which he so desperately sought, the courage with which he revealed in his art his hidden humanity.

Chapter Nine

PAUL GAUGUIN

ALTHOUGH he was born eleven years before Seurat, Paul Gauguin also turned to art after 1880 at the moment of the crisis of impressionism, and he was affected by the consequences of the crisis in a very personal way.

He, too, felt the need for theory. But he did not have Seurat's philosophical calm, and unlike Seurat he did not attain those extremes of refinement at which the intellect seems to hinder the spontaneous flowering of art. Rather, he was violently torn between the sensual violence of the savage and the intellectual order of civilized man, and he succeeded in resolving the conflict in a few perfect pictures, never in a coherent theoretical principle.

An essential aspect of this phenomenon is the impossibility of separating his life from his art. To live artistically is a very different thing from creating art. We could understand the art of Renoir and Cézanne quite well even if we knew nothing of their lives, but this is not true of Gauguin. The facts of his life have interested writers even more than his art, and understanding of his art has suffered in consequence. And although the sacrifice he made for art up until the moment of his death was of heroic proportions, it is difficult to rid oneself of the suspicion that he often confused his art with his thirst for savage and independent life, with his desire to impress upon the world his disgust for civilization. The legend of the "good savage" has flourished ever since Jean-Jacques Rousseau, but no one has paid so high a price as Gauguin to live this legend and assert its reality.

He was unable to become a savage, but he did succeed in stripping the veil from various conventional falsehoods of civilized society and in calling attention to the sense of evil produced in man by conformity to conventions. At the beginning of our century Gauguin's ideas triumphed not only in painting but in other fields, and even today they continue to constitute an important element in ways of seeing and thinking. Thus his importance in the history of taste has been enormous, while the ephemeral quality of certain elements in his art has become apparent over the years.

Paul Gauguin was born in Paris in 1848; his maternal grandmother, Flora Tristan, had been a propagandist for free love and Saint-Simonian humanitarianism, and in a *crime passionel* had been wounded by her husband, who was condemned to twenty years in prison. This ancestry, with its mixture of Spanish and Peruvian blood, has been offered as an explanation of Gauguin's character: he was violent in love, quick to sacrifice himself for an ideal and especially quick to impress his own ideal on others, tender and cynical, ingenuous and calculating, uncertain and strong willed, an artist and a charlatan. Capable of arousing the greatest enthusiasm, of seeming a master even to a person greater than himself like Van Gogh, of obtaining the applause of the literary avant-garde led by Mallarmé, he antagonized most people and was detested by them: in its hatred civilized society avenged itself upon him. A sailor and stockbroker in his youth, his earliest connections with art were as a shrewd collector and a Sunday painter; he was a happy husband and father until, in 1883, he resigned from his bank in order to paint every day; then he fell into poverty, abandoned his family, underwent all kinds of misfortunes and carried them with him halfway round the world.

In 1886 he went to Brittany and founded the school of Pont-Aven; in 1887 he went to Martinique, whence he returned frustrated; in 1888 he went to Arles to work with Van Gogh, and the partnership ended tragically. In 1890–91 he was glorified by Parisian men of letters as the symbolist painter *par excellence;* he decided to found a school of the tropics and went alone to Tahiti to realize his dream of savage life and art. He returned in 1893 and lived for some time on the proceeds of a small inheritance, and when this was exhausted, misunderstood by almost everyone and disgusted with Paris, he returned in 1895 to Tahiti, where his health rapidly deteriorated as the result of hunger and illness. After an attempt at suicide he escaped from Tahiti to the island of Dominica in the Marquesas, where he lived until his death in 1903. It was a continuous flight from inexorable and cruel reality, and although he was convinced that he was right and was always quick to take up the fight, in his last years he considered himself a defeated man.

In Gauguin's life as well as in his art, the opposites which he synthesized only in certain pictures are the result of a centrifugal force which lies like a curse at the heart of his personality. In 1888 he wrote, "There are two natures within me, the Indian and the sensitive plant." For the publication of *Noa-Noa* he sought the collaboration of a "decadent man of civilization," Charles Morice, to give contrast to himself, the "naive and brutal savage." [1] Mallarmé said that Gauguin was "the supreme primitive man." [2] Others considered him an impostor. Actually, the combination of Indian and sensitive plant is misleading and gives rise to a confusion between primitivist and primitive. His egotism gave his art the character of a political manifesto and confused his ideal.

At the end of his life, all his illusions gone, Gauguin wrote with admirable clarity, "I wanted to establish the right to dare everything: my abilities have not produced great results, but the battle is opened. The public owes me nothing, since my pictorial work is only relatively good; but I am owed something by the painters who are profiting today from the liberty I secured for them." [3] He himself thus wrote history's judgement.

His character was that of the polemicist. He complained of lack of affection and tortured himself with a yearning for love, and he gave vent to his feelings in an oath. He knew he was not a poet, because he could not love, and he took refuge in sarcasm. Yet he gave the impression of possessing a high moral sense. Van Gogh said of him, for example, "Gauguin loves to make us feel that a good picture is the equivalent of a good action—not that he says so in so many words, but it is difficult to be near him without becoming aware that he has a certain sense of moral responsibility." [4] The Protestant minister who was with Gauguin during his last days remembered him as follows: "A very amiable man, completely kind and simple with the Marquesans. The latter reciprocated fully.

[1] *Lettres à D. de Monfreid*, p. 339.   [2] Morice, *Gauguin*, p. 54.
[3] *Lettres à D. de Monfreid*, p. 348.
[4] Letter to Aurier, in Aurier, *Oeuvres posthumes*, p. 266.

. . . Very generous and chivalrous, Gauguin had undertaken the defense of the natives. There are numerous examples of his goodness on their behalf." [5]

Intellectually, too, he was a mass of opposites. His culture was not extensive: as he himself tells us, he was "surly at school." But he claimed to create an art of ideas, and in preparation for a picture he wrote a philosophical treatise. His spirit of adventure urged him on to seek the mystery of the universe: this had nothing in common with the mystery of art, which lies in the innermost recess of the artist's soul. His spirit of contradiction urged him on to revolution, but he seems not to have asked himself whether his revolution was a revolution of art. He was not content to create; he wanted to invent. "He invented everything. He had invented his easel, his bizarre costume. He decorated everything."[6] Nor was he aware that the desire for the exotic in art signifies the substitution of unusual subject for artistic motif since, as Renoir said, the primitive and savage style can draw its inspiration from the flowers in one's own garden. Thus, in the violence of his passions Gauguin sinned against life and often against art as well.

Furthermore, this terrible revolutionary allowed himself to be seduced by fashion. Too sincere to play the part of the savage in Paris, he sought primitive life in Brittany, which had become internationally frequented, and in Tahiti, already popularized by Loti. It must be said, however, that the inspiration which Gauguin drew from these places was, in other ways, serious and profound.

[5] Rotonchamp, *Gauguin,* 1906, p. 191.
[6] Armand Séguin, in *L'Occident,* 1903, I, p. 160.

In short, rarely has a human soul been more subject than Gauguin to the dialectic of light and shadow, good and evil.

In his account of the exhibition of the independents in 1881, Huysmans wrote, "Last year, M. Gauguin exhibited for the first time; it was a series of landscapes, a diluted version of Pissarro's still uncertain works. This year M. Gauguin appears with a canvas that is all his own, a canvas that reveals the indisputable temperament of a modern painter. It is entitled *Study of a Nude* [fig. 160] . . . I am not afraid to state that among contemporary painters who have worked with the nude, none has yet struck so vehement, so real a note . . . The flesh cries out to us. . . . How much truth there is in all the parts of this body, in this fattish, sagging belly!" And after indulging in comparisons with the nudes of Rembrandt and in invective against neo-classic nudes, he concluded that Gauguin "has created a daring and authentic canvas."[7]

For Gauguin the stockbroker and Sunday painter, such enthusiastic praise as this, which won him the attention of the public and the artists, was doubtless an encouragement to his abandonment of bourgeois life, his total dedication to painting, which took place a year and a half later.

When we look at the picture today, we see an image composed according to impressionist rules of light and shadow, rather like Pissarro, who for years was his guide, but with evident realistic emphases, as in the folds of the flesh and the distortion of the back; the contrast between lights and darks is more decided than in an impressionist picture, and the

[7] Huysmans, *L'Art moderne,* pp. 262–267.

drawing is inexpert, with no respect for proportions. These deviations are eloquent of realistic intent, but they are an obstacle to the realization of the whole. As to colours, the nude is pink and green with very blue shadows, the linen is pink and sky blue, the stuffs on the right are green and blue, the hair blue black; the wall is purple, the guitar hanging on the wall is black and yellow, the rug is striped in white yellow, blue, and red. The rug and the guitar are perfectly realized in substance. The remainder is somewhat lacking in solidity. The colour is daring and intense, but it is more successful in details than in the whole. In short, this is the work of a daring colourist without much feeling for tone, of a draftsman who has a program but is nonetheless unsure, of an artist who is not very vital, more dialectical than inspired.

About six years later Gauguin painted *The Bathing Party at Pont-Aven* (fig. 161). The style of the picture still belongs to the tradition of Pissarro; the drawing has become surer than in 1880; spatial composition is normal; colours are less intense, the brush stroke is small to emphasize the brilliance of the light: it was not for nothing that Seurat had recently achieved his success among the artists!

But in 1888 he saw Brittany with very different eyes in *The Swineherd, Brittany* (fig. 162). Although a few brush strokes remain, the whole is executed in flat areas of colour, outlined in black, and juxtaposed without transitions or suggestions of space.

The single colours are arbitrary with regard to reality: the forest is red orange purple, the mountain purple brown, the rocks sky-blue pink, the houses white and blue, the pigs yellow, the boy's clothing blue and purple.

The whole is thus coherent in form and colour; it stands alone, at a level which does not coincide with the vision of reality; it is an abstraction from reality to create an object which has an independent life, the life of art. Although a few secondary details still recall impressionism, the style is different, based on a new theory, and this style Gauguin was to develop and carry to much greater heights, but never to change, during the rest of his life.

He called this style *cloisonnisme* or syntheticism. The areas of colour are indeed composed on the surface like the sections of enamel in *cloisonné*: it is the first step he took to pull the scene forward to the surface, to exclude the Cézanne-esque relation between space and volume, and finally to distract attention from the representation of reality and concentrate it on the picture *per se*.

When we study nature out of doors, we receive various sensations which we are tempted to analyse—as the impressionists analysed the effect of light. But if at the moment of executing a picture we draw a curtain over the model and paint from memory, our sensations become simplified and fused, and their expression will lack details and will have an effect of relationships rather than of precise images. Then form will no longer be merely synthetic, as the form of every work of art must be, but *synthetistic*.

In conformance with this Gauguin renounced effects of light and shadow, which had been essential not only to the impressionists but also to the neo-impressionism of Seurat, and he renounced complementary colours, which become fused in light, and employed such combinations as blue and green, which when placed close together remain perfectly distinct, each seen as itself. Gauguin adored the chromatic scale of the sunset, from orange to red and purple. Thus, restoring to colour the value which the impressionists had attributed to light, Gauguin glorified pure colour. He said, "Everything must be sacrificed to pure colour. A tree trunk, whose local colour is bluish grey, becomes pure blue. The same with all colours." [8] The age-old tradition of painting gloried in nuances of colours; the impressionists, giving their chief attention to light in the division of colours, had found the way of obtaining nuances of light without weakening chromatic intensity. And now Gauguin at one blow abolished nuances and sought the harmony of pure colours. This was the principal reason for the antagonism which his art aroused, but it was also his best means of artistic realization.

Pure colours, however, posed a problem difficult to solve. If form is completely subservient to them, the resulting effect is that of a shadow play, that is, of images on the surface without any possibility of suggesting even a minimum effect of volume and space. Gauguin was too much of an artist to be satisfied with this, and only rarely did he dare create the new form suited to pure colour. In general he preferred a compromise. He had studied the drawing of Degas, without knowing how to assimilate its incisive and constructive value. He therefore accepted a generically academic form, with its chiaroscuro, which necessarily attenuated the intensity of pure colour. The drawing became summary rather than synthetic, and the tone became dull. Gauguin was aware of this weakness: "My nature tends to the summary; I hope to reach my perfection at the end of my career." [9]

[8] Rotonchamp, *Gauguin*, 1906, p. 211.   [9] *Lettres à Emile Bernard*, 1926, p. 84.

A composition of images on the surface easily acquires a decorative value. And Gauguin contributed enormously to the decorative taste called the *art nouveau,* which triumphed around 1900. He had the good sense, however, to abstain from what was most displeasing in this taste, because he knew how to include in his decorative surfaces a fantastic content, out of which he created pictorial symbolism.

But to indicate the nature of his fantastic content we must be acquainted with others of his works.

The dependence of Gauguin's new style on inspiration is seen in the pictures which he completed in Martinique, for example, *Around the Huts, Martinique* (fig. 163). It is dated 1887, a year before the *Swineherd,* and in it the synthetistic style is more timid. But the result is superior because of the interest aroused in the artist by the tropical landscape and the Negro boy.

Three pictures of 1889 well illustrate the character and the limits of Gauguin's symbolism: *Jacob Wrestling with the Angel* (fig. 164), *The Yellow Christ* (fig. 165), *La Belle Angèle* (fig. 166). The first two are religious in subject-matter—a rare thing in Gauguin's circle. In this case, too, he was following a fashion, and Pissarro distrusted him and regarded his mysticism as a betrayal. But Brittany and the devout life of the humble women who frequented its churches fascinated Gauguin. He did not renounce his realism, however, the relation between the scene and what he saw, and therefore he did not paint the sacred image but rather the adoration which the Breton women accorded it. They are shown listening to their pastor, who is explaining the meaning of Jacob's struggle with the angel, and Gauguin represents this struggle in an indefinite distance, as in a dream; he does not restrict himself to this theme, however, but allows his attention to wander and makes use of the strange coifs of the Breton women to achieve a pleasing decorative effect. The colour harmony is a failure: flesh tints are not orange, which would accord with the blue and purple, and the coifs are too white to achieve any relationship with the pure red of the earth: Gauguin's difficulty in realizing colours is still apparent.

The same method is followed in *The Yellow Christ*: the scene represents three peasant women in prayer before a *calvaire*—a cross with a crude wood sculpture of the crucified Christ. The summary form of the Christ represents fairly accurately the folk quality of the sculpture, but its very summariness makes it incapable of reinforcing the relationship of the pure colours. The artist's interest is elsewhere, in the yellow colour of the image as it is related to the yellow of the background and the blues of the shadows—for the purpose of expressing the sadness of the country, its barrenness, its autumnal aspect. Symbolism is thus for Gauguin a way of expressing himself indirectly. Scenes of everyday life are an excuse now for decorative rhythm, now for a landscape motif, and in each case there is a hint of sadness appropriate to the religious life.

In *La Belle Angèle* conditions are different. In the first place, this is a portrait, and the beautiful woman interests the painter, who delineates the form not only of her face but also of her hands and dress in perfect harmony with his composition of colours. The pinks, greens, and sky blues are reinforced by blues and reds both in the image and in the background, and they are varied with the yellow gold and yellow orange of the Buddhistic idol. The form gives the impression of being faceted, the better to bring together the areas of pure colour. But the portrait, however much it interested the artist, did not suffice him: it is inscribed in a magic circle and becomes a supernatural apparition, and it is placed to one side in order to afford a glimpse of a vague vision from which emerges the Buddhistic idol—an allusion to the idol-like character of the portrait itself and to the painter's aspiration toward oriental mysticism. All this has no intellectual value, but even today the artist's fancy continues to fascinate us, with its flashing chromatic authority, its plastic affirmation of mystery. It was this picture that caused Mallarmé to say of Gauguin: "It is extraordinary that anyone can put so much mystery into so much brilliance." [10]

Gauguin's voluntary exile in Tahiti was the cause of the progressive disintegration of his life, but it was the salvation of his art.

Shortly after arriving in Tahiti in 1891 he painted a portrait of a girl, with the inscription *Vahine no te Tiare* (fig. 167). Here, suddenly, is a masterpiece. He loved the beauty of the women of Tahiti—a beauty which in the faces is rather square, and which in general is unrefined, confident, strong; he felt a sympathy for their naive naturalness; he was enthusiastic over the warm, rich tones of their flesh. He loved his model too much to sacrifice it to synthetism, and therefore he painted in a synthetic, but not synthetistic, manner. His form is all accents, but nothing of value is omitted, and noth-

[10] Rotonchamp, *op. cit.,* p. 113.

ing is abstract, because every line, every tone is full of admiration and joy. The melancholy, baleful Gauguin has disappeared. Far from civilization, distant even from Papeete, in the depth of the forest, he refound his calm, his humanity, his joy. And with his joy he regained rightness of tone, dark on light, and a calm harmony of colours that was no longer inflamed. The yellow brown of the flesh, the blue black of the hair, and the purple blue of the clothing (barely broken into by an area of pink white) stand out against the light background, deep orange above and red below, strewn with green leaves. And even certain defects of construction, proportion, volume, and light become positive qualities, because they imply freshness or vivacity of expression, creative spontaneity. Gauguin was to create works as beautiful as this but none better.

In *Fishing,* 1891 (fig. 168), the composition is successful, with an easy, abundant, fluent character. His enthusiasm for the reality which was before his eyes prevented him from paying too high a price for his theories, from which, in any case, he derived the synthetic strength of his representation.

The Spirit of the Dead Watching, 1892 (fig. 170), was considered by Gauguin himself of exceptional merit. This, too, had its origin in direct emotion. From his cabin in the forest Gauguin had gone to the town of Papeete and returned in the dead of night. "Motionless, nude, prone on the bed, her eyes huge with fear, Tehura looked at me and seemed not to know me. . . . Her fright became contagious, it seemed to me that a phosphorescent light was flowing from her staring eyes. I had never seen her so beautiful; above all, never had her

168

beauty been so moving." [11] The purple of the background is blended with the orange of the body and the blue of the cover by means of the yellow of the sheet. The harmony is full throated, unexpected, and suggests the phosphorescent light which the natives interpret as the spirit of the dead. Unfortunately symbolist principles led Gauguin to add the figure of a phantom, which serves no purpose and disturbs the effect, which is achieved fully and with very precise feeling by means of chromatic expression. "This explanation is for those who always want to know the why's and wherefore's. Otherwise, the picture is simply a study of an Oceanian nude." [12] In the picture the nude dominates the symbolic and decorative elements by its reality, all the more alive in not being naturalistic or anecdotal. At the last moment, after Gauguin had sacrificed his true motif on the altar of symbolism, his critical awareness told him that what most mattered—not to others but to himself—was the study of the nude in a halo of superstitious fears.

In the Tahitian forest all of Gauguin's instincts came to the surface, even the sadism which we see in *Arii Matamoe,* 1892 (fig. 169). This is the decapitated head of John the Baptist which interested so many painters of the Renaissance. It is more than painted: it is thrown onto the tray with tremendous energy. The cabin, the weeping people, the image of a barbaric god make the composition an elegy.

In *Te aa no Areois,* 1892 (fig. 171), he feels respect for a feminine nude, for its simplicity, its dignity. Here there is no remnant of academic form, but the rigorous simplification of form, which is identified with colour areas. Outlines are

[11] Gauguin, *Noa-Noa,* pp. 92–93.   [12] Rotonchamp, *op. cit.,* p. 220.

schematic, anatomy is barely hinted at: abstraction is thus emphasized, as compared, for example, with the nude in *The Spirit of the Dead Watching,* but it is an abstraction so pervaded with the artist's feeling that it is perfectly justified and indeed perfect and complete, beyond any summariness. The decorative elements are like a display of fireworks in honour of the image, which is given an ample, solemn character by the surrounding space.

The White Horse, 1898 (fig. 172), is of considerable importance because of its happy harmony of colouring and composition. The colours are not harmonized as complementary or similar: it is a harmony of dissonances. In the brook the water is blue verging on purple, with yellow light that verges on orange. Now the purple blue and the orange yellow are complementary. But the yellow is too orange and the blue too purple to be absolutely complementary. They suggest complementary harmony without achieving it, and the intensity of each colour is heightened. Similarly, the green of the field and the red of the horse in the left background are not completely complementary, because the red verges on orange whereas the green does not become blue green. The tonal effect is treated in the same fashion. The "white" horse is of a tender, delicate grey, in which all the surrounding colours are reflected. In this lowering of tone there is a delicacy, made up of refinement and quiet, which is a suggestion of light although the effect of light is not realized. The effect of perspective is also unrealized. The white horse is almost foreshortened, with an undulation that suggests foreshortening; the red horse is foreshortened but contrasts with the field, which is pulled to the surface. The planes of the picture are superimposed on the surface, suggesting depth. And the harmony of planes, which is not realized in perspective, is resolved in serpentine lines accentuated by the branches in the foreground and by the brook. The result is a vagueness which is the vagueness of the warm hours of the day, of lonely places, of vegetative life. And the very intense colours are not exciting but rather dazzling and induce a lethargic calm.

Gauguin's paintings of Tahiti reveal two prevailing interests: one the representation of the slow, inactive life natural to the women of the place, and the other the decorative arabesque, which is intended, under the fire of the colours, to express artistic experimentation. Two pictures of 1894–1896 well express these two diverse tendencies. The title of *No te aha oe riri* (fig. 173) signifies a jibe, "Oh, you're jealous!" But fortunately the title has no relation to the picture, which represents a shaded spot in front of a cabin, with a woman approaching two others who are seated. The standing woman has a form proper to her colour, ample and synthetic, solidly constructed: she is a thing of nature. The slanting line of the foreground intersects that which is parallel to the background of the cabin, that is, the vision is on the surface with a suggestion of deep space. The purple red of the earth and of the roof and the olive orange of the flesh tones harmonize with the blue green of the shadow and with the luminous yellow of the cabin. Here Gauguin is master of his mode of composition and of his colour harmonies, and he paints with naturalness and self-assurance.

Mahana no Atua (fig. 174), on the other hand, has the agitated character of a mystic dance; on the surface are lines that twist and wind, and colours that overflow in numerous rivulets. From top to bottom it is a succession of pink, yellow, purple, blue, green, red, pink, orange, purple, green—a succession rather than a total effect, to which, however, the form of the divinity succeeds in giving a decorative unity. The artist's purpose was unquestionably to achieve a mystical effect, even though the scene appears somewhat theatrical, instructive rather than meditative.

In February, 1897, Gauguin wrote to Daniel de Monfreid that he had completed his greatest canvas: *Where Do We Come From? What Are We? Where Are We Going?* (fig. 175). Not only, he said, did it surpass in value all his previous works, but "I shall never do anything better or anything like it. Into it, before my death, I have poured all my energy, so great a passion of suffering amid terrible circumstances, so clear and unretouched a vision, that hastiness disappears, and life surges out. . . . This whole month I have worked feverishly day and night. . . . Despite the gradations of tone, the aspect of the landscape is constantly, from one end of the picture to the other, blue and Veronese green. Against it, all the nude figures stand out in bold orange." [13] When the picture was exhibited in Paris by Vollard the following year, Fontainas criticized its abstraction and its allegory. And Gauguin wrote him explaining that the title had been given to the picture after it was finished and that it was not a title but a signature. He had wished to express his dream, his oneness with all of nature, his sufferings "induced by feelings of vagueness and ignorance concerning the mystery of our origin and our future." It was thus a day-dream, full of apprehension concerning the mystery of life. But Fontainas also

[13] *Lettres à D. de Monfreid,* pp. 200–201.

criticized "the forms which are the poor product of an awk-wardly metaphysical imagination that is dubious in its sense and arbitrary in its expression." [14] In this he was wrong. For, at least in the two central figures (fig. 176), Gauguin has achieved a more lofty sense of form than ever before.

Tahitian Girl (fig. 167), *The Spirit of the Dead Watching* (fig. 170), *Te aa no Areois* (fig. 171) contain forms that are among Gauguin's happiest, and yet the form of the central figure of *Where Do We Come From?* is presented with even stricter coherence as an ideal model of form constituted of pure colour. If we compare it with that of *The Yellow Christ* (fig. 165), we see the artistic progress that Gauguin has made in nine years, his transition from summary form to synthetic form. He has achieved freedom of fancy and, despite all ad-versities, has learned to create beyond all external limitations, with a supreme urge to beauty.

Escaping in 1901 from hatreds aroused in Tahiti and settling in Dominica, Gauguin resumed work with what can only be called new energy and with a more rapid, sketchy style, full of life. A large painting, *The Call* (fig. 177) and two others of smaller size, *Adoration* (fig. 178) and *Nativity* (fig. 179), all three of 1902, assure us that Gauguin's declin-ing health was not accompanied by any artistic decline. On the contrary, in the desperate struggle to survive, his spirit became ever more serious, more absorbed.

Amid the usual splendour of the colours, the composition of *The Call* is natural, gravely animated, hinting at action. He has arrived at a more spontaneous realization of the world of his fancy.

[14] *Mercure de France,* 1899, XXIX, p. 235 *et seq.*

Adoration and *Nativity* are two religious motifs, revelatory of the artist's meditation. Among savages and their simple psychology he seems to become less savage, more human. The scene of the Nativity is perhaps the most sincere, modest, and intimate that he ever painted. In the face of death he returned to the things he had loved of old.

Let us now consider the spiritual content of Gauguin's art, the character and significance of his symbolism.

Every work of art is, of course, a transposition of impressions of reality to the theoretical plane and hence is at once abstract and concrete. The difference between Gauguin and the impressionists consists in his emphasis on abstraction. He was not the only artist of his time to make this emphasis; as we have seen, Cézanne and Seurat did the same. What distinguishes Gauguin is his manner of achieving abstraction, his pure colours, his synthetism, his decorative line, his relative abandoning of the third dimension. This manner was considered by him, and by the writers around Mallarmé, as the *symbolist style.*

Albert Aurier, who in 1890 praised Gauguin in an enthusiastic article in the *Mercure de France,* was familiar with Hegel and with his definition of symbolic art as that art which represents by means of abstract signs, without the balancing of body and idea which characterizes classic art. And Gauguin is closer to Assyrian and Persian art than to Greek. He was thus not a classic but a symbolic artist. Maurice Denis explained:

We substituted for the idea of "nature seen through a temperament," the theory of equivalence or of the sym-

174

bol: we stated that the emotions or states of mind induced by any sight were accompanied in the imagination of the artist by plastic signs or equivalents capable of reproducing these emotions or states of mind without any need to produce a *copy* of what had originally been seen; that to each state of our sensibility there must correspond an objective harmony capable of translating it.[15]

All this is clear, and we can see it realized in all of Gauguin's best works. It remains to consider the nature of the content which was symbolized in his decorative lines and pure colours.

Precise emotions, man's direct reactions to the life of nature or to the behaviour of other men, are obviously not adapted to expression by means of abstract signs and pure colours. But also known in psychology are the complex emotions, the "condensations of emotions" which lend themselves to symbolic representation. The desolate melancholy of a countryside like that of Brittany may be considered one of these. In Tahiti Gauguin frequently proposed to himself as a theme "the harmony of human life with animal and vegetable life, in compositions in which I assign an important part to the great voice of the earth."[16] As an idea, this can be ridiculed. But who, if he has the soul of a poet, has not experienced something of the sort? This is the origin of that naive animism in which every element of nature speaks with its own voice, and the contemplation of the relationships between the various elements of nature can well be expressed artistically.

[15] M. Denis, *Théories*, p. 259.
[16] Gauguin in *Mercure de France*, XIII, p. 223.

Therefore to say that symbolism loses itself in mysticism does not detract at all from Gauguin's capacity to realize.

The dangers which he carried within himself were of another kind: his contradictions as a man, his indomitable will and his laziness, his violent sensuality and his need for ideal purity, his passion for art, which in its very excess reduces art to an instrument of controversy and of rebellion against everything and everyone.

But synthetism was for him more of a strength than a weakness. Finding himself on the threshold of abstract art, Gauguin crossed it with great courage; in the depths of his own being he perceived his need for abstraction and gave it life.

His unsated desire for beauty, his primitivism which becomes savage, his symbolic equivalences which he is able to keep from becoming cerebral allegories, his abstractions which reveal certain aspects of reality—all these make it possible for him to be an artist whenever he forgets for a moment to be a rebel, a theorist, a reformer, the head of a school. At such times he can paint. Out of the ruin of his life springs the glory of his art.

Chapter Ten

VINCENT VAN GOGH

Van Gogh's letters constitute one of the most fascinating collections of memoirs of the end of the nineteenth century, portraying as they do a human being who burned with passion for the aesthetic and moral life and sacrificed himself for his ideals even to the point of madness and suicide. It is natural that they should have greatly contributed to the world-wide fame which the artist has achieved. And the man in the street who is delighted by the *Sunflowers,* even though he may not be concerned with the artist's burning passion or his supreme sacrifice, feels in the charm of the image something unusual, unique, never before seen. Neither Manet nor Cézanne is as widely popular today as Van Gogh.

The fauve or expressionist painters were the first to understand the exceptional value of Van Gogh's art, and to a certain extent they considered him their master. In general the best of them preferred Cézanne, but they invoked Van Gogh's authority to make their execution rapid, immediate, impulsive, and to employ intense colour harmonies independent of light and shadow.

The writers who have concerned themselves with Van Gogh have plunged into his letters and have exalted the man and the saint but have devoted less attention to the paintings,

177

treating them frequently as a kind of postscript, whose greatness is but a reflection of the artist's human greatness. And some have sneered at the pictures out of prejudice—a prejudice which may be academic or may spring from an admiration for Cézanne's formal structure.

If there is an artist who resembles no one else, who is detached from everything that preceded and surrounded him, that artist is Van Gogh. And the reason for his uniqueness is to be found in his Dutch Protestant way of feeling, foreign to the French atmosphere in which he practised his art from 1886 to his death in 1890. In his case, therefore, more than with any of the other painters mentioned in this book, it is necessary to approach the works with a mind free of prejudices, always remembering that he belongs to one tradition and one only—that invented by himself out of his desperate will.

Born in 1853 at Groot-Zundert, a Dutch village in which his father was a Protestant minister, Vincent Van Gogh became at the age of sixteen a clerk in the art firm of Goupil, where he developed a taste which was that of the firm's customers—bourgeois, traditional, mediocre. He worked in the various branches of the firm, at The Hague, Brussels, London, and Paris, read extensively, and visited museums. Deeply wounded and humiliated as the result of his rejection in a love affair, he became discontented with his situation in life and felt a need for the absolute. He turned to religion and sought to make himself a Protestant minister but, failing in his university studies, became a preacher in the Borinage, the coal-mining region of southern Belgium. He tried to achieve a truly Christian life by becoming poorer than the poor, by sacrificing his own health in the practice of charity for others, but his lack of eloquence in the pulpit made him ineffectual.

Discouraged by this series of failures, he became a vagabond and lived in poverty, but in painting he saw a hope of salvation.

Seriously, even furiously, he studied drawing, anatomy, and perspective at Brussels, at The Hague, where he was given guidance by his cousin the painter Mauve, and at Antwerp, where he developed an enthusiasm for Rubens. But he was intolerant of regular schooling and was incapable of learning; he worked doggedly in his own fashion, and in March, 1886, went to Paris, where he was supported by his younger brother Theodore (Théo), who had also become a print and picture dealer.

In Paris, in the studio of Cormon, Van Gogh met Emile Bernard and later Toulouse-Lautrec; he was given advice by Pissarro, met Gauguin, and witnessed the triumph of Seurat. He was in the midst of everything that was newest and most alive in art, and from that moment he lived only for painting.

What he painted before 1886 can be considered the prehistory of his art.

Perhaps the most important painting of this earliest period (1880-85) is *The Potato Eaters,* 1885 (fig. 180). He painted it at a moment when it was his dream to become "the painter of peasants," and he therefore identified himself with the poverty, the crudity, the awkwardness of his models, and he exaggerated forms and poses to illustrate his theme—not the most propitious attitude for art. Moreover, he was unfortunate in his heavy, coarse drawing and in his rather dark and dirty colour, which lacked energy and vitality. At that time his models were several Dutch realists: Anton Mauve (1838–88), Jacobus H. Maris (1837–99), Willem Roelofs (1822–97). These painters sought preciousness of colour in substance rather than in relationships and were therefore unable to go beyond the landscape painters of 1830 or Courbet. Van Gogh's only original contributions were his exaggerations and his awkwardness.

Shortly before reaching Paris he lightened his palette, following the example of Rubens and the Japanese, but only in Paris did he succeed in understanding what modern painting was.

Still Life with Plaster Statuette (fig. 181) furnishes an idea of the violent change of direction which Van Gogh gave his painting in his new surroundings. Hitherto he had painted with his interest concentrated exclusively on the subject; now he painted a subject without interest, in order that he might concern himself solely with the way of painting it. To extend his colour areas he pulled his motif abruptly to the surface and raised his horizon line. The colours are light and are harmonized with exquisite sensibility: the green yellow of the larger table-cloth, the red of the rose, and the green of the leaves, the yellow and blue of the two books—each colour stands out in turn, in contrast with the neutral purple grey tones of the statuette and of the smaller table-cloth. The form is limited to a few clear-cut outlines and to regular, minute brush strokes, which serve to determine the planes. Paris, Pissarro, and the Japanese were the agents of the change, but the true cause is to be sought in the painter's imagination, which did not gradually evolve but leapt ahead. He was the latest to arrive on the scene, but already he was at the very forefront of the avant-garde of painting.

His rapidity of assimilation is surprising, and *Banks of the Seine* (fig. 182) is an impressionist picture, similar to some that were painted by Pissarro or Sisley in those years, with full mastery of optical synthesis and light-effect, but also with his own particular love of intense colour.

So far, however, he had been an assimilator, not a creator.

If we compare *Small Gardens on Montmartre* (fig. 183), painted in Paris in 1887, with *The Crau* (fig. 187), painted in Arles in June, 1888, we see how very definitely Van Gogh's style was formed between those two dates.

The essential difference between the two pictures lies in the fact that *The Crau* is a considerably more rigorous pictorial synthesis. In *Montmartre* the countless minute brush strokes are still impressionistic, and the whole appears like a kind of intoxication of colour (yellow, green, blue, pink, and purple). It has an atmospheric effect and a rare vital force—joyless but unleashed by the painter in an effort to forget his own torment, and it is seen against a purple-blue sky, which seems to be keeping itself far distant in order not to share in the life of the earth. His first summer in Arles, Van Gogh came to know the sun-baked landscape of Provence, and while he was painting *The Crau* he wrote to Théo, "The entire atmosphere is now golden—one might even call the tone bronze or copper; and that with the green blue of the intensely hot sky gives a delightful colour, completely harmonious." "I am working on a landscape with wheatfields. . . . it is in the style of the two landscapes of Montmartre which were shown at the Independents, but I think it is more solid and has a little more style." [1] When he had finished the picture, he felt that it was superior to the other landscapes which he had hitherto painted.

In *The Crau* the colours, less varied and broken than in *Montmartre,* are in areas which extend in perspective into deep space, and they achieve not only greater intensity and preciousness, but greater calm—that calm which comes of certainty finally arrived at. Although there are still impressionistic brush strokes in the foreground, in the distance the areas give the motif solidity and absolute clarity. The yellow tones, ranging from lemon to orange, barely broken into by a green hedge, extend to the horizon, and this, while lofty, is so distant as to appear infinite against the blue-green sky verging on grey. Vibrancy, nuances, characteristic of northern France, have disappeared, and in their place is the sunny immobility of the South. Van Gogh's art, hitherto extremely subjective, now becomes objective; the artist's soul detaches itself from its creation, annihilates itself in the object, which it makes marvellous in itself, an image to be worshipped.

But anyone who knows Van Gogh knows that this creation has its other side: the immobility of vision necessary for the transformation of a representation into an object of art has as its counterpart renunciation and sacrifice. And it is the undercurrent of this sacrifice that gives life to the object as art.

Another comparison may serve to make us understand the development of Van Gogh's style, that between the *Self-Portrait* dated 1888 (fig. 184) and the other self-portrait en-

---

[1] *Further Letters of Vincent Van Gogh to his brother,* 1886–1889, English edition, 1929, No. 497. *Lettres de Vincent Van Gogh à son frère Théo,* Grasset, pp. 192–193.

titled *The Man with the Pipe,* painted in January-February 1889 (fig. 193).

The first, which was probably painted in January, 1888, still shows the style of the Parisian period, which was to end a month later. Van Gogh certainly had seen Cézanne's self-portrait entitled *Cézanne with his Palette* (Venturi Catalogue No. 516), and like Cézanne he undertook to construct his image of himself in depth, making use of the canvas on the easel as a transverse plane parallel to that of the human figure. But the structural problem is not deeply felt by Van Gogh, and therefore in his picture the image is not firmly related to the plane in which Cézanne had placed it so securely. Nor is Van Gogh at his freest and best in the rhythm of the light and shadows, which is indicated with regular, commalike brush strokes according to the neo-impressionist practise; this prevents him from fully realizing his interest in the expressive sharpness of the glance.

Toward the end of his Arles period, in January and February, 1889, when signs of his psychic disorder were already apparent, in a moment of mental lucidity after leaving the hospital he painted *The Man with the Pipe,* one of his greatest masterpieces. The flesh tones are brown with yellow lights; the bandage is white with yellow and purple reflections; and these mixed colours, tending to neutral, harmonize the pure colours in the rest of the picture—the red and orange of the background, the blue of the cap and the green of the coat—and in some way give them reality. The resulting harmony is full-bodied, solid, sonorous, while the form has remarkable firmness, as in the mouth and the eyes. Van Gogh is too absorbed in the sacrifice of his life to be interested in the problems of painting, in the construction of space, in the representation of himself. His fancy sees an image from which he is completely detached, as if he were someone else; he looks at it sharply, lucidly, with pitiless penetration, and creates it simply, rapidly, synthetically. The image seems to be emerging rapidly out of a fiery sunset—his own sunset, which he was living so dramatically. The desperate wish to create art is barely implicit, but it is the wellspring of the picture's great power.

The Crau and *The Man with the Pipe* illustrate not only Van Gogh's full realization of his art but also his clear-cut departure from the taste of his Parisian period and his affirmation of a personal, well-ordered artistic ideal.

When he arrived at Arles in February, 1888, after so many uncertainties, doubts, and maladjustments, Van Gogh's health, which had always been delicate, improved; he was happy at the coming of spring, rejoicing to see the southern countryside blaze with sunlight and reveal the intensity of its colour.

In September he wrote, "I am beginning to feel completely different from what I was when I came here; I no longer have doubts, I no longer hesitate to attack a problem, and these feelings may well increase." (Letter No. 539.) His feelings of certainty are a reaction against the world of impressionism and divisionism, which he found too complex: he was seeking a more direct form of expression.

The fact is simply that I find that what I learned in Paris is disappearing, and that I am returning to my ideas

184

which had come to me in the country, before I met the impressionists. And I should not be at all surprised if before long the impressionists found something to criticize in my way of painting, which has been fertilized by Delacroix's ideas rather than theirs. For instead of trying to render exactly what I have before my eyes, I make use of colour more arbitrarily in order to express myself strongly. Well, let's leave theory alone, but I am going to give you an example of what I mean. I should like to paint the portrait of an artist friend, who dreams great dreams, who works as the nightingale sings, because that is his nature. This man will be blond. I should like to put into the picture my appreciation, the love I have for him. I shall paint him, therefore, just as he is, as faithfully as I can—to begin with. But the picture will not be finished then. To finish it, I shall proceed to be an arbitrary colourist. I shall exaggerate the blondness of his hair, even using orange tones, chromes, pale lemon. Behind his head, instead of painting the banal wall of the shabby room, I shall paint infinity; I shall paint a simple background of the richest, most intense blue that I can possibly mix; and by means of this simple combination, the blond head illuminated against the rich blue background, I will obtain an effect as mysterious as a star in the deep azure of the sky. (Letter No. 520.)

The entire program of Van Gogh's mature style could not be better expounded: the adherence to reality which was innate in the programs of the impressionists (though not in their works) was abolished, and for it was substituted an ideal that transforms the portrait of a man between four walls into a star in the sky. And this transformation was to be accomplished exclusively by means of the language of colours. Pissarro had opened the way for Van Gogh: "What Pissarro says is true: we should exaggerate the effects which colours produce by their harmonies or dissonances." (Letter No. 500.) But into this abstract program Van Gogh injected a new way of feeling, a new need to become simple and popular: "I am beginning more and more to look for a simple technique, which perhaps is not impressionist. I should like to paint in such a way that, were it necessary, anyone with two eyes could understand." (Letter No. 526.)

Revelation of spirit by means of colour: that was Van Gogh's dream. He concentrated on "the study of colour. I am always hoping to find something in that. To express the love of two lovers by a marriage of two complementary colours, their blending and clashing, the mysterious vibrations of combined tones. To express the thoughtfulness of a brow by the radiance of a light tone on a dark background. To express hope by means of a star. The ardour of a human being by means of a ray of the setting sun. This is certainly not a realist *trompe-l'oeil,* but is it not something that really exists? I should like to paint men or women with an indefinable eternal something about them; the halo used to be the symbol of what I mean, and now we seek it in radiance itself, in the vibrancy of our colouring." (Letter No. 531.)

Is this a dream? Certainly it is a dream which he realized— to a lesser extent than he wished, but to a much greater extent than present-day criticism admits. In fact, it is enough to compare a mature work by Van Gogh—that is, one painted in the

summer of 1888 or later—with one by Gauguin, to understand how Van Gogh succeeds in revealing his own spiritual
impulses in a magic way.

Under Gauguin's influence Van Gogh tried to paint from
imagination: "I do not find it disagreeable to try to work
from imagination." (Letter No. 560.) "Gauguin gives me the
courage to imagine, and the things of the imagination certainly have a more mysterious character." (Letter No. 562.)
But that method was one that was suited to Gauguin, not to
Van Gogh, and the latter soon revised his ideas: "Aurier's
article[2] would encourage me, if I dared let myself go, to run
greater risks in leaving reality behind, and in creating a kind
of tonal music with color, as in certain works by Monticelli.
But the truth is so dear to me, and the effort to create what is
true! After all, I really believe that I should rather be a shoe-
maker than a musician in color." (Letter No. 626.) Van
Gogh's great moral conscience, the great seriousness of his
character, made it impossible for him to seek an aesthete's
escape. He had to keep in close touch with reality in order to
attain to truth. What his truth was, he naturally did not
know. It is not for artists to know this: for them the truth
is a desire for truth, a transcending of all their experiences
to realize their desire in a work of art. And in his paintings
Van Gogh realized his desire in the glorious way we all know.

In Provence he felt the truth of Cézanne's forms and tones
and lamented having seen too few pictures by him. But he
was well acquainted with Delacroix and Monticelli, whom he
accepted as masters because of their "suggestive" colour.
"Without wishing to, I am obliged to use thick pigment,

[2] Aurier, *Oeuvres posthumes*, p. 257 et seq.

like Monticelli. At times I really believe that I am that man's continuation." (Letter No. 541.) He adored Hokusai, with his flat colours and his freedom with respect to objective representation of nature; in fact, he took an idealized Japan as his model in his escape from the frantic, too intellectual life of Paris. "The art in which we are working has, we feel, a long future ahead of it, and we must therefore be settled, like those who are calm, and not live like decadents. Here I shall lead more and more the life of a Japanese painter, living quietly and respectably in the very midst of nature. You see, don't you, that this is less dismal than the decadents' way?" (Letter No. 540.)

His need for calm and joy, for a simplicity of life that can be reflected in simplicity of art, clearly distinguishes Van Gogh among the artists. Gauguin made a display of his agitation and carried it with him to Tahiti. Van Gogh kept his conflicts hidden within himself until they drove him mad.

He dreamed of founding at Arles something more solid than Gauguin's school of Pont-Aven, and with the help of the faithful Théo he succeeded in persuading Gauguin to join him. But their life together soon proved impossible; their disagreements became violent; and Van Gogh, undernourished and generally disorganized, revealed his alarming mental state by pursuing Gauguin with a razor. In his repentance he cut off the lobe of one of his ears. He entered the hospital, left it several times only to return following new breakdowns, and in May, 1889, took voluntary refuge in the asylum of Saint-Rémy.

At Saint-Rémy he worked between attacks, continuing to produce the paintings which were his consolation, one might say his catharsis. He even modified his style still further, but the principle underlying this new change he never put into words, and we must seek them in the works themselves. An earlier letter from Arles, to Emile Bernard, gives a foretaste of the Saint-Rémy style: "Is it not intensity of thought that we seek, rather than a calm brush? And in the conditions of spontaneous work, work done on the scene in the immediate presence of nature, is a calm and well-controlled brush always possible? To me it seems no more possible to be calm at such times than when lunging with a foil." [3]

In May, 1890, Van Gogh's health seemed better. His stay at Saint-Rémy had begun to weigh upon him, and he returned to Paris. Théo made it possible for him to live in Auvers-sur-Oise, under the surveillance of Dr. Gachet, the friend of so many painters. He arrived in Auvers May 21, 1890, and began to work as usual; two months later, on July 29, he killed himself.

Let us now consider others of the pictures which he painted in Provence.

Springtime at Arles made Van Gogh happy and optimistic. When he painted *The Flowering Tree*, April, 1888 (fig. 185), he was still using an impressionist brush stroke, but already his colours were his own. He has discovered the joy of tender and pure colour; the pink of the peach-blossoms against the blue and white of the sky, the lilac of the earth against the orange of the fence are marvels. It is a tribute to the memory of his master Mauve, which he expressed at the same time in joyful lines:

[3] *Lettres de Vincent Van Gogh à Emile Bernard,* Paris, 1911, p. 116.

Do not think the dead are dead.
As long as there are living men
The dead will live, the dead will live. (Letter No. 472.)

His gradual separation from impressionism, together with a curious discovery of a Japanese motif in Provence, can be seen in *The Drawbridge,* May, 1888 (fig. 186). Broken tones become increasingly rare: the blue of the water is dominant against the yellow and green of the earth, and the dark blue of the cypresses is dominant against the light blue of the sky. These tones are made effective by means of delicate gradations which detract not at all from the splendour of the colours.

Van Gogh's most popular picture is unquestionably the *Sunflowers,* August, 1888 (fig. 188). He painted several versions of this to decorate his room at Arles, "with the gusto of a Marseillais eating bouillabaisse." (Letter No. 526.) "I am thinking of decorating my studio with half a dozen pictures of Sunflowers, a decoration in which raw or broken chromes will burst out against various backgrounds of blue, from the palest Veronese to royal blue, framed in narrow strips of lath painted in lead orange. Effects like the stained glass windows of Gothic churches." [4] The success of these pictures is due to the relationships of the yellows, which go from lemon to orange, with the blues. And yet anyone can see that they are more than mere plays of colour. A human zeal makes itself felt, not in the sense of sentimental participation but in the artist's compelling drive to make himself objective. To create beauty the Greeks and the Italians of the Renaissance

[4] *Lettres à E. Bernard, op. cit.,* p. 139.

190

discovered proportions; Van Gogh explodes the colours of the August sun of Arles. The way is different, but the goal is the same: creation of an object beautiful in itself, detached from its creator. Van Gogh's concentration in creation, his joy that is too profound to be gay, his vague presentiment that the sun which is beating on these flowers is driving him mad, his faith in this bit of nature, as though it were an idol— all these give the character of art to the beautiful object.

Vincent's House at Arles, September, 1888 (fig. 189), is also a beautiful object, thanks to the relationship of the lemon yellows with the dark blue of the sky. But we sense that the time of mental torment is near: something menacing is unleashed by this beauty.

A month later, in October, 1888, he painted *Van Gogh's Bedroom at Arles* (fig. 190), of which he made a replica now in the Art Institute of Chicago. This, too, is one of his most famous pictures, and he speaks of it at length in his letters. "This time, it is simply my bedroom; but here the colour must do the trick, and in giving a greater style to things by its simplification must be suggestive of rest or sleep in general. In short, the sight of the picture must rest the mind, or rather the imagination. The walls are pale purple. The floor is of red tiles. The bedstead and chairs are fresh butter yellow, the sheet and pillows very light lemon green. The blanket scarlet. The window green. The dressing-table orange, the wash-bowl blue. The doors lilac. And that is all—there is nothing in this room with its closed shutters. The sturdiness of the furniture must once again express complete rest. The portraits on the wall and a mirror and a hand-towel and a few clothes. The frame—since there are no whites in the picture—will be white. This is to take my revenge on the enforced rest which I have been obliged to take. I shall work at it all day tomorrow, but you see how simple the conception is. Shadows and cast shadows are eliminated; it is coloured in flat tints like Japanese prints." (Letter No. 554.)

This is a new type of still life—an interior which would be inanimate but for the participation of the artist. He reveals his intent—to express by means of simplified colour a state of calm and repose—and all the other notations serve only to make this intention precise. Unwittingly he lets slip the fact that the picture is indeed a *revenge* on rest: the revenge is more strongly expressed than the rest. Van Gogh was melancholy and discouraged at this time, clinging tenaciously to work as to an anchor of safety. He wished to represent sleep and could not. The tragedy of his mind was approaching, heralded by signs of derangement, and it allowed him neither rest nor sleep. Calm reigns in the abandoned room, but it is a calm without hope and without pity. It is an empty room and is so not by mere chance: it is abandoned forever, because of departure or death. The colours are brilliant and pure, without shadows, but they do not suggest joy—only sadness. It is a rest that is born of despair. The colours reveal the artist's state of mind without his knowing it. He is not aware of what he feels, either in his letter or in his picture, and thus his feeling, his heavy-hearted humility, is expressed spontaneously. And extending even beyond his feeling is his faith in pure colours, which give his expression a mediate, indirect quality, the quality of art.

At Arles Van Gogh often complained that he had too few models to be able to satisfy his desire to paint figures. He often speculated concerning the relationship between his areas of pure colour and the formal limits necessary to the human image, and he was convinced that only the human figure could give his art greater profundity.

In August, 1888, he painted *Roulin the Letter Carrier* (fig. 191). The blue of the uniform on the light background and the form, which preserves a certain amount of light and shadow, realize an effect of tone and volume. The vivacious —indeed violent—image impresses the beholder with its reality and monumentality. In his letters Van Gogh describes the character of his friend Roulin with verve and perspicacity, but in the picture he renounces any description of the physical or spiritual reality of his model and concerns himself only with the energy and presence of the image.

Roulin the Letter Carrier is a halting-place, perfect in itself, on the road to a style more completely detached from the painting of the past, more purely Van Gogh's own.

The masterpiece which personifies this utter individuality is *The Woman of Arles,* November, 1888 (fig. 192). The impressionists avoided black, but Van Gogh takes the black of the dress and of the hair as his basis, to contrast it with the yellow of the background. A few reds (in a book and in the chair), a few light or dark greens, a few pink greys accompany the principal motif. But when we say black or yellow we speak of tints; in Van Gogh they are colours, not only because of their composition, but especially because of their form. It is indeed the form which acts upon the colours, making them sharper and more expressive. This is almost the first picture in which Van Gogh discovers for a human image a form consisting entirely of impetuous strokes and accents, without relief, without gradations, simplified to the extreme. This is the only form that is suited to Van Gogh's colour. And just as his colours are at the opposite extreme from impressionist colour, so his form is at the opposite extreme from that of Cézanne. This picture is on the plane of the popular image, but raised by genius to the level of sublime art. Anyone who wishes to be convinced of the "necessity" of this form has only to look at the various pictures of the same woman of Arles which Van Gogh painted after a drawing by Gauguin: [5] when the form necesary to his colour is lost, the colour itself fails. And yet he knew himself so little that when two friends admired his first *Woman of Arles* he attributed its merit to the model and not to his own painting. (Letter No. 595.)

At Saint-Rémy Van Gogh was only intermittently lucid, but when he was able to paint, he did so with particular intensity, continuing to create masterpieces. His style changed from that of the Arles period not because he adopted new theoretical principles, but because his new eagerness for life and his sense of oncoming tragedy called for a new form, and his powerful fancy was equal to the demand made upon it.

If with the *Sunflowers* we compare the *Iris* of May, 1889 (fig. 194), or the *White Roses* of May, 1890 (fig. 195), we immediately see a new vibrancy in the line and a new reserve in the intensity of the colour. Drawing seems once again to take the upper hand. No longer, as in the *Bedroom,* is the task of expression confided to the colour alone.

[5] De la Faille, *Vincent Van Gogh,* 2nd ed., pp. 710–13.

In the *Iris* the relationship of the blue and green is magnificent, but it is no longer detached, isolated, imposed, as is the colour relationship in the *Sunflowers*. And the texture of the lines has a value in itself, quite independent of its representational value. If instead of flowers the subject happened to be a slab of rock, the linear texture would be very much the same.

If these lines be taken to represent the artist's torment, in the *White Roses* the torment is overcome, and there appears a certain serenity, even though joyless and pervaded with a tender tremulousness. The representation is more natural and more refined than in the *Sunflowers,* though at the same time less magical. The roses are now white, now pink white, now white with a few touches of red, outlined in blue and blue green on a background of green veined with pink. The nervous outline suggests an accent of light in the colour, and the mass of the motif, despite the white, has a darker tone than the light background.

It was in November, 1889, that Vincent wrote to Théo of his need to adhere to the reality which he saw, to avoid the fanciful quality in the art of Gauguin and Bernard, and he quoted as examples of his patient studies of the truth his paintings of olive groves and cypresses. *The Olive Grove,* which is autumnal (fig. 196), and the summery *Yellow Wheat and Cypresses* (fig. 197) are two typical examples of Van Gogh's new style.

Rocks (as we shall see) and olive trees are the natural motifs most suited to express Van Gogh's tragic passion. With their serpentine lines the olive trees give a sense of the struggle which they have undergone to free themselves from the earth and push their branches toward the sky: they are like roots, penetrating the air with as much effort as they would make to penetrate the earth. There is no better mirror of Van Gogh's spirit: he feels his own drama projected not only in the trees, but also in the earth. Everything throbs in an invocation to life, in a struggle against evil. And the style of this struggle is found in the strips of colour following one another like waves tormented by the wind, like accents which alone form entire words.

As soon as Van Gogh can face a far-off horizon, he responds quickly to the beauty of nature, and then his tormented lines become calm, as in *Yellow Wheat and Cypresses*. Here the colour once again takes on the splendour of *The Crau,* and the composition is successfully organized, beginning at the cypresses and developing in distance, with the fiery yellow of the fields and the green of the shrubs against the light blue of the mountains and the lilac white of the sky. In the foreground the earth is burning, and the cypresses have the form of flames; in the distance is the desire for space and peace.

As in his olive trees, and to a greater extent than in his cypresses, Van Gogh projects his torment in rocks, as in *The Ravine (Les Fontettes)*, December, 1889 (fig. 198), and *At the Edge of Les Alpines,* May, 1890 (fig. 199).

Concerning *The Ravine* Vincent wrote to Emile Bernard, "I am working on a large canvas of a ravine . . . two extremely solid bases of rock, between which flows a thin stream of water, a third mountain closing the ravine. These motifs certainly have a beautiful melancholy about them, and besides it is amusing to work in very wild places where you have to bury your easel in the stones so that the wind doesn't blow everything down." [6]

The romantic motif is furnished by the blue mass of the rocks against the green sky, but since the blue contains green touches and the green contains blue touches the effect of contrast is not as clear as in the Arles period. Furthermore the artistic value is in the form, the commalike form, which is not concerned so much with volumes as with vibrancy. The chromatic vibrancy of the impressionists is here fully transformed into a formal vibrancy. The distant rock is for Van Gogh majestic and rigid, but the more the rocks are drawn forward to the foreground, the more tormented their life becomes, to the point of being awesome and demoniacal in the arching rock corroded by the torrent. Rarely has the violence of the struggle between the elements of mineral nature been felt with such passion. It is as though in this ravine the artist had had a Dante-esque vision of hell.

Moreover, despite Van Gogh's urge to portray reality faithfully, his style acquired an ever clearer autonomy, as is shown in *At the Edge of Les Alpines*. A comparison with any one of Cézanne's paintings of rocky Provençal hills will show more clearly than words the unbridgeable gap between the two painters. Van Gogh does not paint the rocks, but his own torment, which he projects into a legendary upheaval of gigantic rocks as though he were witnessing the chaos that preceded the creation of the world.

In *Starry Night*, June, 1889 (fig. 200), his contemplation of the night sky is a vision of the moon, of the stars, of fanciful comets, as though the sky, transmuted by his yellows

[6] De la Faille, *op. cit.*, p. 142.

and blues, were becoming an explosion of lights, bringing panic fear to human beings in touch with the mystery of nature.

Even in a portrait, the *Portrait of Dr. Gachet,* painted in June, 1890, one month before his suicide (fig. 201), he employs the style in undulating strips, which had had its beginning at Saint-Rémy. His interest in the formal motif distracts Van Gogh's attention from colour contrast: both the coat and the background are blue green, and only the neutral and orange tones of the face detach themselves from the rest in order to suggest, in the calligraphy of the style, a sudden, magic apparition. Van Gogh himself understood the tragic quality of this image: for him it was the expression of the conditions of his epoch. (Letter No. 643.) It is evident that this picture was painted by a sick man. But the sick man achieves such intensity of expression that by any standards his work is art.

It is not easy to evaluate Van Gogh's art objectively in the midst of the beautiful French taste of the period, so full of the restraint, the balance, the refinement that he did not possess. Still, no one who looks at *The Crau* or *The Woman of Arles* can deny that the artist has created a colour harmony of a type previously unknown, and that with a power of expression all his own he has found in this harmony a new quality of the image *per se,* the quality of an image to be worshipped. Further, in *The Olive Grove* and in *The Ravine* he has created a new form, filled with commalike shapes, devoid of volume but capable of infusing into the images his aspirations to freedom from tradition and from evil, in order that he may attain a more synthetic and immediate mode of artistic expression.

These are great things, and however his work may shock our habits of feeling and thinking, we cannot but admire it as that of a human conscience burning with desire for goodness, for beauty, for freedom of fancy. Out of his mistakes and his sufferings, out of the sacrifice of his life, Van Gogh succeeded in creating a few pictures of absolute perfection, sufficient in themselves to ensure his glory. And we must not forget how seminal his work has been in encouraging other artists to dare everything in the world of colour and in the expressive intensification of synthetic form. Over and above his art, he left a message that was acclaimed by the fauvists and the expressionists, and which sixty years after his death is still alive in the art of the world.

Chapter Eleven

HENRI DE TOULOUSE-LAUTREC

O F THE great artists who flourished in the last thirty years of the nineteenth century Henri de Toulouse-Lautrec was the youngest, born in 1864, and together with Van Gogh he was the farthest removed from the tradition that began with Manet.

Only Degas, for whom Lautrec had a particular veneration, can be considered his ideal master, both with respect to his form, which tended more to drawing than to colour, and with respect to his subjects, which were taken from the life of the theatre, the dance, and the cafés of Paris—not from the outdoors. Unlike Degas, Lautrec concentrated his attention on the demi-monde, on the life of the café-concerts and brothels. There is nothing of this kind in Cézanne, who re-created in painting the eternal values of the outdoors; or in Renoir, who when he depicted popular dance-halls saw only their wholesome aspect and the youthful grace of those who frequented them; or in Seurat, who tested the values of his theory in circus scenes; or in Gauguin, who sought the good life among savages, far from Paris; or in Van Gogh, who used his colours to attain to a God of his own. Lautrec was the first among the great artists to specialize in the representation of vice; he understood perfectly its nature as vice, but he had a spontaneous need to enjoy himself which was basically a way of escape.

In attempts to explain his art too much emphasis has been placed upon his noble birth and his unfortunate physical condition. Nevertheless, these must be mentioned, since nothing in a man is extraneous to his activity as an artist. Toulouse-Lautrec was a descendant of the counts of Toulouse, whose fame goes back to the time of Charlemagne. Perhaps his destiny was to live in a fashion that was arbitrary, capricious, and bizarre, like his father, without the discipline and the devotion to an ideal that are prerequisites to important accomplishment. But when he was a child two fractures of the thigh, which never knit properly because of his fragile health, made him a dwarfish cripple. The extraordinary development of his intelligence was the compensation for his physical deformity. His intense need for kindness and affection found a response only in his mother, who was, however, too religious and severe to become his confidante. As for his social environment, he could not remain in it without feeling humiliated, particularly since in those circles intelligence was not highly valued. Moreover, he had inherited a capricious, proud character, with a passion for freedom and sincerity and with an urge to action which his physical condition did not permit him to indulge. It was natural, therefore, that, being abnormal, he should seek a world apart, where his genius would be appreciated and where his crippled condition would not cause comment—and in which his aristocratic refinement would be considered attractive because of its rarity. Romain Coolus has said, "Paradoxical though it may seem, Toulouse-Lautrec was attractive because of his strange physical appearance.[1]

[1] *L'Amour de l'Art*, April, 1931, p. 137.

Whatever the significance of his social origin and his physical condition may be, they are at the periphery, not at the center, of the direction taken by his taste. A natural disposition, which cannot be explained since it was inherent in the depth of his character but merely stated, was the primary impulse of his art. His intense need for truth and sincerity could be satisfied only beyond the pale of social conventions, either out of doors, where he did not care to live, or in the world of vice, where there was nothing to hide and which afforded any number of occasions for enjoyment. And about 1890 vice in Paris lost its hypocrisy, was in fact displayed on the stage so that everyone could admire it, and was given many embellishments—not by way of apology, but for the purpose of endowing it with imaginative as well as physical attractiveness.

In 1881, when he was barely seventeen, Lautrec wrote to a friend, "I have tried to create the true, not the ideal. It is a defect, perhaps, for warts find no favor in my eyes and I like to adorn them with stray hairs and make them round and give them a shiny tip. I don't know whether you can control your pen, but when my sketching pencil moves I must let it go its own way, or—bang! there's an end to everything." [2] Thus at seventeen he believed that to create the true and not the ideal was to place a touch of light upon a wart. It was natural that later he should seek models with warts, physical and spiritual. The problem is to understand how, out of that interpretation of warts—so to speak—he succeeded in creating for himself the style of a great artist, or, which is to say the same thing, how he succeeded in giving a style to the Parisian

[2] Maurice Joyant, *Henri de Toulouse-Lautrec, Peintre,* 1926, p. 50.

demi-monde in which he lived. For one fact is clear: the Parisian demi-monde has always existed, before and after the years 1890–1900, but in those years it acquired an almost fairy-tale quality due to Lautrec's art. Just as Saint Augustine admits that perfect beauty exists in the monkey, so Lautrec created the perfect form of a type of vice and thus gave it an ideal value.

After studying for a time with Bonnat, in 1883 he entered the studio of Cormon, where he benefited not from the academic instruction but from the contact with painters of the new generation, among them Emile Bernard. Later he met Van Gogh, who greatly admired him. It was the moment of Seurat's neo-impressionism, followed by Gauguin's synthetism and symbolism, and everywhere there was a keen admiration for Japanese prints and drawings. The effects of light and shadow that had been the glory of the impressionists were of no interest to one who like Lautrec detested landscape painting. He had a passion for drawing, for line in movement, for expressive outline, and his decorative line and flat colour were at first close to Degas, then to Gauguin. But his temperament, considerably more concentrated and less extensive than Gauguin's, soon transformed everything he had learned into a completely personal style. By about 1890 his style was definitively formed.

Without question this style became an end in itself—that is, it acquired the autonomy of art—but in its beginnings the desire to illustrate was predominant. Lautrec owed his first successes to his posters, which were commissioned by impressarios and other members of the theatrical circles which he frequented. And the poster, it need scarcely be said, must combine decorative quality with effective illustration. Coloured posters had recently come into fashion: the first, by Chéret, dates from 1869.[3] In his very first attempts Lautrec showed his artistic superiority in a simplification and exaggeration of forms which allowed the observer to grasp immediately both the meaning of the poster and its decorative scheme. Lautrec's form long bore the mark of his posters, and he has unquestionably been identified with this type of art. Before him everything in this field had been tentative, and although after him there were many developments, it can be said that with few exceptions the poster as we know it is his product.

It would be a mistake, however, to consider Lautrec chiefly a maker of posters: his art found its greatness in painting, between the years 1889 and 1897. After that he began to drink to excess and to suffer from a persecution mania, and in 1899 he had to enter a sanitarium near Neuilly. He returned to Paris, but he was doomed and in 1901 died of paresis.

What Lautrec's art was in 1887 can be seen in the portrait of *Countess Adèle de Toulouse-Lautrec, Mother of the Artist* (fig. 202). The dress and the hair are in blues, which stand out in tone against the background of a room filled with light and with reflections in green, sky blue, and pink. There are isolated touches of red on the sofa and on the table, and the flesh tones are pale and greenish, with blue shadows. The most beautiful part of the picture is the airy background, conceived in an impressionistic manner but with a sharpness and nervousness which are Lautrec's own. The figure is less

[3] R. J. Goldwater, "L'affiche moderne," *Gazette des Beaux-Arts,* December, 1942.

successful, because it is confined and isolated within outlines which are the result of study rather than creation. We feel the painter's timidity: his respect for the figure of his mother prevents him from being daring in his art. This portrait seems to contain hints of the not very dissimilar kind of painting being done by Edouard Vuillard, who was barely four years younger than Lautrec.

The quickness of his maturing, and the use of models better suited to his style, made it possible for him to achieve more personal results in 1889 with *Young Woman Sitting at a Table* (fig. 203), and *The Laundress* (fig. 204).

In the *Young Woman* we are aware of the sure placing of the figure in space and of a perfect coherence of form and colour. There is still the desire for atmosphere, seen in the nuances of the colours and in the various motifs, but the tone is right: a haze of tiny purplish particles envelops the entire picture with the exception of the dark blue skirt and the red powder box. The drawing, on the other hand, has become sharp, incisive, simple. The need for sincerity is felt in the position of the image, face to face with the spectator, in her flabby beauty, glassy as the result of alcohol, and in the pitiless vision that is at the same time sufficiently delicate to do justice to what remains of the woman's beauty despite her besotted condition. The motif is completely realistic, but the delicacy of the image and of the purple is a touch of poetry.

The Laundress represents a step forward in stylistic development, though not in artistic realization. Here for the first time we see the silhouette that has an important function in Lautrec's style: it allows him to emphasize his line and express the raffish aspect of the image. Although the brown background is not all in one tone it seems to be so, so clearly does the image stand out, with its white shirt-waist shaded with green and with pink reflections. The drawing is fine and meticulous; chiaroscuro gives a hint of the plastic; and yet the sharpness of the silhouette gives us a foretaste of the artist's future manner of seeing images in flat colours.

In a picture called *Gabrielle the Dancer,* painted in 1890 and now in the museum at Albi, there is still a certain fluctuation between the vibrancy of impressionistic light and linear emphasis. But in another picture with the same motif painted a year later (fig. 205) the coherence of style is absolute. There are a few light-effects, but they are obtained by means of lines rather than colours, so that it is impossible to say where drawing stops and painting begins. Drawing holds a possibility of immediacy of effect, of expression entirely by means of accents, that is unknown in painting, and thus it is easy to understand the effectiveness of a Lautrec image, its utter truth, and at the same time (when the painter's deeper feelings are aroused) its fascinating new type of beauty, at once human and animal. Colour that has the quality of drawing and line, this is Lautrec's "discovery," his "secret." By means of it he preserves some of the formal necessities bequeathed him by impressionism, and above all he fully realizes his ideal and his form, both of which are far removed from impressionism.

The works so far mentioned have been portraits, and they contain no element of caricature. The raffish emphasis of *The Laundress* is in the theme more than in the style, and the biting acidity of the style of *Gabrielle the Dancer* produces a result which is the exact opposite of caricature, in fact, the exact opposite of the type of beauty which has become synonymous with Lautrec.

In the picture called *At "The Sweetheart,"* 1891 (fig. 206), a motif inspired by Degas's *Absinth* (fig. 39), the artist's aim is to represent a Parisian scene of genre—an old prostitute sitting drinking with her pimp. There is in existence a photograph of the two models, taken when they were posing for the painter: the "pimp" is a pleasant young man, Maurice Guibert, and the "prostitute" a graceful model. Lautrec has deformed them, vilified them, accused them of imaginary crimes, although there is a lightness of touch that reveals his liking for bringing off a *tour de force,* for turning a social motif into a theatrical trick. As an illustration of the material and spiritual poverty of the dregs of Parisian society the scene is an undoubted success, but it is more difficult to distinguish what it contains of pure art. The composition is harmonious, with the bottle (added by the painter—not present in the photograph) balancing the woman's body. The image of the man is pulled forward to bring the surface arabesque into conformity with the representation of deep space. The wall of the background, characterless in the photograph, plays a definite rôle in the picture, its brush strokes being symbolically identical with those used in the figures: like them, it is tainted with vice. The colour harmony is based on a relationship of green and purple, in which the red of the woman's hair forms a contrast. That is, the painter expresses his vision not merely by realistic comment, but artistically—in the very power of his brush stroke, in his lines, in his colours.

Lautrec's transformation of his friend into a pimp is caricature, and not very successful caricature, because in the exaggeration the human character is lost and only the mask remains. The artist is not sufficiently detached from his motif (the sense of the dregs of Paris) and is therefore incapable of creating a vital image: it is insufficiently individualized and remains a type rather than a reality. The woman, on the other hand, although repugnant, is full of life. Her left hand is expressive of the vulgarity of her entire existence; her pose and her glance reveal her mind, her natural baseness, her habitual drunkenness: the whole figure has immense vividness. Where does the illustration end and the art begin? This is a work that reveals the painter in a moment of irony against social conventions, and yet beneath his sharp wit we sense his desperate sadness.

The Bed, 1892 (fig. 207), is one of a series of Lesbian scenes painted by Toulouse-Lautrec as decorations for a brothel. Yet it contains neither pornography nor a moralistic judgement. The placing of the elements of the picture is in itself a masterpiece. The foreshortening, which is translated into surface arabesque; the representation, which becomes a vivid communication of undulating rhythm gives life by points and angles; the scene of vice, which is touched on with such delicacy as to acquire an aspect of childlike eccentricity; the frankness with which the light area (white, green, pink) is juxtaposed with the wine red of the bed-cover and the background; and finally the linear character of the colour, which gives it a witty, hinting quality—all this makes for artistic perfection and reveals Lautrec's attitude, which is disillusioned and yet amused and sympathetic.

In the Salon, Rue des Moulins, 1894 (fig. 208), represents

208

a kind of official parade of brothel life. It is a descriptive picture, like something out of Maupassant or the Goncourts, and it gives an absurd, comical impression of pomp and dignity. The room has the sumptuousness of a palace, with a suggestion of filth. Some of the women display the pretentious airs of high society; the madam, prim in her high-necked gown, sits beside a half-undressed figure; while in the background, half cut off by the frame, another woman displays her bare buttocks. This last half image is the comic key to the scene. Lautrec does not laugh; he sees and represents the absurd situation lucidly, by means of a few sharp, incisive figures. The colour adds the fanciful to the absurd: broad areas of purple, green, and pink, of an acid harmony, transport the scene onto an unreal plane.

Of a very different power of fancy are Lautrec's scenes taken from the night life of the Moulin Rouge. *La Goulue, between Her Sister and a Dancer,* 1892 (fig. 209), and *At the Moulin Rouge: the Female Clown Cha-U-Kao,* 1895 (fig. 210), are two of the best examples of this type of composition.

La Goulue is shown entering the Moulin Rouge. She is framed between the images of her two companions, that of her sister being cut off by the edge of the picture; the execution of these images is summary with flat tones; like the background, they are in dark colours with a light touch or two in their bizarre ornaments. The *raison d'être* of the picture is the image of *La Goulue* herself, entirely in light colours; unlike the rest of the picture, she is not merely indicated, but painted, rich in gradations of tone, sky blue, yellow, and pink; the colour is not applied in posterlike areas, but is linear, with a suggestion of atmosphere. The image is comic, portrayed with a fanciful and witty humour: she is an authentic queen of the café-concert.

Even more clearly the work of a genius is *Cha-U-Kao*; the fullness of the artist's inspiration is evident in the space surrounding the image, in its transverse direction, which is the very embodiment of space, in the background images, which seem casual and give such perfect balance to the principal figure. The colour is fuller and richer than in *La Goulue*: Cha-U-Kao is dressed in green and yellow, and these two colours recur, more or less darkened, more or less mixed with brown or sky blue, throughout the canvas, except for the large pink spot of the woman on the right. But all this is an accompaniment to, or a variation on, the central figure: the ideal type of female clown, vulgar and natural.

When La Goulue lost the favor of the public and was dethroned as queen of Montmartre, she had to seek a living in the booths of suburban fairs, and although she had at first despised Toulouse-Lautrec, she now sought his aid. Always quick to kindness, he painted two displays for her booth at the Foire du Trône, one of them *The Dance of La Goulue, or, the Oriental Dancing Girls,* 1895 (fig. 211). It is one of the most beautiful, if not the most beautiful, of Lautrec's compositions, a fanciful vision, worthy of a primitive, expressing an atmosphere of comic oriental religiosity appropriate to a booth in a suburban fair. La Goulue is shown dancing in oriental costume, beautiful as an idol. To have idealized her when she was the rage of Paris would have seemed to Lautrec hypocritical; but to do so now, when she was no longer glamorous, was an act of generosity.

Two pretended orientals assist her on the stage, the pianist pounds desperately at the keys, and we have a rear view of spectators flocking to the booth. These are portraits of friends of Lautrec and La Goulue. In the right-hand corner is the profile of *Félix Fénéon* (fig. 212), the earliest champion of neo-impressionism; all in luminous greys, it is one of Lautrec's most powerful portraits, the transformation of a face into a legend.

The *Portrait of Cipa Godewski*, 1896 (fig. 213), shows us the extreme vivacity and vitality of a sketch by Lautrec. Godewski was a Pole, a song-writer, one of whose volumes Lautrec had illustrated. On the surface, therefore, the painting of his portrait would seem a perfectly innocent project. But Lautrec's style imprints on the jovial fellow's face something not caricature and not malicious but belonging to the world of the diabolical and the monstrous. The brush strokes, the features of the face, the pose, everything partakes of the vitality, and this escapes vulgarity thanks to the great power infused into it by the artist's overwhelming fancy.

The *Portrait of Paul Leclercq,* 1897 (fig. 214), is more correct; the figure's surroundings are indicated, and it is a complete picture. Leclercq, who later published his memoirs of Lautrec, tells how the painter worked: "He aimed his eye-glass at me, squinted, and took up his brush; and after seeing what he wanted to see he put a few light touches of very thin paint on his canvas. . . . Then he . . . said, peremptorily: 'Enough work. . . . Too beautiful outside.' And we would go for a walk in the neighborhood." Elsewhere he says, "Toulouse-Lautrec spoke a language all his own. He even had his friends adopt it. He loved to omit verbs and even whole phrases: one concise expression summed up all his thought. . . . For those of us who knew him, the way he expressed himself with his pencil can never make us forget the brief way he expressed himself in words; nothing was stronger or more pungent than his conversation in terms of images sketched in an acid phrase, picturesque and vivid; nothing was more powerful than his disconcerting expressions." [4]

Looking at the portraits of Godewski and Leclercq, we feel the truth of those reminiscences. Lautrec's art, too, is colloquial, abridged, improvised. It is an art of a few strokes, but in it the expression of his vision and feeling, at once so objective and so deforming, is realized to perfection.

Miss May Belfort, 1895 (fig. 215), is shown singing on the stage, holding a cat in her arms. May Belfort was a young Irish woman, a singer in café-concerts; she had a cunning grace, aping girlish naiveté. Lautrec was one of her enthusiasts and portrayed her many times. His enthusiasm was not for her beauty as a woman but for her mock girlishness, and he interpreted this falseness in the pose, in the face, in the costume. The colours, yellow and white in the costume and green in the background, have their accompaniment in the purple shadows. The yellow lights waft the notes of Lautrec's song into the air, and the purple shadows give them hints of irony. And the irony is as necessary to the lyricism as the shadows are to the light. Their unity creates a free image, real and ideal, a masterpiece.

Lautrec felt an enthusiasm for beauty when he painted *The Female Clown Cha-U-Kao,* 1895 (fig. 216), perhaps his most lofty ideal expression. This picture is probably a preparatory

[4] Paul Leclercq, *Autour de Toulouse-Lautrec,* 1921, pp. 14 and 23.

study for the composition reproduced in Figure 210, which is also very beautiful, but the image in the latter is vulgar as compared with that in Figure 216.

Baudelaire, speaking of Delacroix's women, mentions their "sickly beauty of heart and mind," and the "supernatural intensity" of their glance. That was the romantic ideal of woman in 1855, but forty years later beauty was considered an escape, an amusement. Being a clown, Cha-U-Kao found her naturalness in her artificiality, and Lautrec's communication of this strange result is a miracle of art, evident in the perfect naturalness of the woman and of the style and in the exceptional grace of the image, of her extraordinarily individual features, of her bizarre costume, of the comic touches, and of the theatrical surroundings. The colour harmony is tenuous. The purple of the dress is surrounded by the sky blue and white of the background, by the lemon yellow of the scarf, by the white of the wig and the light yellow of the flesh tones. Everywhere there is lightness of touch, a phantomlike quality, but the face has a fullness of form in which all the elements of the picture are concentrated and recapitulated, and this is the perfection of art.

In the last years of his life Lautrec seems to have dreamed of a less abridged style, a more complex type of painting in which he could include light and shadow effects which he had neglected for his linear colour.

The English Girl at "The Star" in Le Havre, 1899 (fig. 217), is perhaps the best example of this aspiration. The background is in green and blue geometric areas; the dress is blue with touches that are not linear but pictorial in the manner of Cézanne; the collar is pink and the hair yellow. The ensemble of these colours produces an effect in which once again, after almost ten years, there is the shine of natural light. It is not a realization but a great promise, and Lautrec's death at the age of thirty-seven left it unfulfilled.

But he had found his perfection in his unreal lines, which combine lyrical ingenuousness and the irony of the *grand seigneur,* and in his artificial colours, which are pure amusements of the spirit and yet belong to the supreme realm of art.

Epilogue

TWENTY-ONE years ago I published an essay on Manet (*L'Arte*, 1929) which I intended as a first attempt at a critical interpretation of the major painters of the nineteenth century. Other essays followed; then monographs on *Cézanne* (1936) and *Pissarro*;[1] then *Les Archives de l'Impressionnisme* (1939) and the first volume of *Modern Painters* (American Edition, 1947), from Goya to Courbet; and finally *La Peinture Contemporaine* (1948), from Matisse to the young painters of our own day. This second volume of *Modern Painters,* from Manet to Toulouse-Lautrec, the first planned and the last of all to appear, illustrates the most glorious moment of modern art, the creative activity which realized age-old aspirations and laid the bases for the best painting being done in our day.

The chapter on Manet in this volume has few affinities with the essay published in 1929, due to the many intervening years devoted to study of the problems of modern art, but the critical method remains approximately the same. My purpose is still to indicate to my readers which of the works of each artist are perfect, and which are less than perfect, according to a judgement based on a norm which is not fixed once and for all and applied to every work and to every artist, but which is derived from a reconstruction of each artistic personality. Each artist's way of feeling, of imagining, of thinking, and of

[1] This in collaboration with Rodo Pissarro (Paris, 1939).

desiring, has a unity which gives his work its fundamental tone; and in this tone are to be found his spontaneous impulse to creation and his reaction to his surroundings—to his masters, to his companions, to his followers, to his critics, to his public—in other words, his freedom of imagination and the elements of his taste which limit that freedom. Hence, fidelity to his essential tone signifies the artist's consistency with respect to himself and his own ideals, while a straying away from it signifies a momentary deviation resulting from influences extraneous to art.

In this book the reader will have found no praise of a "classical renaissance" nor of the value of realism or impressionism or symbolism: his attention has been directed to the absolute value of the individual artists. Their desires, theories, or programs and those of their period have been interpreted as historical conditions of their individual activity, as the accompaniment to their song—necessary, but secondary like any accompaniment.

If, before bringing my long labour to a close, I pause momentarily to contemplate the activity of those famous years between 1870 and 1900, I marvel again at the works that are so varied and numerous and excellent and am once again convinced that this period must be counted among the greatest epochs in the history of painting. And I find myself wondering whether from these individual works and these individual artists, so different among themselves, we can derive one all-inclusive message, a chorus of voices which will be revelatory of the character of a particular civilization.

Among the painters mentioned in the first volume, personalities like Goya or Corot or Daumier are of magnificent stature. And as between one of the earlier men, such as Corot, and one of the later, such as Manet, it would be futile to discuss which is the greater. Still, we feel that Manet not only created several perfect works, as did Corot also, but that he gave us something different, something which does not fall completely within the realm of art but goes beyond, into that of theory. Not that he wished to formulate a theory—of that he had no thought whatever—but out of a surging impulse against age-old conventions he created a form which is distinct not only because it is his own but also because it belongs to a civilization different from that of his immediate predecessors, Corot or Courbet. In other words, he initiated a new civilization of art, which Monet and Renoir, Cézanne and Van Gogh, and all the others developed in their different ways.

For an even approximate indication of the character of this civilization, the terms impressionism and symbolism are insufficient, and still less helpful are the data of vision, such as optical synthesis and decoration. Rather, it is important to emphasize the attitude assumed by the painters from Manet to Lautrec towards the physical and spiritual world, towards nature and subject—an attitude which is one of detachment and which shows a new consciousness of the autonomy of art. Not out of any desire for a program, but with their innermost artistic conscience, which was at times in opposition to their own intentions, all these painters concentrated their chief attention on lines, on forms, and on colours, rather than on the reality of the human beings and landscapes which their forms represented.

In different ways—relying upon sensibility, or placing full confidence in the powers of the imagination, or possessing precise theoretical consciousness—they profited from their study of nature and from their literary and aesthetic culture to construct a picture as one would an object of art, justified by its form-colour values rather than by its representational effectiveness. If we look at the total development of art over the centuries, we can confidently say that the shift of attention on the part of the painters from Manet to Lautrec has changed tradition but little, because every great artist has felt the presentation of images to be more important than the representation of facts. And yet that slight shift was enough to constitute a new condition of art, to generate a new force which changed not only painting but also sculpture, architecture, music, literature, and even criticism. And even today, eighty years after the beginning of the new era in painting, the efforts of our artists are concentrated on the attainment of the autonomy of art. Today this seems to us natural and necessary, but at that time it prevailed only after struggles, scandals, and decades of suffering. For this reason let us call the era of painting between 1870 and 1900 *the period of the struggle for autonomy.*

218

Bibliography and Index

Bibliography[1]

1873– Galerie Durand-Ruel, Ed. Durand-Ruel, Paris.

1885– Théodore Duret, *Critique d'avant-garde*, Paris.

1892– Georges Lecomte, *L'Art Impressionniste*, Paris.

1893– G. Albert Aurier, *Oeuvres Posthumes*, Paris.

1894– Gustave Geffroy, *La Vie Artistique, III, Histoire de l'Impressionnisme*, Paris.

1902– Emile Zola, *Mes Haines*, Paris.

1903– Roger Marx, *Etudes sur l'Ecole Française*, Paris.

1904– Camille Mauclair, *L'Impressionnisme*, Paris.

1904– J. K. Huysmans, *Certains*, Paris.

1904– Robert De La Sizeranne, *Les questions Esthétiques*, Paris.

1906– Camille Mauclair, *Trois Crises de l'Art Actuel*, Paris.

1913– Maurice Denis, *Théories*, Paris.

1913– Charles Louis Borgmeyer, *The Master Impressionists*, Chicago.

1914– Charles Morice, *Quelques Maîtres Modernes*, Paris.

1919– Théodore Duret, *Les Peintres Impressionnistes*, Paris.

1919– Jacques-Emile Blanche, *De David à Degas*, Paris.

1920– Gustave Coquiot, *Les Indépendants*, Paris.

1922– Maurice Denis, *Nouvelles Théories*, Paris.

1922– André Salmon, *Propos d'Atelier*, Paris.

1922– Octave Mirbeau, *Des Artistes*, Paris.

1923– Jules Laforgue, *Mélanges Posthumes*, Paris.

1923– Max Deri, *Die Malerei im XIX. Jahrhundert*, Berlin.

1924– Octave Mirbeau, *Des Artistes, Deuxième Série*, Paris.

[1] This bibliography makes no claim to be complete. It lists merely publications of which the author has made use.

BIBLIOGRAPHY

1924– Gustave Coquiot, *Des Peintres Maudits,* Paris.

1926– Madeleine Octave Maus, *Trente Années de lutte pour l'Art,* Brussels.

1926– Roger Fry, *Transformations,* London.

1926– Karl Scheffler, *Geschichte der Europäischen Malerei,* Berlin.

1927– Elie Faure, *Histoire de l'Art, L'Esprit des Formes,* Paris.

1927– Emile Verhaeren, *Sensations,* Paris.

1928– Henri Focillon, *La Peinture aux XIX° et XX° Siècles,* Paris.

1929– Adolphe Basler et Charles Kunstler, *La Peinture Indépendante en France,* Paris.

1930– Walter Friedlaender, *Hauptströmungen der Französischen Malerei von David bis Cézanne,* Leipzig.

1931– Robert Rey, *La Renaissance du Sentiment Classique,* Paris.

1931– Jacques-Emile Blanche, *Les Arts Plastiques,* Paris.

1933– André Lhote, *La Peinture,* Paris.

1934– Paul Jamot, *La Peinture en France,* Paris.

1934– Alfred Leroy, *Histoire de la Peinture Française,* Paris.

1936– Lionello Venturi, *History of Art Criticism,* New York.

1937– Pierre Francastel, *L'Impressionnisme,* Paris.

1938–49 Les Trésors de la Peinture Française, Ed. Albert Skira, Paris-Geneva.

1939– R. H. Wilenski, *Modern French Painters,* New York.

1939– Anna Maria Brizio, *Ottocento Novecento,* Turin.

1939– Lionello Venturi, *Les Archives de l'Impressionnisme,* Paris.

1943– Bernard Dorival, *Les Etapes de la Peinture Française Contemporaine,* Paris.

1946– André Lhote, *De la Palette à l'écritoire,* Paris.

1946– John Rewald, *The History of Impressionism,* New York.

1947– Charles Chasse, *Le Mouvement Symboliste dans l'art du XIX Siècle,* Paris.

1947– C. L. Ragghianti, *Impressionismo,* Turin.

1947– Germain Bazin, *L'Epoque Impressionniste,* Paris.

1948– Thadée Natanson, *Peints à leur tour,* Paris.

222

BIBLIOGRAPHY

1948–   Lionello Venturi e Rodolfo Pallucchini, *Gli Impressionisti alla XXIV Biennale di Venezia,* Venice.

1948–   Jean Leymarie, *Manet et les Impressionnistes au Musée du Louvre,* Paris.

I. MANET.

Principal works: Etienne Moreau-Nélaton, Paris (Laurens), 1926; Paul Jamot et Georges Wildenstein, Paris (Beaux-Arts), 1932; Adolphe Tabarant, Paris (Gallimard), 1947.

Other works: Emile Zola, *Edouard Manet,* 1867; republished in *Mes Haines,* Paris, 1902; Edouard Bazire, *Manet,* Paris, 1884; George Moore, *Confessions of a Young Man,* London, 1888; Théodore Duret, *L'Histoire d'Edouard Manet et de son oeuvre,* Paris, 1902; several times republished; Joseph De Nittis, *Notes et souvenirs,* Paris, 1912; Antonin Proust, *Souvenirs,* Paris, 1913; Jacques-Emile Blanche, *Propos de peinture. De David à Degas,* Paris, 1919; Hugo v. Tschudi, *Edouard Manet,* Berlin, 1920; Jacques-Emile Blanche, *Edouard Manet,* Paris, 1924; Léon Rosenthal, *Manet aquafortiste et lithographe,* Paris, 1925; Marees Gesellschaft, *Manet,* Munich, 1928. Album with fifteen plates in color; Jean Guiffrey, *Lettres illustrées d'Edouard Manet,* Paris, 1929; Edouard Manet, *Lettres de jeunesse,* Paris, 1929; Adolphe Tabarant, *Manet, Histoire Catalographique,* Paris, 1931; Robert Rey, *Manet,* Paris-London, 1938; Adolphe Tabarant, *Manet* ("Trésors de la peinture française," Paris, 1939, with eight plates in color); Gotthard Jedlicka, *Edouard Manet,* Erlenbach-Zurich, 1941; Marcel Guérin, *L'oeuvre gravée de Manet,* Paris, 1944; Pierre Courthion et Pierre Cailler, *Manet raconté par lui-même et par ses amis,* Paris, 1945; John Rewald, *Edouard Manet, Pastels,* Oxford, 1947; Maurice Bex, *Manet,* Paris, 1948; Waldemar George, *Manet et la carence du Spirituel,* Paris, n. d.

Articles: Théodore Duret, "Quelques lettres de Manet," *Revue Blanche,* March 15, 1899; Gabriel Séailles, "Edouard Manet," *Revue de Paris,* February, 1910; Paul Jamot, "Le Fifre et Victorine

223

Meurend," *Revue de l'Art Ancien et Moderne,* January, 1927; Lionello Venturi, "Manet," *L'Arte,* July-August, 1929, p. 145 *et seq.;* Paul Jamot, "La Poésie de Manet," *L'Amour de l'Art,* May, 1932; Germain Bazin, "Manet et la Tradition," *L'Amour de l'Art,* May, 1932; René Huyghe, "Manet Peintre," *L'Amour de l'Art,* May, 1932; Paul Valéry, "Sur un portrait de Berthe Morisot, par Edouard Manet," *L'Art Vivant,* June, 1932; Jacques-Emile Blanche, "Manet ou le Mystère en Plein Jour," *L'Art Vivant,* June, 1932; Florent Fels, "Notes sur Manet," *L'Art Vivant,* June, 1932; Jacques Guenne, "La Grandeur de Manet," *L'Art Vivant,* June, 1932; Claude-Roger Marx, "Les Eaux Fortes et les Lithographies de Manet," *L'Art Vivant,* June, 1932; Adolphe Tabarant, "Une correspondance inédite d'Edouard Manet," excerpt from *Mercure de France,* 1935.

Catalogues of Manet Exhibitions: Galerie Matthiessen, Berlin, 1928; Musée de l'Orangerie, Paris, 1932.

II. DEGAS.

Principal works: Paul André Lemoisne, *Degas et son oeuvre,* Paris, 1946. (Four volumes so far published, with catalogue raisonné of paintings and pastels.)

Other works: Georges Grappe, *Degas,* Paris, 1911; Degas, *98 reproductions signées par Degas,* Galerie A. Vollard, Paris, 1914; Paul Lafond, *Degas,* Paris, 1918 (2 volumes); Vente Degas (Sale catalogue of contents of Degas's Studio; his own works and his collection. Paris, 1918 and 1919, 6 volumes); Loys Delteil, *Edgar Degas,* Vol. IX of "Le Peintre Graveur Illustré," Paris, 1919; Henri Hertz, *Degas,* Paris, 1920; Max Liebermann, *Degas,* Berlin, 1922; Georges Rivière, *Les dessins de Degas,* Paris, 1922 and 1923 (two series); Paul Jamot, *Degas,* Paris, 1924; Ambroise Vollard, *Degas,* Paris, 1924; Gustave Coquiot, *Degas,* Paris, 1924; Julius Meier-Graefe, *Degas,* Munich, 1924; J. B. Manson, *Edgar Degas,* London, 1927; Marcel Guérin, *Les Lettres de Degas,* Paris, 1931; Georges Rivière, *M. Degas, bourgeois de Paris,* Paris, 1935; M. Rebatet, *Degas,* Paris,

1944; John Rewald, *Degas. Works in Sculpture,* New York, 1944; Denis Rouart, *Degas à la recherche de sa technique,* Paris, 1945; Jean Leymarie, *Les Degas du Louvre,* Paris, 1947.

Articles: Walter Sickert, "Degas," *Burlington Magazine,* November, 1917; George Moore, "Memories of Degas," *Burlington Magazine,* January-February, 1918; Paul André Lemoisne, "Les carnets de Degas," *Gazette des Beaux-Arts,* April, 1921; Charles Du Bos, "Remarques sur Degas," *Revue critique des Idées et des Livres,* 1922, T. 34, pp. 262–277; J. Raunay, "Degas," *Revue de France,* 1931. Année II, tome 2; Jacques-Emile Blanche, "Portraits de Degas," *Formes,* February, 1931; Waldemar George, "La Jeunesse de Degas," *Formes,* May, 1931; Etienne Moreau-Nélaton, "Deux heures avec Degas," *L'Amour de l'Art,* July, 1931; René Huyghe, "Degas ou la fiction réaliste," *L'Amour de l'Art,* July, 1931; Germain Bazin, "Degas sculpteur, Degas et l'objectif," *L'Amour de l'Art,* July, 1931; Jules Chialiva, "Comment Degas a changé sa technique du dessin," *Bulletin de la Société d'Histoire de l'Art Français,* February, 1932; Enrico Piceni, "Degas uomo cattivo," with three unpublished letters. *Illustrazione Italiana,* April, 1932; Marcel Gromaire, "L'Exposition Degas," *L'Art Vivant,* January, 1933; Georges Jeanniot, "Souvenirs sur Degas," *Revue Universelle,* October 15 and November 1, 1933; Paul Valéry, "Chez Degas," *Nouvelle Revue Française,* January 1 and October 1, 1935; Ernest Rouart, "Degas," *Le Point,* February, 1937.

Catalogues of Degas Exhibitions: Georges Petit, 1924; Musée de l'Orangerie (portraitiste et sculpteur), 1931; Pennsylvania Museum of Art, Philadelphia, 1936; Musée de l'Orangerie, 1937.

III. MONET.

Principal work: Gustave Geffroy, *Claude Monet,* Paris, 1922. Another edition in 2 volumes, 1924.

Other works: Théodore Duret, *Claude Monet.* Preface to

an exhibition, 1880. (Republished in *Critique d'avant-garde,* 1885). Octave Mirbeau, *Les "Venise" de Claude Monet,* Paris, 1912; Arsène Alexandre, *Claude Monet,* Paris, 1921; Marc Elder, *A Giverny, chez Claude Monet,* Paris, 1924; Camille Mauclair, *Claude Monet,* Paris, 1924; Florent Fels, *Claude Monet* (Albums Druet), Paris, 1927; François Fosca, *Claude Monet,* Paris, 1927; Louis Gillet, *Trois variations sur Claude Monet,* Paris, 1927; Georges Clemenceau, *Claude Monet. Les Nymphéas,* Paris, 1928; Léon Werth, *Claude Monet,* Paris, 1928; Charles Leger, *Claude Monet,* Paris, 1930; Gaston Poulain, *Bazille et ses amis,* Paris, 1932; Pierre Francastel, *Monet, Sisley, Pissarro,* Paris, 1939; Georges Grappe, *Claude Monet,* n. d.

Articles: A. De Lostalot, "Claude Monet," *Gazette des Beaux-Arts,* 1883, I; Octave Mirbeau, "Claude Monet," *L'Art dans les Deux Mondes,* March, 1891; G. Albert Aurier, "Claude Monet," published in *Oeuvres Posthumes,* 1893, p. 221 *et seq.*; Thadée Natanson, "Claude Monet," *Revue Blanche,* 1895; Gustave Kahn, "L'Exposition Claude Monet," *Gazette des Beaux-Arts,* 1904, II; Roger Marx, "Les Nymphéas de Claude Monet," *Gazette des Beaux-Arts,* 1909, II; Louis Vauxcelles, "Claude Monet," *L'Amour de l'Art,* August, 1922; Walter Sickert, "French Pictures at Knoedler's Gallery," *Burlington Magazine,* July, 1923; Waldemar George, "Hommage à Claude Monet," *L'Amour de l'Art,* December, 1926; Georges Rouault, "Claude Monet," *L'Amour de l'Art,* June, 1927; Thiebault-Sisson, "Les Nymphéas de Claude Monet," *Revue de l'Art,* 1927, II, pp. 41–52; Max Liebermann, "Claude Monet," *Kunst und Künstler,* 1927, t. 25, pp. 163–173; P. Gsell, "Claude Monet," *Renaissance,* 1927, pp. 79–82; Arsène Alexandre, "Claude Monet," *Renaissance,* 1927, pp. 43–47; Georges Grappe, "Claude Monet," *L'Art Vivant,* 1927, pp. 1–6; Robert Rey, "Claude Monet et l'Impressionnisme," *L'Art Vivant,* 1927, pp. 13–14; Willi Wolfradt, "Monet und der Impressionismus," *Cicerone,* February, 1928; Raymond Regamey, "La formation de Claude Monet," *Gazette des Beaux-Arts,* 1927, I; Florent Fels, "L'Atelier de Claude Monet au Musée de l'Orangerie," *Formes,* May, 1931.

IV. PISSARRO

Principal works: Ludovic Rodo Pissaro et Lionello Venturi, *Camille Pissarro, Son art—Son oeuvre*, Paris, 1939. (The catalogue raisonné is by L. R. Pissarro, the monograph on the artist by L. Venturi); Camille Pissarro, *Letters to his son Lucien*. (Edited by John Rewald and translated by Lionel Abel), New York, 1943.

Other works: Julius Elias, *Camille Pissarro*, Berlin, 1914; Georges Lecomte, *Camille Pissarro*, Paris, 1922; Loys Delteil, *C. Pissarro*, Vol. XVII of "Le Peintre Graveur Illustré," Paris, 1923; Adolphe Tarabant, *Pissarro*, Paris, 1924; Leo Koenig, *Camille Pissarro*, Paris, 1927; Claude Roger-Marx, *Camille Pissarro*, Paris, 1929; Charles Kunstler, *Camille Pissarro*, Paris, 1930; Pierre Francastel, *Monet, Sisley, Pissarro*, Paris, 1939.

Articles: Octave Mirbeau, "Camille Pissarro," *L'Art dans les Deux Mondes,* January 10, 1891; G. Albert Aurier, "Le Néo-Impressionniste: Camille Pissarro," published in *Oeuvres Posthumes,* 1893; André Fontainas, "Camille Pissarro," *Mercure de France,* XXVII, 1898, XXX, 1899; Gustave Geffroy, "Camille Pissarro," *La Vie Artistique,* VI, 1900; Georges Lecomte, "Exposition Camille Pissarro," *Revue Populaire des Beaux-Arts,* June, 1898; Maurice Denis, "Camille Pissarro," *Occident*, December, 1903, republished in *Théories,* 1913; Henry Stephens, "Camille Pissarro," *Brush and Pencil,* March, 1904; Théodore Duret, "Camille Pissarro," *Gazette des Beaux-Arts,* May, 1904; Charles Morice, "Exposition Pissarro," *Mercure de France,* May, 1904; Julius Meier-Graefe, "Camille Pissarro," *Kunst und Künstler,* II, September, 1904; Octave Mirbeau, *Préface au catalogue de l'exposition C. Pissarro,* Durand-Ruel, Paris, 1904; J. B. Manson, "Camille Pissarro," *The Studio,* May, 1920; Waldemar George, "Pissarro," *L'Art Vivant,* March, 1926; J. C. Holl, "Pissarro," *L'Art et les Artistes,* February, 1928; Georges Lecomte et Charles Kunstler, "Un fondateur de l'Impressionnisme," *Revue de l'art ancien et moderne,* March, 1930; Gustave Kahn, "Camille Pissarro," *Mercure de France,* March 15, 1930; Jacques de Laprade,

"Camille Pissarro d'après des documents inédits," *Beaux-Arts,* April 17-24, 1936; John Rewald, "Oeuvres de jeunesse inédites de Camille Pissarro," *L'Amour de l'Art,* April, 1936; John Rewald, "Camille Pissarro," *Burlington Magazine,* June, 1938; Jules Joëts, "Lettres inédites de Pissarro à Claude Monet," *L'Amour de l'Art,* 1946, f.3; Jules Joëts, "Camille Pissarro et la période inconnue de St. Thomas et de Caracas," *L'Amour de l'Art,* 1947, f.2.

V. SISLEY

Principal works: Gustave Geffroy, *Sisley,* Paris, 1927; Pierre Francastel, *Monet, Sisley, Pissarro,* Paris, 1939; Pierre du Colombier, *Sisley au Musée du Louvre,* Paris, 1947; Loys Delteil, *Alfred Sisley,* Vol. XVII of "Le Peintre Graveur Illustré," Paris, 1923.

Articles: Octave Mirbeau, "Le Salon du Champ de Mars," *Le Figaro,* May 25, 1892; Adolphe Tavernier, "Sisley," *L'Art Français,* VI, March 18, 1893; Arsène Alexandre, "Exposition Alfred Sisley," *Le Figaro,* February 7, 1897; Théodore Duret, "Quelques lettres de Manet et de Sisley," *Revue Blanche,* March 15, 1899; Adolphe Tavernier, "L'Atelier de Sisley," (Preface to catalogue of an exhibition at *Bernheim Jeune,* 1907); R. H. Wilenski, "The Sisley Compromise," *Apollo,* 1928, I, pp. 69–74; Pierre Berthelot, "Exposition Sisley," *Beaux-Arts,* March, 1930; Deborde de Montcorin, "A. Sisley" (Lecture, printed by *Les Amis de Moret,* 1930); René Huyghe, "Lettres inédites de Sisley," *Formes,* November, 1931, pp. 151–4; Hans Heilmeier, "Alfred Sisley," *Kunst,* t. 63, 1931, pp. 131–144; Maximilien Gauthier, "Hommage à Sisley," *L'Art Vivant,* March, 1933, pp. 116–17; Galerie D'Art Braun et Cie. (Letters from Sisley to Duret, Monet, Viau), *Bulletin des expositions,* II, 1933.

VI. RENOIR

Principal works: Octave Mirbeau, *Renoir,* Paris, 1913; Ambroise Vollard, *La vie et l'oeuvre de P. A. Renoir,* Paris, 1919; Ardengo Soffici, *Scoperte e Massacri* (containing a chapter on

Renoir), Florence, 1919; Elie Faure, *Renoir,* Paris, 1920; Georges Rivière, *Renoir et ses amis,* Paris, 1921; François Fosca, *Renoir,* Paris, 1923; G. Duthuit, *Renoir,* Paris, 1923; Gustave Coquiot, *Renoir,* Paris, 1923; Loys Delteil, *Renoir,* Vol. XVII of "Le Peintre Graveur Illustré," Paris, 1923; Théodore Duret, *Renoir,* Paris, 1924; Albert André, *Renoir,* Paris, 1928; Adolphe Basler, *Renoir,* Paris, 1928; Julius Meier-Graefe, *Renoir,* Leipzig, 1929; Albert André et Marc Elder, *L'Atelier de Renoir,* 2 vol., Paris, 1931; Georges Besson, *Renoir,* Paris, 1932; Claude Roger-Marx, *Renoir,* Paris, 1933; Albert C. Barnes and Violette de Mazia, *The Art of Renoir,* New York, 1935; Michel Florisoone, *Renoir,* Paris, 1938; Germain Bazin, *Renoir,* Paris, 1939; André Lhote, *Peintures de Renoir,* Paris, 1944; Michel Drucker, *Renoir,* Paris, 1944; Rosamund Frost, *Renoir,* New York, 1944; Enrico Piceni, *Auguste Renoir,* Milan, 1945; Claude Renoir, *Souvenirs sur mon père,* Paris, n. d. [1947].

Articles: Teodor de Wyzewa, "Renoir," 1891 (Reprinted with additions in *Peintres de jadis et d'aujourd'hui,* 1903); G. Albert Aurier, "Renoir," published in *Oeuvres Posthumes,* Paris, 1893, p. 226 *et seq.*; Thadée Natanson, "Renoir," *Revue Blanche,* I, 1896; André Fontainas, "Art Moderne," *Mercure de France,* July, 1898; March, 1900; July, 1902; Jean Carré, "Notes sur Renoir," *La Vie,* 1912, pp. 408–410; Arsène Alexandre, "Renoir sans phrases," *Les Arts,* May, 1920; Georges Besson, "Renoir à Cagnes," *Cahiers d'Aujourd'hui,* November, 1920; Paul Jamot, "Renoir," *Gazette des Beaux-Arts,* 1923, II; J. G. Goulinat, "Les sources du métier chez Renoir," *L'Art Vivant,* February and April, 1925; Léon Werth, "La Collection Gangnat," *L'Amour de l'Art,* February, 1925; Elie Faure, "La Collection Gangnat," *Renaissance,* April, 1925; Christian Zervos, "Reflexions sur l'oeuvre de Renoir," *Cahiers d'art,* 1927, p. 45; Germain Bazin, "Les sanguines de Renoir," *Formes,* May, 1930; André Fontainas, "La rencontre d'Ingres et de Renoir," *Formes,* March, 1931; Jules Joëts, "Les impressionnistes et Chocquet," *L'Amour de l'Art,* April, 1935; Michel Florisoone, "Renoir et la famille Charpentier," *L'Amour de l'Art,* February, 1938.

BIBLIOGRAPHY

Collections and Catalogues of Exhibitions: Arsène Alexandre, *La Collection Canonne,* Paris, 1930; Catalogue of the Collection Maurice Gangnat, Paris, 1925. Théodore Duret, Preface to the *Catalogue des oeuvres de Renoir,* Paris, 1883; Arsène Alexandre, *Exposition Renoir,* 1892; Paul Jamot, *Exposition Renoir à l'Orangerie,* Paris, 1933; Centennial Loan Exhibition—Renoir, New York, 1941.

VII. CEZANNE.

Principal work: Lionello Venturi, *Cézanne. Son art. Son oeuvre,* Paris, 1936. (With catalogue raisonné of the oeuvre, and bibliography up to 1936.)

Important publications since 1936: Cézanne, *Correspondance* (edited by John Rewald), Paris, 1937; F. Novotny and L. Goldscheider, *Cézanne,* New York, 1937; Adrien Chappuis, *Dessins de Paul Cézanne,* Paris, 1938; Fritz Novotny, *Cézanne und das Ende der Wissenschaftlichen Perspektive,* Vienna, 1938; Albert C. Barnes and Violette De Mazia, *The Art of Cézanne,* New York, 1939; Raymond Cogniat, *Cézanne,* Paris, 1939; Gotthard Jedlicka, *P. Cézanne,* Zurich and Leipzig, 1939; Marcel Provence, *Cézanne au Tholonet,* Aix-en-Provence, 1939; John Rewald, *Cézanne, sa vie, son oeuvre, son amitié pour Zola,* Paris, 1939; Lionello Venturi, *Cézanne Water-colours,* London, 1943; Rainer Maria Rilke, *Lettres sur Cézanne,* Paris, 1944; Gerard Schildt, *Cézanne,* Stockholm, 1946; Erle Loran, *Cézanne's Composition,* Berkeley, California, 1946; Bernard Dorival, *Cézanne,* Paris, 1948.

Articles: John Rewald, "A propos du catalogue raisonné de l'oeuvre de Cézanne et de la chronologie de cette oeuvre," *Renaissance,* March-April, 1937; Alfred Barr, "Cézanne d'après les lettres de Marion à Morstatt," *Gazette des Beaux-Arts,* t. 138, 1937, pp. 37-57; John Rewald, "Achille Emperaire," *L'Amour de l'Art,* May, 1938; D. Le Blond-Zola, "Paul Alexis, ami des peintres," *Mercure de France,* March 1, 1939; John Rewald, "Paul Cézanne: New Documents for the Years 1870–1871," *Burlington Magazine*, April, 1939, p. 163 *et seq.*; F. B. Deknatel, "Manet and the formation of Cézanne's art," *College Art Journal*, March, 1942.

Among the Monographs before 1936 the following are worthy of note: Ambroise Vollard, *Paul Cézanne*, Paris, 1914; Octave Mirbeau and others, *Cézanne*, Paris, Bernheim-Jeune, 1914; Gustave Coquiot, *Cézanne*, Paris, 1919; Joachim Gasquet, *Paul Cézanne*, Paris, 1921; Julius Meier-Graefe, *Cézanne und sein Kreis*, Munich, 1922; H. v. Wedderkop, *Paul Cézanne*, Leipzig, 1922; Georges Rivière, *Le maître Paul Cézanne*, Paris, 1923; Tristan Klingsor, *Cézanne*, Paris, 1923; André Salmon, *Cézanne*, Paris, 1923; Emile Bernard, *Sur Paul Cézanne*, Paris, 1925; Léo Larguier, *Le dimanche avec Paul Cézanne*, Paris, 1925; Elie Faure, *Paul Cézanne*, Paris, 1926; Roger Fry, *Cézanne, a study of his development*, London, 1927; Kurt Pfister, *Paul Cézanne*, Potsdam, 1927; Gerstle Mack, *Paul Cézanne*, London and New York, 1935.

VIII. SEURAT.

Monographs and Books: Félix Fénéon, "Les Impressionnistes en 1886," Paris, 1886; J. Cristophe, *Georges Seurat*, Paris, 1890; André Salmon, *La Révélation de Seurat*, Brussels, 1921; Lucie Cousturier, *Georges Seurat*, Paris, 1921 and 1926; André Lhote, *Georges Seurat*, Rome (Valori Plastici), 1922; Walter Pach, *Georges Seurat*, New York, 1923; Gustave Coquiot, *Seurat*, Paris, 1924; Gustave Kahn, *Les Dessins de Seurat*, Paris, 1926; Roger Fry, *Transformations* (containing a chapter on Seurat), London, 1926; Waldemar George, *Seurat*, Paris, 1931; Claude Roger-Marx, *Seurat*, Paris, 1931; D. Catton Rich, *Seurat and the evolution of "La Grande Jatte,"* Chicago, 1935; John Rewald, *Georges Seurat*. English editions, New York, 1943, 1946. French edition, Paris, 1948 (with complete bibliography); Jacques de Laprade, *Georges Seurat*, Monaco, 1943; Germain Seligman, *The Drawings of Georges Seurat*, New York, 1947; André Lhote, *Seurat*, Paris, 1947.

Essays and Articles: Teodor de Wyzewa, "L'Art Contemporain," *Revue Indépendante,* November-December, 1886; J. K. Huysmans, "Chronique d'art," *Revue Indépendante,* April, 1887; Félix Fénéon, "Le Néo-Impressionnisme," *L'Art Moderne,* May 1, 1887; Gustave Kahn, "Georges Seurat," *L'Art Moderne,* April 5, 1891; Anonymous (F. Fénéon), Note on Seurat in *Entretiens Politiques et Littéraires,* 1891, Vol. 2, n. 13; Teodor de Wyzewa, "Georges Seurat," *L'Art dans les Deux Mondes,* April 18, 1891; J. Cristophe, "Georges Seurat," *La Plume,* September 1, 1891; Thadée Natanson, "Un primitif d'aujourd'hui: Georges Seurat," *Revue Blanche,* April 15, 1900; Félix Fénéon, "Notes inédites de Seurat sur Delacroix," *Bulletin de la Vie Artistique,* April 1, 1922; Félix Fénéon, "Les carnets d'H. E. Cross," *Bulletin de la Vie Artistique,* May 15-October 15, 1922; A. Ozenfant, "Seurat," *Cahiers d'art,* September, 1926; O. Sitwell, "Les Poseuses," *Apollo,* 1926; Emile Verhaeren, "Georges Seurat," Société Nouvelle, April, 1891; reprinted in *Sensations,* 1928; Meyer Schapiro, "Seurat and 'La Grande Jatte'," *Columbia Review,* XVII, 1935; W. Grohmann, "Seurat," *Allgemeines Künstler-Lexicon,* Vol. 30, 1936; A. Watt, "The art of Georges Seurat," *Apollo,* March, 1936; Jean Helion, "Seurat as a Predecessor," *Burlington Magazine,* July, 1936; Robert J. Goldwater, "Some aspects of the development of Seurat's style," *The Art Bulletin,* June, 1941; Benedict Nicholson, "Seurat's 'La Baignade'," *Burlington Magazine,* November, 1941; Lionello Venturi, "The Art of Seurat," *Gazette des Beaux-Arts,* July-December, 1944; John Rewald, "Félix Fénéon," *Gazette des Beaux-Arts,* July-August, 1947; February, 1948.

IX. GAUGUIN

Writings of Paul Gauguin: *Lettres à Daniel de Monfreid,* Paris, 1920; *Lettres à André Fontainas,* Paris, 1921; *Avant et Après,* Paris, 1923; *Noa Noa,* Paris, 1924; *Lettres à Emile Bernard,* Paris, 1926; *Lettres à sa femme et à ses amis,* Paris, 1947; *Lettres à Schuffenecker* (published by Alexandre in the monograph listed below);

BIBLIOGRAPHY

Racontars d'un Rapin et Diverses Choses (Extracts published by Rotonchamp in the monograph listed below).

Monographs: Jean de Rotonchamp, *Paul Gauguin,* Weimar, 1906; Jacques Rivière, *Etudes* (published by the *Nouvelle Revue Française*), Paris, 1911; Charles Morice, *Paul Gauguin,* Paris, 1920; Charles Chasse, *Gauguin et le Groupe de Pont-Aven,* Paris, 1921; John Gould Fletcher, *Paul Gauguin,* New York, 1921; E. Wiese, *Paul Gauguin,* Leipzig, 1923; Robert Rey, *Gauguin,* Paris, 1924; Marcel Guérin, *L'oeuvre gravée de Paul Gauguin,* Paris, 1927; Jean Dorsenne, *La vie sentimentale de Paul Gauguin,* Paris, 1927; Arsène Alexandre, *Paul Gauguin,* Paris, 1930; Robert Burnett, *The Life of Paul Gauguin,* London, 1935; Louis Hautecoeur, *Gauguin,* Paris, 1938; John Rewald, *Gauguin,* Paris, 1938; Pola Gauguin, *Paul Gauguin, mon père,* Paris, 1938; Emile Bernard, *Souvenirs inédits sur l'artiste Paul Gauguin et ses compagnons,* Paris, 1939; René Hamon, *Gauguin le solitaire du Pacifique,* Paris, 1939; Charles Kunstler, *Gauguin Peintre maudit,* Paris, 1942; Antony de Witt, *Paul Gauguin,* Milan, 1945; W. G. Russell Allen, *Gauguin,* New York, 1946; Raymond Cogniat, *Gauguin,* Paris, 1947; René Jean, *Gauguin,* Paris, 1948; Maurice Lamingue, *Gauguin,* Paris, 1948; F. Elgar, *Gauguin,* Paris, 1949.

Articles: G. Albert Aurier, "Le Symbolisme en peinture: Paul Gauguin," *Mercure de France,* March, 1891; Octave Mirbeau, Preface to the catalogue of the Gauguin Exhibition, Paris, 1891; G. Albert Aurier, "Gauguin," *Revue Encyclopédique,* April, 1892; Armand Seguin, "Gauguin," *L'Occident,* March, April, May, 1903; Daniel de Monfreid, "Sur Paul Gauguin," *L'Ermitage,* December, 1903; Charles Morice, "Quelques opinions sur Paul Gauguin," *Mercure de France,* November, 1903; Maurice Denis, "Gauguin," *Mercure de France,* January, 1904; Victor Segalen, "Gauguin dans son dernier décor," *Mercure de France,* June, 1904; Louis Vauxcelles, "La Sculpture de Paul Gauguin," *L'Art Décoratif,* January, 1911; Charles Chasse, "Gauguin et Mallarmé," *L'Amour de l'Art,* August, 1922; Gustave Kahn, "Paul Gauguin," *L'Art et les Artistes,* November, 1925; Gaston Varenne, "Les bois gravés et sculptés de Paul Gauguin," *Renaissance,* December, 1927; Henri Hertz, "Paul Gauguin," *Art in America,* April, 1927; Robert Rey, "Les bois sculptés de Paul Gauguin," *Art et Décoration,* February, 1928; Louis Vauxcelles, "De Gauguin," *Formes,* February, 1931; Lionello Venturi, "Gauguin," *L'Arte,* March, 1934; Charles Chasse, "De quand date le symbolisme de Gauguin," *L'Amour de l'Art,* April, 1938; R. Brest, "Gauguin," *Ver y Estimar,* Buenos Aires, October-November, 1948; Jean Leymarie et René Huyghe, *Gauguin* (Catalogue de l'Exposition du Centenaire, Paris, 1949); Jean Leymarie, "L'Exposition Gauguin," *Bulletin des Musées de France,* June, 1949.

X. VAN GOGH.

Principal works: G. Albert Aurier, "Vincent Van Gogh," *Mercure de France,* December 1, 1889 (The only article published during the life of the artist. Republished in Aurier's *Oeuvres Posthumes,* 1893); Vincent Van Gogh, *Lettres à Emile Bernard,* Paris, 1911; Vincent Van Gogh, *Lettres à son frère Théo*; complete Dutch edition, Amsterdam, 3 vol., 1914-25; English edition, London-Boston-New York, 3 vol., 1927-29. Edited by J. Van Gogh-Bonger; J. B. de La Faille, Vincent Van Gogh; two editions, Paris and Brussels, 1928 and Paris, 1939 (Catalogue raisonné; drawings are included in the first edition); Theo Van Gogh, *Lettres à son frère Vincent,* Amsterdam, 1932; Vincent Van Gogh, *Letters to Anton Ridder van Rappard,* London, 1936; Vincent Van Gogh, *Lettres à son frère Théo*; selection made by P. Philippart, Paris, 1937; and by A. Hamilton-Barr, New York, 1935.

Other works: Julius Meier-Graefe, *Vincent,* Munich, two editions, 1910 and 1922; Théodore Duret, *Vincent Van Gogh,* Paris, 1916 and 1919; F. M. Huebner, *Vincent Van Gogh,* Leipzig, 1921; Kurt Pfister, *Vincent Van Gogh,* Potsdam, 1922, Berlin, 1929; Emile Bernard, *Vincent Van Gogh,* Paris, 1923; Gustave Coquiot, *Vincent Van Gogh,* Paris, 1923; Oskar Hagen, *Vincent Van Gogh* (Mappe),

BIBLIOGRAPHY

Munich, 1924; Roche Grey, *Vincent Van Gogh,* Munich, 1924; Paul Colin, *Vincent Van Gogh,* Munich, 1925; Waldemar George, *Vincent Van Gogh,* Munich, 1927; Florent Fels, *Vincent Van Gogh,* Munich, 1928; Charles Terrasse, *Vincent Van Gogh,* Munich, 1930 and 1935; G. F. Hartlaub, *Vincent Van Gogh,* Berlin, 1930; T. W. Earp, *Vincent Van Gogh,* London, 1934; Walter Pach, *Vincent Van Gogh,* New York, 1936; Lamberto Vitali, *Vincent Van Gogh,* Milan, 1936 (with bibliography); G. L. Luzzatto, *Vincent Van Gogh,* Modena, 1936; Jean de Beucken, *Vincent Van Gogh,* Liège, 1938; Louis Hautecoeur, *Vincent Van Gogh,* Monaco, 1943; Jean de Beucken, *Vincent Van Gogh,* Brussels, 1945; Antoine Artaud, *Vincent Van Gogh,* Paris, 1947; Wilhelm Uhde, *Vincent Van Gogh,* Paris, 1947; W. Muensterberger, *Vincent Van Gogh; Dessins, Pastels, Etudes,* Paris, 1948; Hans Tietze, *Vincent Van Gogh,* Vienna, n. d.

Principal articles: Emile Bernard, "Vincent Van Gogh," *La Plume,* III, 1891, p. 300; Octave Mirbeau, "Vincent Van Gogh," *Echo de Paris,* March 31, 1891; Charles Saunier, "Les Peintres symbolistes," *Revue Indépendante,* 1892, p. 394; H. Meier-Riefstahl, "Vincent Van Gogh," *Burlington Magazine,* XVIII, 1910–11, pp. 9 and 155; W. Trübner, "Van Gogh und die neuen Richtungen der Malerei," *Die Kunst,* XXI, 1915, p. 130; C. Glaser, "Vincent Van Gogh," *Allgemeines Lexicon der Bildenden Künstler,* XIV, Leipzig, 1921; Jacques-Emile Blanche, "A propos de l'exposition Van Gogh," *L'Art Vivant,* July 15, 1927; Elie Faure, "A propos des faux Van Gogh," *L'Art Vivant,* April 1, 1930.

Catalogues of Van Gogh Exhibitions: Paul Cassirer Exhibition, Berlin, 1928; Stedelijk Museum, Amsterdam, 1931; Museum of Modern Art, New York, 1935 (Alfred H. Barr, *Vincent Van Gogh*); Exposition Internationale de 1937, Paris. Huyghe-Florisoone-Rewald, *Vincent Van Gogh;* Wildenstein Exhibition, New York, 1943 (Catalogue: Georges de Batz); Van Gogh Exhibition, Amsterdam, Brussels, Paris, 1947; Kröller-Müller Museum, Otterlo.

BIBLIOGRAPHY

XI. TOULOUSE-LAUTREC.

Principal work: Maurice Joyant, *Henri de Toulouse-Lautrec, Peintre,* Paris, 1926; *Dessins, Estampes, Affiches,* Paris, 1927.

Other works: H. Esswein, *Toulouse-Lautrec,* Munich, 1904; Gustave Coquiot, *Toulouse-Lautrec,* Paris, 1913; Théodore Duret, *Toulouse-Lautrec,* Paris, 1920; Loys Delteil, *Toulouse-Lautrec,* Vol. X and XI of "Le Peintre Graveur Illustré," Paris, 1920; Paul Leclercq, *Autour de Toulouse-Lautrec,* Paris, 1921; Paul de Lapparent, *Toulouse-Lautrec,* Paris, 1927; Pierre Mac Orlan, *Lautrec, peintre de la lumière froide,* Paris, 1934; Emile Schaub-Koch, *Psychanalyse d'un peintre moderne,* Paris, 1935; Gerstle Mack, *Toulouse-Lautrec,* London and New York, 1938; Gilles de la Tourette, *Lautrec,* Paris, 1938; Jacques Lassaigne, *Toulouse-Lautrec,* Paris, 1939; Leonardo Borgese, *Toulouse-Lautrec,* Milan, 1945; Irene Brin, *Images de Lautrec,* Rome, Bestetti-Tumminelli, 1947; Ole Vindig, *Toulouse-Lautrec,* Copenhagen, 1947; Daniel Catton Rich, *Henri de Toulouse-Lautrec "Au Moulin Rouge,"* London, n. d. [1949].

Articles and catalogues: Thadée Natanson, "Oeuvres de Toulouse-Lautrec," *Revue Blanche,* February 16, 1893; Arsène Alexandre, Preface to catalogue of the *Exposition Toulouse-Lautrec* at the Galerie Durand-Ruel, Paris, 1902; André Fontainas, "Rétrospective et exposition de Toulouse-Lautrec," *Mercure de France,* May and June, 1902; Jean Louis Renaud, Preface to *Catalogue de l'exposition de Henri de Toulouse-Lautrec,* Toulouse, 1907; Louis Thomas, "Henri de Toulouse-Lautrec," *La Nouvelle Revue,* July 1, 1913; Charles Saunier, "Henri de Toulouse-Lautrec," *La Grande Revue,* June, 1914; Arsène Alexandre, Preface to catalogue of the *Exposition Toulouse-Lautrec* at the Galerie Manzi-Joyant, Paris, 1914; Louis Vauxcelles, "Toulouse-Lautrec," *L'Amour de l'Art,* 1921, pp. 271–3; Arsène Alexandre, "Toulouse-Lautrec au musée d'Albi," *Renaissance,* January, 1922; Gustave Geffroy, "Toulouse-Lautrec," *Gazette des Beaux-Arts,* August, 1922; Auguste Marguillier, "Le musée Toulouse-Lautrec à Albi," *Mercure de France,* August 1, 1923;

BIBLIOGRAPHY

H. Hertz, "Toulouse-Lautrec," *Art in America,* 1925–6, p. 250 *et seq.*; Robert Rey, "Toulouse-Lautrec," *L'Art Vivant,* 1927, pp. 254–257; G. Duthuit, "Toulouse-Lautrec," *L'Amour de l'Art,* 1929, p. 146 *et seq.*; *Catalogue de l'exposition Toulouse-Lautrec au Musée des Arts décoratifs,* Paris, 1931; Tristan Bernard, Vuillard, Romain Coolus, René Huyghe (Group of articles dedicated to Toulouse-Lautrec), *L'Amour de l'Art,* April, 1931; Arsène Alexandre, "Toulouse-Lautrec," *Renaissance,* XVI (1931), pp. 140–145, 173–179; Fritz Neugass, "Toulouse-Lautrec," *Apollo,* 1931, pp. 163–65; François Gauzi, "Souvenirs sur Henri de Toulouse-Lautrec," *Catalogue de la XXIIIe Exposition des Artistes Méridionaux,* Toulouse, 1932; James Greig, "Toulouse-Lautrec and the Circus," *The Studio,* May, 1934; Giuseppe Marchiori, "Toulouse-Lautrec," *Ateneo Veneto,* Venice, February, 1935; Edouard Julien, *Catalogue du Musée d'Albi,* Albi, 1939; Robert J. Goldwater, "L'Affiche moderne," *Gazette des Beaux-Arts,* December, 1942; Catalogue, Toulouse-Lautrec Exhibition, Wildenstein, New York, 1946; M. G. Dortu, Preface to catalogue of the *Exposition Toulouse-Lautrec* at Brussels, 1947; Lionello Venturi, "Henri de Toulouse-Lautrec," *Les Arts Plastiques,* n. 7, 1947; Claude Roger-Marx, *The Lithographs of Toulouse-Lautrec,* New York, n. d.

Index

239

INDEX

240

INDEX

INDEX

INDEX

Plates

Fig. I. MANET: *The Picnic*, 1863.

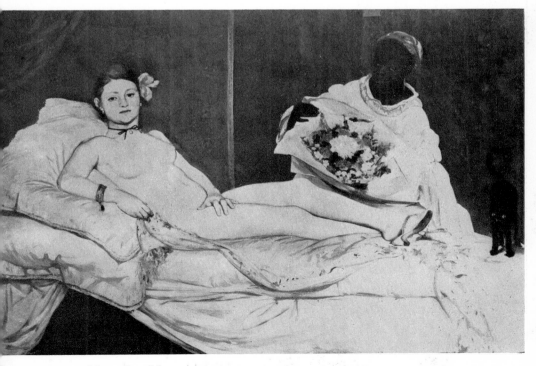

Fig. 2. MANET: *Olympia*, 1863.

Fig. 3. MANET: *Concert in the Tuileries Gardens*, 1860.

Fig. 4. MANET: *Lola de Valence*, 1862.

Fig. 5. MANET: *Soldier Examining His Rifle*, 1867 (from The Execution of Maximilian).

Fig. 6. MANET. *The Fifer*, 1866.

Fig. 7. MANET: *Lunch in the Studio*, 1868.

Fig. 8. MANET: *Portrait of Zola,* 1868.

Fig. 9. MANET: *Berthe Morisot with a Muf*
1869.

. 10. MANET: *Bordeaux Harbor*, 1871.

11. MANET: *Races at Longchamp*, 1864.

Fig. 12. MANET: *The Croquet Game,* Paris, 1873.

Fig. 13. MANET: *On the Beach,* 1873.

Fig. 14. MANET: *The Good Beer*, 1873.

Fig. 15. MANET: *The Grand Canal, Venice*, 1875.

Fig. 16. MANET: *The Road-Menders, rue Mosnier*, 1878.

Fig. 19. MANET: *The Restaurant of Père Lathuile*, 1879.

Fig. 20. MANET: *In the Boat*, 1874.

Fig. 21. MANET: *The Waitress*, 1878.

Fig. 22. MANET: *A Bar at the Folies-Bergère,*
1881.

Fig. 23. MANET: *The Model for A Bar at the
Folies-Bergère,* 1881.

Fig. 24. DEGAS: *The Bellelli Family,*
1860-62.

Fig. 25. DEGAS: *Portrait of a Young
Woman,* 1867.

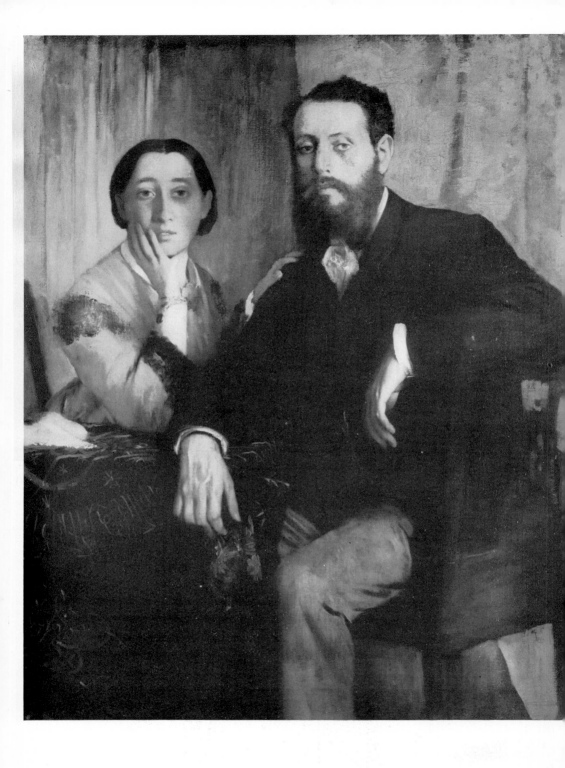

Fig. 26. DEGAS: *M. and Mme. Morbilli,* 1867.

Fig. 27. DEGAS: *War Scene in the Middle Ages*, 1865.

Fig. 28. DEGAS: *The Office of a Cotton Firm*, 1873.

Fig. 29. DEGAS: *The Carriage at the Races,* 1870-73.

Fig. 30. DEGAS: *At the Races,* 1877-80.

Fig. 31. DEGAS: *The Orchestra of the Paris Opera*, 1868-69.

Fig. 32. DEGAS: *Café-Concert, Les Ambassadeurs*, 1876-77.

Fig. 33. DEGAS: *Ballet Classroom, Paris Opera*, 1872.

Fig. 34. DEGAS: *Ballet Rehearsal*, 1875-77.

ig. 35. DEGAS: *Rehearsal in the Ballet Classroom*, 1875.

ig. 36. DEGAS: *Ballet Dancers Trying Their Slippers*, after 1890.

Fig. 37. DEGAS: *Women Combing Their Hair*, c. 1876-78.

Fig. 38. DEGAS: *Diego Martelli*, 1879.

Fig. 39. DEGAS: *Absinth*, 1876.

. 40. DEGAS: *Women Outside a Café, Evening,* 1877.

Fig. 41. DEGAS: *Women Ironing, c.* 1884.

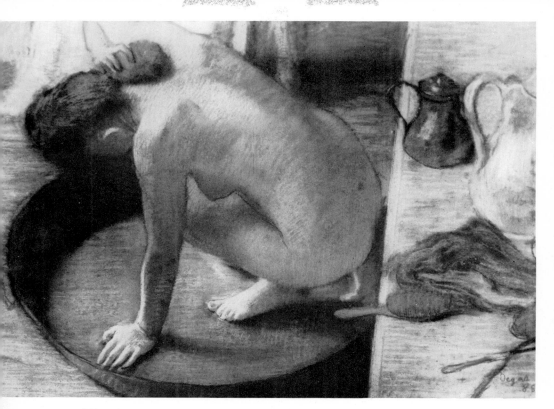

ig. 42. DEGAS: *The Tub*, 1886.

Fig. 43. DEGAS: *End of
the Bath*, c. 1895

Fig. 44. DEGAS: *Breakfast after the Bath*, c. 1895-98.

Fig. 45. DEGAS: *After the Bath,* 1899.

Fig. 46. MONET: *Mouth of the Seine at Honfleur*, 1864.

Fig. 47. MONET: *Camille, or The Lady
in the Green Dress*, 1866.

Fig. 48. MONET: *St. Germain l'Auxerrois*, 1866.

Fig. 49. MONET: *Women in the Garden,* 1867.

Fig. 50. MONET: *Argenteuil-sur-Seine,* 1868.

Fig. 51. MONET: *La Grenouillère*, 1869.

Fig. 52. MONET: *Sailboat at Argenteuil*, 1873.

Fig. 53. MONET: *The Bridge at Argenteuil*, 1874.

Fig. 54. MONET: *Riverbanks*, 1874.

Fig. 55. MONET: *Boats at Argenteuil*, 1875.

Fig. 56. MONET: *The St. Lazare Station, 1877.*

Fig. 57. MONET: *The Breaking of the Ice, 1880.*

58. MONET: *Boats in Winter*, 1885.

59. MONET: *Haystacks, Late Summer*, 1891.

Fig. 60. MONET: *Poplars Beside the River Epte,* 1890.

Fig. 61. MONET: *Rouen Cathedral, West Facade,* 1894.

Fig. 62. MONET: *Pool with Waterlilies. Harmony in Pink,* 1900.

Fig. 63. PISARRO: *The Côte du Jallais at Pontoise,* c. 1867.

Fig. 64. PISARRO: *The Locks at Bougival,* c. 1869.

Fig. 65. PISARRO: *Road near Louveciennes*, 1871.

Fig. 66. PISARRO: *The Route d'Osny, Pontoise*, 1872.

Fig. 67. PISARRO: *The Haystack*, 1873.

Fig. 68. PISARRO: *Village Street, Auvers-sur-Oise,* 1873

Fig. 69. PISARRO: *The Little Bridge, Pontoise,* 1875.

ig. 70. PISARRO: *Peasant Woman Pushing a Wheelbarrow*, 1874.

Fig. 71. PISARRO: *The Côte des Bœufs, Pontoise*, 1877.

Fig. 72. PISARRO: *Vegetable Garden and Flowering Trees, Spring, Pontoise,* 1877.

Fig. 73. PISARRO: *Sunken Road, View over Epluches,* 1881.

Fig. 74. PISARRO: *Mère Larcheveque,* 1880.

Fig. 75. PISARRO:
Bathing Women,
1894.

Fig. 76. PISARRO: *The Grand Pont, Rouen,* 1896.

Fig. 77. PISARRO: *The Rue de l'Epicerie, Rouen, Morning, Grey Weather*, 1898.

Fig. 78. PISARRO: *The Place du Théâtre Français, Sunshine*, 1898.

Fig. 79. SISLEY: *The Edge of the Forest of Fontainebleau,* 1865.

Fig. 80. SISLEY: *The Canal St. Martin, Paris,* 1870.

Fig. 81. SISLEY: *Little Square, Argenteuil*, 1872.

Fig. 82. SISLEY: *Port-Marly*, 1873.

Fig. 83. SISLEY: *Louveciennes, Heights of Marly*, 1873.

Fig. 84. SISLEY: *Snow at Louveciennes*, 1874.

Fig. 85. SISLEY: *The Route de la Princesse, Louveciennes, Evening,* 1875.

Fig. 86. SISLEY: *Landscape,* 1876.

Fig. 87. SISLEY: *The Boat during the Flood*, 1876.

Fig. 88. SISLEY: *The Seine at Suresne, 1877.*

Fig. 89. SISLEY: *A Cottage at Les Sablons, 1885.*

Fig. 90. SISLEY: *Sunset on the River Loing, St. Michel, Moret*, 1889.

Fig. 91. SISLEY: *The Bridge at Moret*, c. 1894.

Fig. 92. RENOIR: *Portrait of Mlle. Romaine Lacaux,* 1864.

Fig. 93. RENOIR: *Lise*, 1867.

Fig. 94. RENOIR: *La Grenouillère,* c. 1867.

Fig. 95. RENOIR: *The Pont Neuf,* 1872.

Fig. 96. RENOIR: *Bathing Woman*, 1876.

Fig. 97. RENOIR: *The Moulin de la Galette*, 1876.

Fig. 98. RENOIR: *Child with a Watering Pot*, 1876.

Fig. 99. RENOIR: *Woman with a Parasol*, c. 1876.

Fig. 100. RENOIR: *The First Time at the Theatre*, c. 1876.

Fig. 101. RENOIR: *Portrait of M. Chocquet*, 1876.

Fig. 102. RENOIR: *At La Grenouillère*, 1879.

Fig. 103. RENOIR: *Woman in a Straw Hat*, c. 1879.

Fig. 104. RENOIR: *Madame Charpentier and Her Children*, 1878.

Fig. 105. RENOIR: *The Boating Party at Lunch*, 1881.

Fig. 106. RENOIR: *L'Estaque,* 1882.

Fig. 107. RENOIR: *Bathing Woman,* 1881.

Fig. 108. RENOIR: *The Grandes Baigneuses*, 1887.

Fig. 109. RENOIR: *Young Girl,*
c. 1890.

Fig. 110. RENOIR: *Bathing Girls Playing with a Crab*, c. 1897.

Fig. 111. RENOIR: *Paul Durand-Ruel*, 1910.

Fig. 112. RENOIR: *Landscape*, c. 1910.

Fig. 113. RENOIR: *Woman's Torso*, 1905.

Fig. 114. RENOIR: *After the Bath*, 1913.

Fig. 115. RENOIR: *Gabrielle at the Mirror*, c. 1910.

Fig. 116. RENOIR: *Bathing Women*, c. 1918.

Fig. 117. CEZANNE: *Portrait of a Monk*, 1865-67.

Fig. 118. CEZANNE: *Pastoral*, 1870.

Fig. 119. CEZANNE: *Melting Snow at L'Estaque*, c. 1870.

Fig. 120. CEZANNE: *The House of the Hanged Man, Auvers-sur-Oise*, 1872-73.

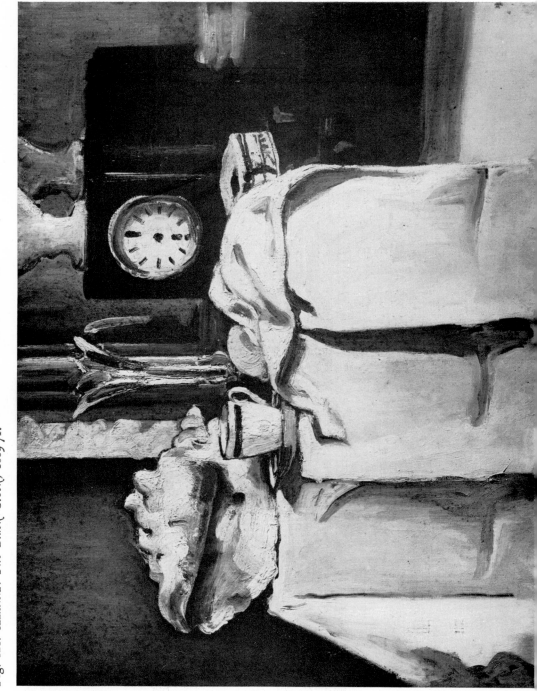

Fig. 121. CEZANNE: *The Black Clock*, 1869-71.

Fig. 122. CEZANNE: *The Boundary Wall*, 1875-76.

Fig. 123. CEZANNE: *Still Life*, 1873.

Fig. 124. CEZANNE: *Portrait of Victor Chocquet*, 1876-77.

Fig. 125. CEZANNE: *The Little Bridge*, 1882-85.

Fig. 126. CEZANNE: *The Bridge over the Marne at Créteil*, c. 1888.

Fig. 127. CEZANNE: *Houses at L'Estaque,* 1882-85.

Fig. 128. CEZANNE: *The Montagne Sainte-Victoire, near Gardanne,* 1885-86.

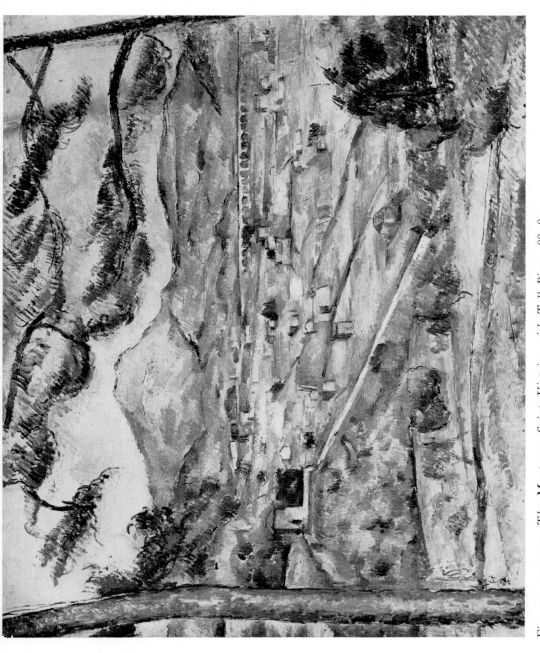

Fig. 129. CEZANNE: *The Montagne Sainte-Victoire with Tall Pine*, 1885-87.

Fig. 130. CEZANNE: *The Bay of Marseilles, Seen from L'Estaque*, 1883-85.

Fig. 131. CEZANNE: *The Montagne Sainte-Victoire,* 1894-1900.

Fig. 132. CEZANNE: *The Kitchen Table,* 1888-90.

Fig. 133. CEZANNE: *Portrait of Paul Cézanne*, 1890-94.

Fig. 134. CEZANNE: *Madame Cézanne in the Greenhouse*, c. 1890.

Fig. 135. CEZANNE: *Woman with a Coffee-Pot*, 1890-94.

Fig. 136. CEZANNE: *The Card Players*, 1890-92.

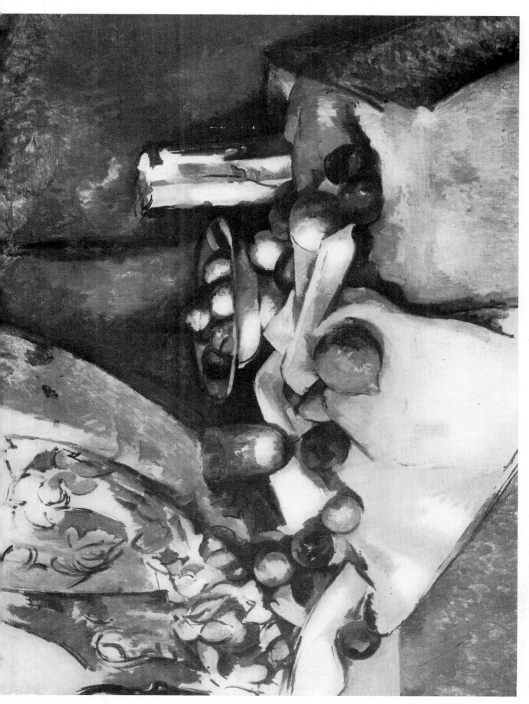

Fig. 137. CEZANNE: *Still Life*, 1895-1900.

Fig. 138. CEZANNE: *Lake of Annecy*, 1896.

Fig. 139. CEZANNE: *The Montagne Sainte-Victoire*, 1904-06.

Fig. 140. CEZANNE: *Portrait of Vallier* (water-color), 1906.

Fig. 141. CEZANNE: *Bathing Women,* 1900-06.

Fig. 142. SEURAT: *Suburb*, 1883.

Fig. 143. SEURAT: *Peasant with a Hoe*, c. 1884.

Fig. 144. SEURAT: *A Bathing Party, Asnières*, 1883-84.

Fig. 145. SEURAT: *The Seine at Courbevoie*, 1885.

Fig. 146. SEURAT: *The Island of the Granáe Jatte, Study for the Picture*, 1884.

Fig. 147. SEURAT: *Sketch for the Grande Jatte*, 1884-85.

Fig. 148. SEURAT: *A Sunday Afternoon on the Island of the Grande Jatte*, 1884-86.

Fig. 149. SEURAT: *The Roadstead at Grandcamp*, 1885.

Fig. 150. SEURAT: *Sunset, Grandcamp*, 1885.

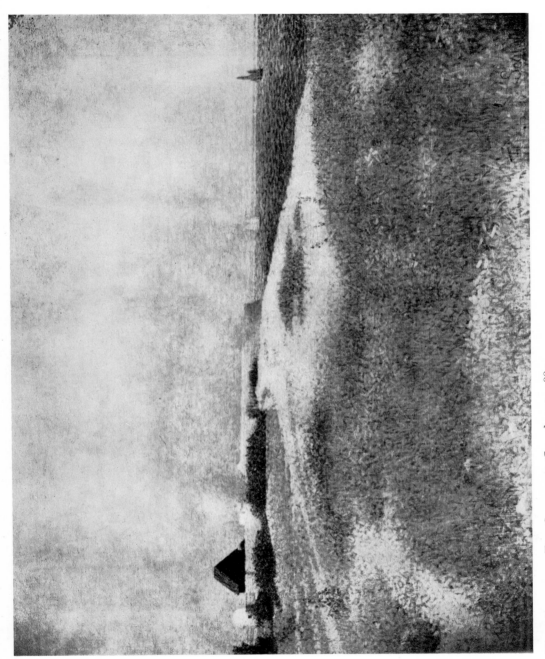

Fig. 151. SEURAT: *Fort Samson at Grandcamp*, 1885.

Fig. 152. SEURAT: *Fishing Boats at Port-en-Bessin*, 1888.

Fig. 153. SEURAT: *Le Crotoy, Looking Downstream*, 1889.

Fig. 154. SEURAT: *Le Crotoy, Looking Upstream*, 1889.

Fig. 155. SEURAT: *The Channel at Gravelines, Little Fort Philippe*, 1890.

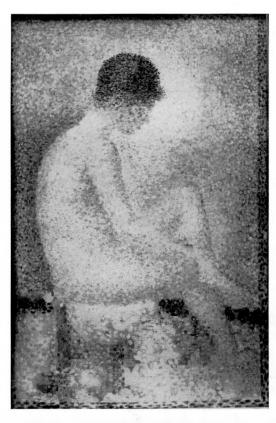

Figs. 156, 157, 158. SEURAT: *Three Studies for "The Models,"* 1887.

Fig. 157.

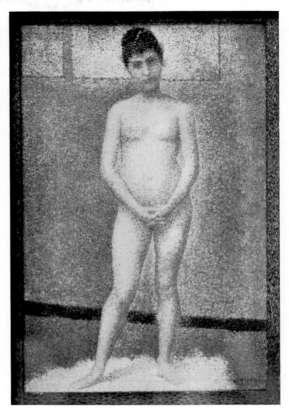

Fig. 158.

Fig. 159. SEURAT: *The Circus*, 1890-91.

Fig. 160. GAUGUIN: *Study of a Nude*, 1880.

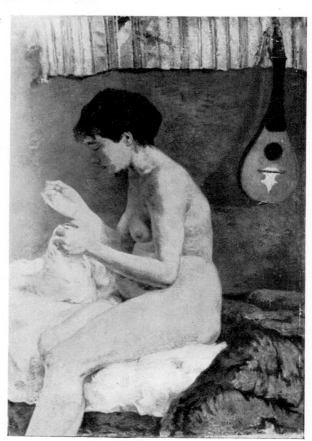

Fig. 161. GAUGUIN: *The Bathing Party at Pont-Aven*, c. 1886.

Fig. 162. GAUGUIN: *The Swineherd, Brittany*, 1888

Fig. 163. GAUGUIN: *Around the Huts, Martinique,* 1887.

Fig. 164. GAUGUIN: *Jacob Wrestling with the Angel,* 1889.

Fig. 165. GAUGUIN: *The Yellow Christ,* 1889.

Fig. 166. GAUGUIN: *La Belle Angèle*, 1889.

Fig. 167. GAUGUIN: *Tahitian Girl, Vahine no te Tiare*, 1891.

Fig. 168. GAUGUIN: *Fishing*, 1891.

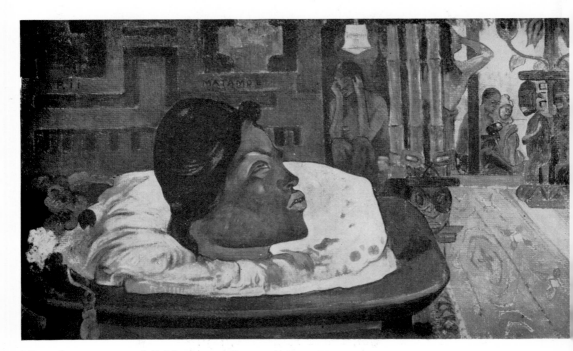

Fig. 169. GAUGUIN: *Arii Matamoe*, 1892.

Fig. 170. GAUGUIN: *The Spirit of the Dead Watching*, 1892.

Fig. 171. GAUGUIN: *Te aa no Areois*
(*The seed of the Areois*), 1892.

Fig. 172. GAUGUIN: *The White Horse*,
1898.

Fig. 173. GAUGUIN: *No te aha oe riri (Oh, you're jealous!)*, 1896.

Fig. 174. GAUGUIN: *Mahana no Atua (The Day of God)*, 1894.

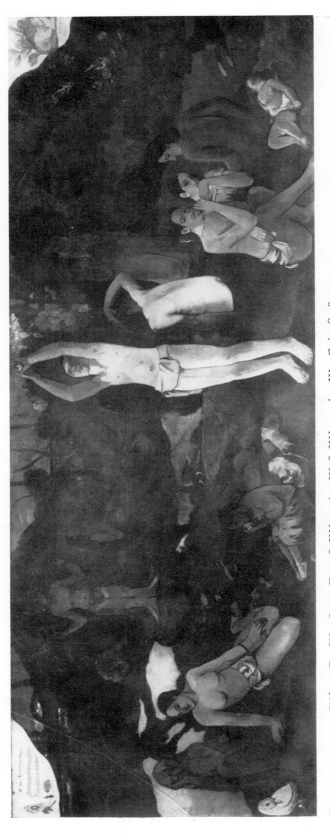

Fig. 175. GAUGUIN: *Where Do We Come From? What Are We? Where Are We Going?* 1897.

Fig. 176. GAUGUIN: *Detail of the preceding.*

Fig. 177. GAUGUIN: *The Call*, 1902.

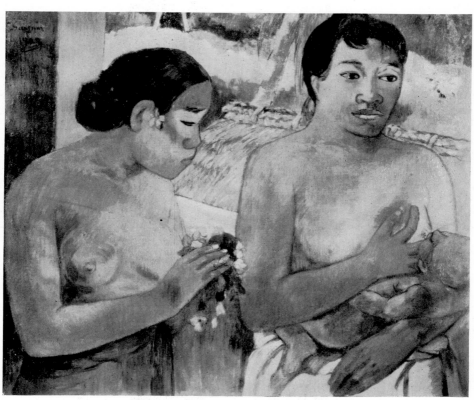

Fig. 178. GAUGUIN: *Adoration*, 1902.

Fig. 179. GAUGUIN: *Nativity*, 1902.

Fig. 180. VAN GOGH: *The Potato Eaters*, 1885.

Fig. 181. VAN GOGH: *Still-Life with Plaster Statuette* (Between March 1886 and February 1888).

Fig. 182. VAN GOGH: *Banks of the Seine* (Between March 1886 and February 1888).

Fig. 183. VAN GOGH: *Small Gardens on Montmartre*, 1887.

Fig. 184. VAN GOGH: *Self-Portrait*, 1888.

Fig. 185. VAN GOGH: *The Flowering Tree, Arles,* April 1888.

Fig. 186. VAN GOGH: *The Drawbridge,* May 1888.

Fig. 187. VAN GOGH: *The Crau*, June 1888.

Fig. 188. VAN GOGH: *Sunflowers, Arles, August* 1888.

Fig. 189. VAN GOGH: *Vincent's House at Arles,* September 1888.

Fig. 190. VAN GOGH: *Van Gogh's Bedroom at Arles,* October 1888, Arles.

Fig. 191. VAN GOGH: *Roulin, the Letter Carrier*, August 1888.

Fig. 192. VAN GOGH: *The Woman of Arles* (*Mme. Ginoux*), November 1888.

Fig. 193. VAN GOGH: *The Man with the Pipe (Portrait of the Artist)*, January-February 1889.

Fig. 194. VAN GOGH: *Iris, St. Rémy*, May 1889.

Fig. 195. VAN GOGH: *White Roses, St. Rémy*, May 1890.

Fig. 196. VAN GOGH: *The Olive Grove, St. Rémy,* November 1889.

Fig. 197. VAN GOGH: *Yellow Wheat and Cypresses,* September 1889.

Fig. 198. VAN GOGH: *The Ravine (Les Fontettes)*, December 1889.

Fig. 199. VAN GOGH: *At the Edge of Les Alpines, St. Rémy*, May 1890.

Fig. 200. VAN GOGH: *Starry Night, St. Rémy*, June 1889.

Fig. 201. VAN GOGH: *Portrait of Dr. Gachet, Auvers*, June 1890.

Fig. 202. TOULOUSE-LAUTREC:
Countess Adèle de Toulouse-Lautrec, Mother of the Artist,
1887.

Fig. 203. TOULOUSE-LAUTREC:
Young Woman Sitting at a Table, 1889.

Fig. 204. TOULOUSE-LAUTREC:
The Laundress, 1889.

Fig. 205. TOULOUSE-LAUTREC:
Gabrielle the Dancer, 1891.

Fig. 206. TOULOUSE-LAUTREC: *At "The Sweetheart,"* 1891.

Fig. 207. TOULOUSE-LAUTREC: *The Bed*, 1892.

Fig. 208. TOULOUSE-LAUTREC: *In the Salon, rue des Moulins*, 1894.

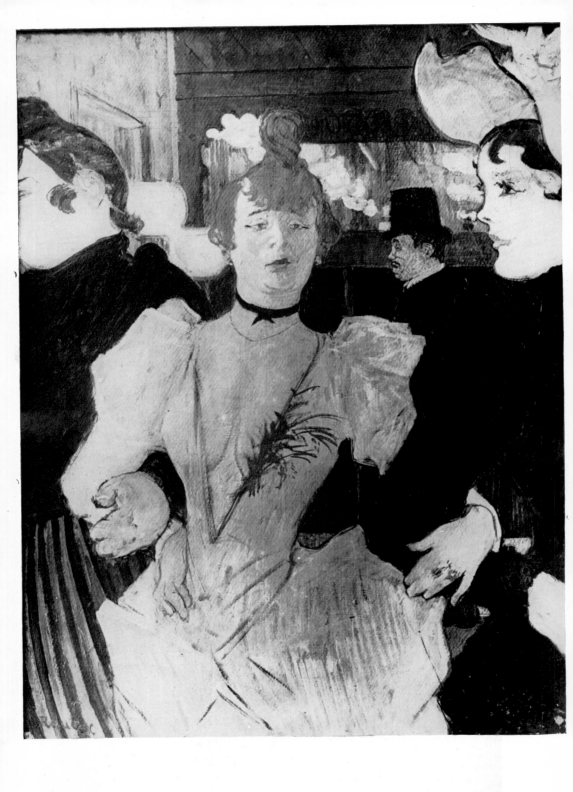

Fig. 209. TOULOUSE-LAUTREC: *La Goulue between Her Sister and a Dancer*, 1892.

Fig. 210. TOULOUSE-LAUTREC: *At the Moulin Rouge: The Female Clown Cha-U-Kao*, 1895.

Fig. 211. TOULOUSE-LAUTREC: *The Dance of La Goulue*, or *The Oriental Dancing Girls*, 1895.

Fig. 212. TOULOUSE-LAUTREC: *Portrait of Félix Fénéon* (detail of Fig. 211).

Fig. 213. TOULOUSE-LAUTREC: *Portrait of Cipa Godewski*, 1896.

Fig. 214. TOULOUSE-LAUTREC: *Portrait of Paul Leclercq*, 1897.

Fig. 215. TOULOUSE-LAUTREC: *Miss May Belfort*, 1895.

Fig. 216. TOULOUSE-LAUTREC: *The Female Clown Cha-U-Kao,* 1895.

Fig. 217. TOULOUSE-LAUTREC: *The English Girl at "The Star" in Le Havre,* 1899.